Introduction to
Technical Illustration

Introduction to Technical Illustration

George C. Beakley
College of Engineering
and Applied Sciences
Arizona State University

Donald D. Autore
College of Engineering
and Applied Sciences
Arizona State University

David W. Hudgins
Government Electronics Group
Motorola, Inc.

Bobbs-Merrill Educational Publishing
Indianapolis

Copyright © 1983 by George C. Beakley

Printed in the United States of America. All rights reserved. No part of this book shall be reproduced or transmitted in any form or by any means, electronic or mechanical, including photocopying, recording, or by any information or retrieval system, without written permission from the Publisher:

The Bobbs-Merrill Company, Inc.
4300 W. 62nd Street
Indianapolis, Indiana 46268

First Edition

First Printing 1983

Cover Design by Gregg Butler

Acquisitions Editor: Therese Zak
Copy and Production Editor: Sara Bernhardt

Library of Congress Cataloging in Publication Data

ISBN: 0-672-97993-4
83 - 5993

Photograph and illustration credits

Alpha Merics Corp.: Fig. 466; Arco Publishing Co., Inc.: Fig. 111; *The Arizona Republic*: Figs. 27, 318; Arizona State University: Fig. 2A; Auto-trol Technology Corporation: Figs. 480, 483, 485, 486; The Bendix Aerospace Systems Division: Figs. 121, 164; Berol U.S.A.: Figs. 170, 390, 391, 392, 398 (*compass*), A-4 (*templates*), A-7, A-9 (*compass*); Caterpillar Tractor Co.: Fig. 115; Chrysler Corp.: Figs. 114, 117, 305, 306, 421, 450; Digital Equipment Corporation: Fig. 484; Formsprag Company: Fig. 11; Garrett Pneumatic Systems Division: Fig. 307; General Dynamics: Fig. 129; Gramercy; Fig. A-4 (*compass and accessories*); Graphic-Standard Instruments Co.: Figs. 169, 274, 279, 303; Miles Hardiman: Figs. 488–502; IBM Corporation: Fig. 32; Keuffel & Esser Co.: Figs. A-3, A-4 (*irregular curve*), A-5A, A-35B, A-36; Koh-I-Noor Rapidograph, Inc.: Fig. 398 (*technical pens*), 465, A-9 (*technical pens*), A-35A; Kroy, Inc.: Fig. 463; Lockheed Missiles and Space Company, Inc.: Fig. 69; Maine Department of Economic Development: Fig. 39; Martin Instrument Co.: Figs. A-1B, A-2; Motorola, Inc.: Figs. 118, 119, 316, 317; North American Rockwell: Fig. 51; North Texas State University: Fig. 2B; Pratt & Whitney Aircraft Group: Figs. 116, 302; Century Strand: Fig. 95; J. S. Staedtler, Inc.: Figs. 399, 401, 487, A-1A, A-5B, A-6, A-9 (*compass*), A-10; Volkswagen of America, Inc.: Fig. 1 (*photograph*); Carl Zeiss, Inc., New York: Fig. 108

Table of Contents

Preface

We wrote this book to introduce students to the basic concepts involved in the professional practice of technical illustration. The illustration techniques we describe emphasize the quickest, most convenient methods used today to satisfy the everyday needs of industry. Seldom-used, more exact techniques that are complicated and time consuming are avoided as much as possible. We favor those methods that professionals use most of the time to achieve acceptable results at minimum cost. After learning these everyday techniques, more theoretical books may be consulted to solve special problems. There has long been a need for a textbook that would adequately provide beginning students with the fundamental knowledge and skill training that is most needed when entering the professional world. This book fills that need. We have combined our knowledge of the needs and practices of industry with teaching methods found effective in the classroom.

Since this is a book dealing with technical illustration, we have made a special effort to ensure that the text illustrations were instructionally clear and effective. The artwork in the illustrations has been prepared by professional illustrators actively employed in industry. We use the same unique method of illustrating sequential steps in important drawing construction techniques as we have used with success in our other texts. In these sequences, lines drawn for each new step are shown in color. In the next step, the color lines revert to black, and the new lines are again in color. As another important aid, we use brief comments to accompany each illustration. These comments summarize the more extensive explanation in the written portion of the text. In this way the sequence of illustrations and comments form an effective "mini-text." This is valuable not only when first reading the text but especially when reviewing for tests or looking up special procedures.

The text is arranged in three main divisions—freehand drawing and visualization, technical illustration systems and procedures, and illustrating techniques. We are convinced that sketching is an effective tool in planning technical illustrations; this has been confirmed by the comments received from many of our colleagues. In keeping with their requests, a complete division on freehand drawing and visualization has been incorporated in the early part of the text. The use of sketching is also strongly encouraged throughout the text. Perforated underlay grids are printed in Appendix C for all the illustration systems to save time and to help maintain proportions in sketching. The first 31 sections of this text were originally prepared by the authors with the assistance of William E. Sadler and Todd T. Smith. This work was published under the title *Freehand Drawing and Visualization*, Bobbs-Merrill, 1982.

When technical illustration systems and procedures are introduced, the basic principles common to all types of axonometric drawing are thoroughly discussed first, using the isometric system as a basis, before proceeding to dimetric and trimetric. Commonly used methods of drawing pictorial representations of circles, cylinders, and curved surfaces are well described. The use of an ellipse protractor has been included for those instructors who prefer this technique. Emphasis is placed throughout the book on drawing systems and techniques that are most commonly used by professional illustrators.

The portion of the book on illustrating techniques covers the popular methods of adding realism to illustrations using line variations, shading techniques, and rendering. The basic principles of using an airbrush are included. The preparation of artwork for publication both in black and white and in color is described. A section is also included highlighting the new developments in computer aided illustration. The book concludes with a portfolio of work done by one of the nation's most prominent technical illustrators to acquaint students with the variety of illustration applications and the quality of work that can be achieved.

Many instructors have requested a complete set of problems to use in practicing the various illustration systems and techniques described. In Sections 1 through 31 covering freehand drawing and visualization, the objects used in each exercise are incorporated in the description of each exercise. In later sections, the exercises use a common set of 100 objects shown in Section 90. In this way different projection systems and illustration techniques can be tried on the same object and comparisons made as to effectiveness and cost (time). Overlay grids are printed on all of the problem objects to facilitate their transfer to the student's paper.

One especially important feature of the appendix is a complete summary of drawing fundamentals. This will be especially valuable to instructors in those technical illustration courses where the background of some entering students is weak or incomplete. Drawing instruments, drawing techniques, lettering, various types of multiview drawing, intersections, developments, dimensioning, and charts and graphs are among the topics reviewed.

Another valuable appendix feature for beginning students or for review is the summary of geometric construction techniques. These are illustrated in sequential steps for ease of understanding. Appendix C has a scale ratio chart that is useful in dimetric and trimetric drawing where different reducing scales are frequently needed. Perforated underlay grids for sketching in orthographic, isometric, dimetric, trimetric, perspective, and oblique are included as well as a set of commonly used ellipse protractors. Appendix D has a pictorial description of common product features to help students become familiar with terminology used in describing manufactured products. A table of geometric shapes and associated formulas is also included along with decimal-inch/millimeter conversion charts.

We appreciate our many colleagues who have responded to our surveys and provided many helpful suggestions. We are also grateful to those who reviewed the manuscript. Professors Stanley N. Alf of Mesa Community College and John H. Matson of Arizona State University have been especially helpful in this regard.

George C. Beakley
Donald D. Autore
David W. Hudgins

Preparation for Drawing

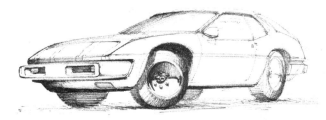

Sketches record ideas . . .

FIG. 1

. . . and help bring them to reality.

The twentieth century has established its position in history as an age of technological creativity. Developments such as manned flight, radio, television, nuclear power, solid state electronics, and space exploration have all changed the communication patterns of people and made possible a standard of living that heretofore was beyond imagination. It is in this era that a new communication profession, *technical illustration*, has had its genesis. This text introduces this field.

A technical illustration is the ultimate graphic form for conveying an idea. Most technical illustrations are developed from freehand drawings. In fact, it is probable that few of this century's innovative designs would have been completed without the extensive use of freehand drawings [1]. The first 31 sections of this text will help you gain proficiency in this essential skill. Later sections will describe the formal drawing techniques used by technical illustrators.

Several language forms
can be used . . .

. . . each has its advantages.

FIG. 2

1. DRAWING AS A LANGUAGE

Drawing is a form of language that uses lines and symbols to convey meaning. Written language, spoken language, and body language are other forms of idea communication. Each has its own application [2]. In some situations their usefulness may overlap and a combination of two or more may be appropriate.

Freehand drawings are frequently called **sketches.** In many respects the sketch is a superior representational system as compared with other types

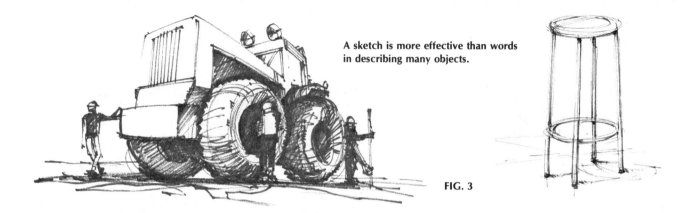

A sketch is more effective than words in describing many objects.

FIG. 3

of language. For example, it might be difficult to describe in words a tractor or a simple drafting stool to a person who had never seen one. On the other hand, a quick sketch could easily describe the object and its form, mass, and proportion [3]. A sketch has the additional quality of being easy to learn and understand compared to a new foreign language.

Sketches are also particularly useful in idea development. A basic concept may be added to other ideas, changed, or expanded to become a new, more potent idea. Since the mind works more quickly than the hand, ways of improving and modifying the sketch can be fed to the eye-hand system even as the first marks are being drawn on paper.

Freehand sketching is an important means of communicating with oneself [4]. However, sketching is most often used as a means of communicating complicated ideas from one person to another [5]. The recall of events, ideas, facts, or procedures can be effectively accomplished by making a sketch, especially if it can be done quickly, accurately, and comfortably. Sketching is also a natural method of recording a mental image for further study, for clarification or modification, or for idea transmission to others. Keep a sketchbook and record your ideas for later reference.

Since sketching is a *symbolic* representation of reality, it is not completely perfect. For example, the dimension of depth is missing because the image is drawn on a flat piece of paper. Natural color and the awareness of true size and true relationships between objects are also lost. To some degree these characteristics can be restored to the paper surface by means of various forms of illusion. These illusions and how to use them are the bases of this study of sketching.

In the following material we will discuss general guidelines for freehand sketching, explore methods of increasing your ability to visualize a three-dimensional object as an image, and develop the means to translate this image onto a two-dimensional piece of paper. In the process of gaining proficiency in sketching, your awareness and perception of the world around you will very likely increase. You may also become more visually aware of how one idea reproduced in sketch form can lead to or generate other creative thoughts.

Sketches are used to communicate with ourselves . . .

FIG. 4

. . . and also with others.

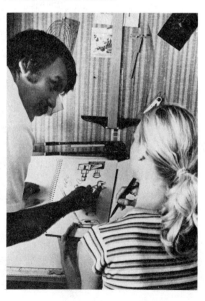

FIG. 5

A word has no size, color, or smell, but by previous agreement it can convey meaning.

FIG. 6 # camel

Lines of a sketch can relate visually to a camel.   FIG. 7

2. SKETCHES AS SYMBOLS

A symbol is a sign by which we know or infer something. Symbols either provide meaning through societal agreement [6] or are representational of objects or ideas they portray [7]. In this sense, sketches are symbols. An examination of children's sketches provides us with a better understanding of this fact [8]. The sketch in [9] more completely describes a specific house and captures some of its character. Note that while the sketch does not have the depth, size, and color of the original house, these basic elements are restored somewhat through illusion. Sketches most often employ the illusions of depth, shape, and proportion. The loss of color does not generally hinder our acceptance of a sketch as being representational.

If [9] were shown to someone from a foreign culture, the person might have some difficulty in recognizing it as a home, because the viewer must compare what is seen in the sketch with prior experiences. If there are none, there is no communication. Thus the person making the sketch must make use of the viewer's preconceptions about reality to convey the desired meaning. The sketcher and viewer must be tuned to the same frequency for understanding to be complete.

A child can represent "house" with a few simple lines.

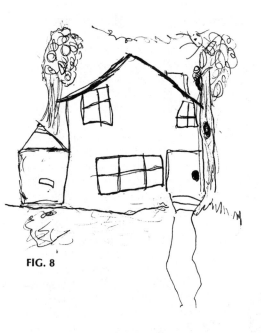

FIG. 8

This sketch captures more of the true character of the house.

FIG. 9

FIG. 10

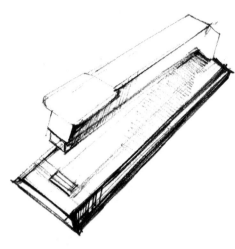

Sketches are accurate representations . . .
but are not expected to convey fine detail.

3. AN ATTITUDE FOR SKETCHING

You will learn a number of procedures and techniques that will improve the quality of your sketches, but the most important of all factors is **attitude.** And the most important ingredient in attitude is **confidence.** Draw confidently, not timidly! Remember that the objective in making a sketch is to produce a ''representation'' of reality—not a copy. You want the sketch to be accurate, but do not be concerned with the fine detail [10]. ***Do not be afraid to make a mistake!*** Allow your arm to move freely and with rhythm [11]. Use a large piece of paper and draw boldly.

Mental and physical exercise can better prepare you for sketching. To relax, take a few deep breaths. Cover your eyes with your hands to block out all light and make your mind a blank. Form a mental picture of a very dark, starless night; open your eyes and relax. You might stretch your arms toward the ceiling and then reach down and touch your toes. Dangle your arms at your waist. Flex the muscles in your arms, hands, and fingers. Relax your neck muscles and tilt your head forward. Slowly rotate your head in a circular motion. ***Loosen up!*** This loosening up will come naturally and automatically as experience is gained in sketching.

4. THE MARKER AND THE DRAWING SURFACE

Sketches can be made using various types of markers and drawing surfaces. For the beginner it is advisable to use a combination that encourages freedom of movement and discourages self-criticism. First try a

Move the arm freely and with rhythm . . .

. . . as in professional sports.

FIG. 11

Marking tools for sketching . . .

Don't use drafting instruments.

FIG. 12

FIG. 13

broad point felt-tip pen, preferably one using black ink [12]. Use a large size piece of inexpensive paper such as newsprint for a drawing surface. As confidence is gained, other tools such as soft charcoal, fine point felt-tip pens, and soft lead pencils may be used. Other surfaces such as tracing paper, textured cardboard, or fine-grain paper may be chosen later.

5. AVOID DRAFTING TOOLS IN SKETCHING

The common drawing instruments, guides, rules, triangles, templates, and so on **should not** be used in freehand sketching [13]! Their use should be reserved for technical drawing. The use of an eraser should also be avoided. This is one reason that a felt-tip ink pen is recommended—to avoid the temptation to make adjustments with the aid of an eraser. Correct errors in a freehand sketch by drawing over the original lines. If the error is too serious for this remedy, discard the paper and begin again [14]. Don't hesitate to discard an undesirable sketch. If you have been approaching sketching with vigor and speed, as you should, you will have invested only a very little time in the drawing.

No sketch should become "too precious."

FIG. 14

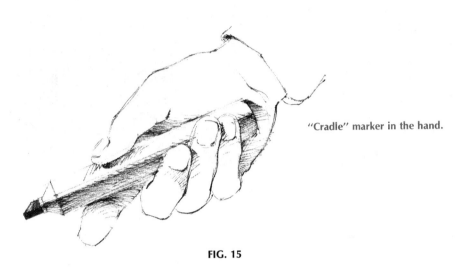

"Cradle" marker in the hand.

FIG. 15

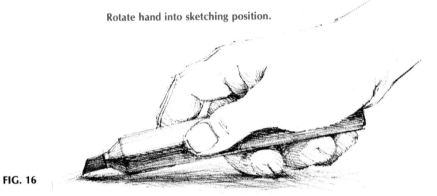

Rotate hand into sketching position.

FIG. 16

6. HOLDING THE MARKER

The way in which you hold the marker determines the accuracy and "looseness" of the final result. Unlike writing, where the fingers are important in guiding the writing instrument, sketching involves the free use of the hand and arm. The marker is held by the hand so that one end rests in the palm [15]. The thumb and forefinger are used loosely to steady the marker as shown. Rotate your hand into a sketching position and make a few random marks on a large piece of paper [16]. At first the hand position will be awkward, and the feeling will not be natural. With practice you will feel comfortable in this new position.

Most people are tempted to return to the writing position. Don't let this happen to you! Draw with your arm,

not your fingers. Imagine that your wrists and hand are bound together in a cast and that you cannot move them separately. This encourages full arm movement and emphasizes a boldness of stroke.

Where possible it is advisable to stand rather than sit at the drawing table. This position helps keep you energetic and your arm free to move. If sitting is required, don't get lazy and allow your hand or elbow to rest on the table.

7. PREPARATION FOR SKETCHING

Just as an athlete "warms up" prior to a race, the sketcher should complete some drawing exercises prior to sketching. The exercises de-

scribed here should be completed in a *minimum* amount of time. Make the strokes as rapidly as your muscles will allow. Do not be concerned with accuracy. It will improve with practice. Use a separate large piece of newsprint (18 × 24 inches approximately) for each of the following exercises.

Exercise 1

(a) With the paper horizontal in front of you, stroke a series of lines from left to right (using the full width of the paper), and then right to left [17]. The lines should be straight and horizontal. It is usual for them to be slightly arched at first, and for one end of the lines to sag. Keep practicing until the sheet of paper has been filled on both sides. Strive to make

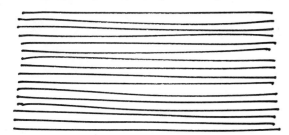

FIG. 17

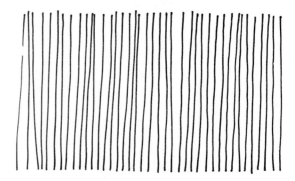

FIG. 18

the lines rapidly and accurately. (Time limit of thirty seconds)

(b) Using another piece of paper, stroke lines vertically—first from top to bottom, and then from bottom to top [18]. Ideally the lines will be straight and vertical. Don't be discouraged if at first the lines tend to be shaky and to fan out at the edges of the paper. Don't slow down in an attempt to increase accuracy! (Time limit of thirty seconds)

(c) On a piece of newsprint lay down a series of circular coil strokes horizontally across the paper [19]. On another piece of paper lay down a series of different sized ellipses. Experiment with differences in stroke "weight." Make some strokes with a light pressure, some with a heavy pressure. Notice the differences in line qualities that result. Now make a series of lines that have a variation in line weight. (Time limit of two minutes)

(d) Contour exercises develop confidence and understanding. Select a common object in the room, such as a chair or a telephone. With the object located in front of you, place your marker on a piece of paper. After this initial contact between the marker and paper **do not** look at the paper again. Look only at the object. Convince yourself that you are touching it. Then slowly follow the lines of the object with your eyes and make corresponding moves with your arm, marking the paper. **Do not** look at the paper! Continue to draw until you believe that you have captured the lines of the object. Now look at your image [20]. (Time limit of one minute)

The contour exercise points out a very important fundamental of drawing. A good visual familiarity with the subject is essential. Consequently, ***more time should be spent in looking at the subject than at the surface of the paper.***

FIG. 19

Sketch coils and ellipses . . . try varying line weights.

Contour exercises develop eye–hand coordination.

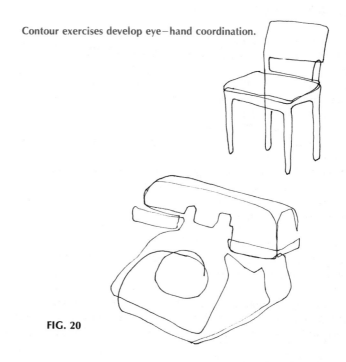

FIG. 20

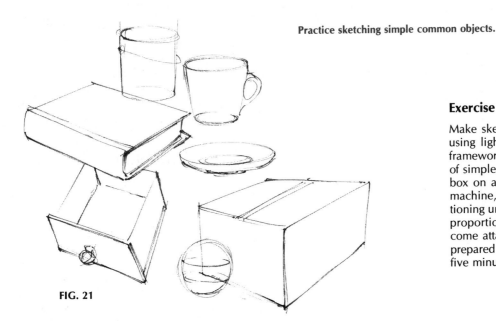

FIG. 21

Practice sketching simple common objects.

Exercise 2

Make sketches of five common objects using light construction lines to form a framework for each. Select large objects of simple shape such as (1) a cardboard box on a table, (2) a beverage vending machine, (3) a garage, or (4) an air conditioning unit. Concern yourself with basic proportions. Avoid details. Don't become attached to your sketches and be prepared to discard them. (Time limit of five minutes for each object)

8. BEGINNING THE SKETCH

Proficiency in sketching will improve with practice. The important thing is to begin and not to be overly concerned with the apparent quality of the first sketches. Whenever you get a chance, practice making simple sketches of common objects—a book, a cup, a wastebasket, a box, a drawer, and so on [21]. Sketch each object as your mind first perceives it. Omit decorative surface designs and minor details such as screws and other fasteners. No attempt should be made to portray surface texture or color. Only the overall shape should concern you at this stage.

Many beginners believe that every line drawn in a sketch will be a part of the finished work. This is not so. Some lines may be drawn lightly. In this way they may serve as the initial framework for the final heavier lines, just as an outline is used in writing a story. These lightweight lines are called construction lines [22]. They help identify errors while laying out the sketch. Generally these errors are the result of initial inaccuracies in judgment. They can be corrected by simply drawing more heavily over the original line work [23]. Avoid using an eraser. The construction lines are retained on the finished sketch [24].

Construction lines act as an initial framework.

Some new information added . . . some errors corrected.

The finished sketch retains construction lines.

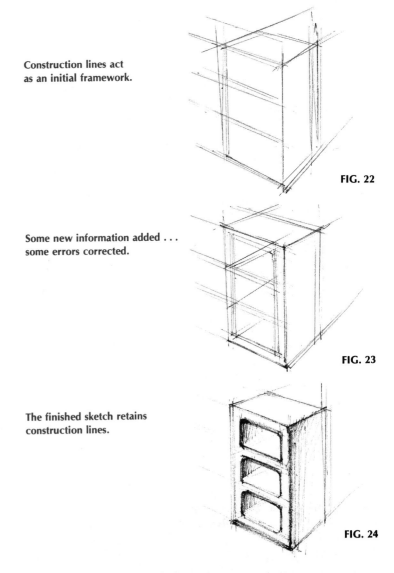

FIG. 22

FIG. 23

FIG. 24

Depth Illusion

In drawing an object as though it were real, you are creating a two-dimensional illusion of three-dimensional space. There are several conditions that will assist you in adding the quality of realism to two-dimensional sketches. Several of these are discussed in the following paragraphs.

9. OVERLAPPING SHAPES

The quality of **depth** in a sketch is important in creating the illusion of three-dimensional space. Overlapping shapes are often used for this purpose. When an object or part of an object is hidden behind another object, it is interpreted by your mind as being located farther away than the shielding object [25]. However, it is not always evident just how far away the object is located. You might not know, for example, whether a few millimeters or several meters separate the shapes [25].

Exercise 3

Sketch a circle, a square, and a diamond. All three should be of approximately equal size. Using the principle of overlapping shapes, sketch the circle in front of the square with the diamond in back of the square. Repeat this exercise twice, changing the order of the shapes each time. Remember to use arm movement—not your fingers. Make the sketches quickly, and keep them "free and loose." No drafting tools such as compasses or straightedges should be used. (Total time limit—five minutes)

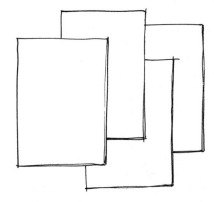

Overlapping shapes create the illusion of depth . . . but how far apart are they?

FIG. 25

10. RELATIVE SIZE

If the sizes are identical . . .
then the larger one must be closer.

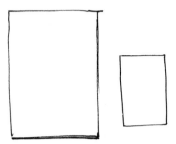

FIG. 26

If you see two objects that you know to be identical, and one appears to be larger than the other, it is natural to assume that the one appearing larger is closer [26]. This illustrates the conditions of relative size. You are not always aware of your brain's work since it functions automatically and frequently beyond the level of consciousness. Your mind stores a large amount of information concerning the relative size of objects and is particularly adept in making instantaneous judgments about the size of the objects that your eye sees. For example, if you see a traffic sign and an airplane at the same time, and the sign appears to be larger,

you ordinarily will assume that it is closer to you [27]. The cumulative effect of overlapping shapes and relative size increases the illusion of depth [28].

Exercise 4

Use a circle, square, and diamond as in Exercise 3. Place the circle in front of the square but diminish the size of the square. Place the square in front of the diamond, but diminish the size of the diamond. Repeat the sketches of Exercise 3, but in each case diminish the size of each overlapped shape. (Total time limit—five minutes)

FIG. 28

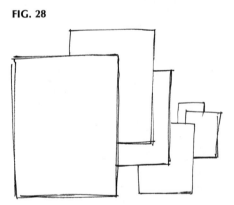

Combining overlapping shapes
and relative sizes . . . increases
the illusion of depth.

FIG. 27

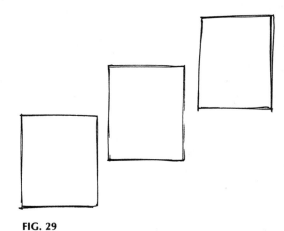

Aerial positioning . . . closer objects appear lower in the field of vision.

FIG. 29

11. AERIAL POSITIONING

Another condition affecting the illusion of depth is aerial positioning. This condition is based on the fact that humans are constructed with their eyes located about 1.6 meters [63 inches (in)] above the ground. This gives the human an advantage over most animals by providing an increased ability to see over objects and into the distance. Closer objects therefore appear lower in your field of vision and objects farther away appear higher [29]. Look across the room. The chairs that are close appear lower in your field of vision and those farther away appear higher [30].

The cumulative effect of overlapping shapes, relative size, and aerial positioning further increases the illusion of depth [31]. You can make good use of these conditions to supply realism to your sketches.

FIG. 30

Combining overlapping shapes, relative size, and aerial positioning . . . further increases the illusion of depth.

Exercise 5

Sketch a circle, square, and diamond. Position them with the square in front of the diamond and the diamond in front of the circle. Obtain depth illusion using the conditions of overlapping shapes, relative size, and aerial positioning. Repeat the exercise using other shape sequences.

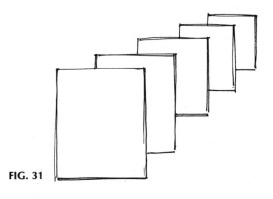

FIG. 31

FIG. 32

More distant objects appear less distinct.

FIG. 33

12. ATMOSPHERIC EFFECTS

The feeling of space and depth is also influenced by the clarity of the atmosphere. This includes the effects that air, smoke, fog, and haze have on the appearance of objects. As an object recedes into the distance, detail becomes less defined and more obscure [32]. This principle provides you with yet another means of adding depth illusion to your sketches.

If the light level remains constant, distant surfaces appear as middle-tone grays. Careful visualization of grass on a golf course will help us to understand this principle. In the near foreground, you can see individual blades of grass with contrasting dark shadows and brightly lit surfaces. Some 10 meters away, the grass surface appears as a uniform, fine texture with suggestions of darks and lights. As the fairway recedes, continues on to the next hill, and approaches the horizon, the individual grass blades are no longer identifiable and only shades of green-gray appear. Taking these atmospheric effects into account will help to add depth quality to your sketches [33]. It is most effective, however, when combined with the other conditions of overlapping shapes, relative size, and aerial positioning [34].

Exercise 6

Make a sketch of a diamond, circle, and square. Arrange them so that the diamond is in front and the square is farthest away. Achieve the illusion of depth using the condition of atmospheric effects. Repeat the exercise using other sequences of the shapes.

Which depth illusion techniques are used here?

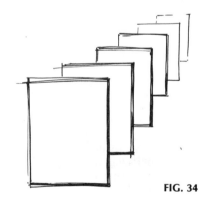

FIG. 34

13. PERSPECTIVE

Perspective is probably the most effective method used to add the illusion of depth to a sketch. This procedure follows fundamental principles of vision because the lines you draw on paper appear to your eye as they do in life situations [35]. A technical discussion of perspective drawing is beyond the scope of this material. However, it will be helpful to describe some basic principles of perspective which will assist you in adding realism to your sketches.

Many forms in our society are basically rectangular. This permits most perspective sketches to be drawn using a few basic principles. It is only when inclined planes, intersecting planes, circles, and other variations are added that perspectives are complex to draw.

The sense of reality evidenced in the photograph . . .

FIG. 35

. . . can be achieved in perspective sketching.

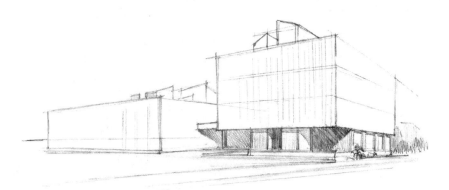

Perspective Sketching

An object appears to grow smaller as it recedes into the distance.

FIG. 36

14. BASIC PRINCIPLES OF PERSPECTIVE

In perspective an object appears to grow smaller in a determinable way as it recedes into the distance. This effect may be referred to as *fore-shortening.* The top and the bottom edges of any vertical surface, when represented by lines, disappear toward each other. If extended to the extreme, they will eventually meet [36]. The location of the point where these lines meet is critical. It is called the *vanishing point* [37]. This is the point where the surface bounded by these lines vanishes.

For the moment you may assume that vanishing points are always lo-

FIG. 37

The vanishing point is the distant point where lines meet.

Vanishing points are located on the horizon.

HORIZON LINE

FIG. 38

cated on the **horizon line** [38]. The horizon is an imaginary line that represents the apparent meeting point of the earth and sky. Mountains and valleys are ignored and the earth is assumed to be flat. If you stand on a beach and look out to sea, you will see a true horizon line [39]. The horizon line is always assumed to be straight and horizontal. It accompanies you wherever you go—whether you sit, stand, or climb stairs. The horizon line's position in relation to what you are viewing can be determined by imagining that the line is located straight ahead from your eyes and that it cuts horizontally across the scene that you are viewing.

A true horizon line is seen when looking out to sea.

FIG. 39

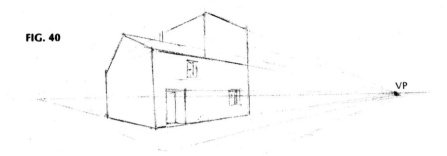

FIG. 40

Extensions of the horizontal edge lines meet on the horizon at the vanishing point.

15. LOCATING VANISHING POINTS

The first step in locating a vanishing point is to imagine that the parallel horizontal top and bottom-edge lines of an object extend toward the horizon line until they appear to merge into a single point [40]. This technique requires practice. It is frequently helpful to close one eye and

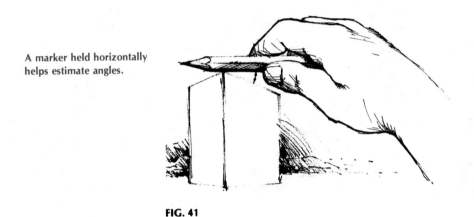

A marker held horizontally helps estimate angles.

FIG. 41

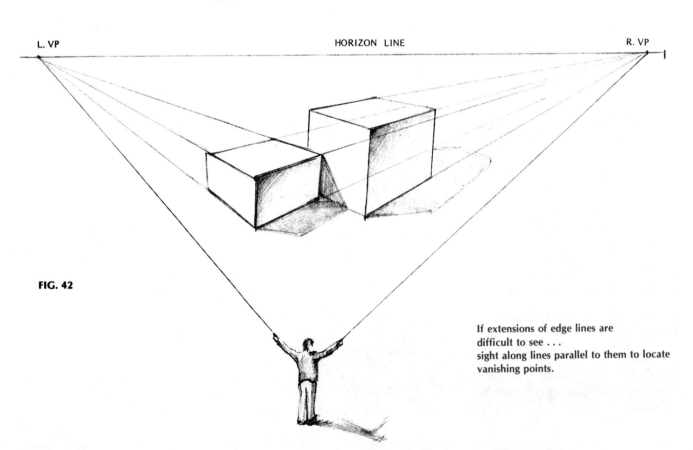

L. VP   HORIZON LINE   R. VP

FIG. 42

If extensions of edge lines are difficult to see . . .
sight along lines parallel to them to locate vanishing points.

hold a marker in a horizontal position in front of your eye so that the marker appears to rest on the top and then on the bottom of the closest vertical line of the object [41]. This makes it easier to judge the angles of the top and bottom lines as they lead to vanishing points on the left and on the right.

In some cases the size or location of an object may make it particularly difficult to locate the vanishing points. If it is not possible to extend directly an edge line of the object to locate a vanishing point, you can sight along an imaginary line running parallel to it [42]. Your imaginary sight line will intersect the horizon line at the same vanishing point as the object lines that are parallel to it. All parallel lines disappear to the same vanishing point.

16. CONSTRUCTION OF A SIMPLE PERSPECTIVE SKETCH

The horizon line is the foundation of the sketch [43]. Always draw it first (assuming it is located on the paper). In some instances it may be well above or below the object. The next construction line drawn should be one representing the closest vertical edge of the object [44]. Establish the height of the object by marking points on the vertical line to designate the top and bottom of the object [45]. If the horizon line passes through the object, proportion the height of the object above and below the horizon as it appears to your eye.

Estimate the angular relationships of the top and bottom edges of the object to the horizon line. Using these angles, extend light angular construction lines to the right and left from the top and bottom of the front edge of the object to the horizon line [46]. The vanishing points will be established where these pairs of receding lines meet at the horizon. Finally, make a judgment about the comparative width and depth dimensions of the object and represent them with vertical construction

FIG. 43

HORIZON LINE

The horizon line is the foundation of the sketch . . . draw it first.

FIG. 44

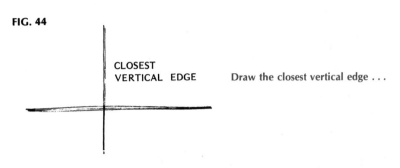

CLOSEST VERTICAL EDGE

Draw the closest vertical edge . . .

FIG. 45

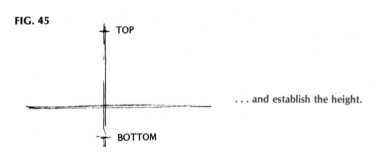

TOP

BOTTOM

. . . and establish the height.

FIG. 46

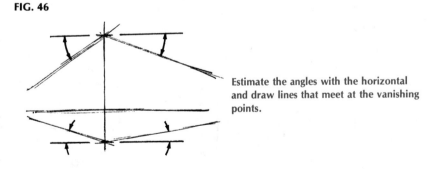

Estimate the angles with the horizontal and draw lines that meet at the vanishing points.

FIG. 47

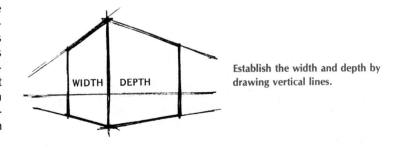

WIDTH DEPTH

Establish the width and depth by drawing vertical lines.

lines drawn to the left and right of the front edge line [47]. Figure [48] shows the sequence of steps used in sketching a more complicated object in perspective.

Steps in sketching a more complex object.

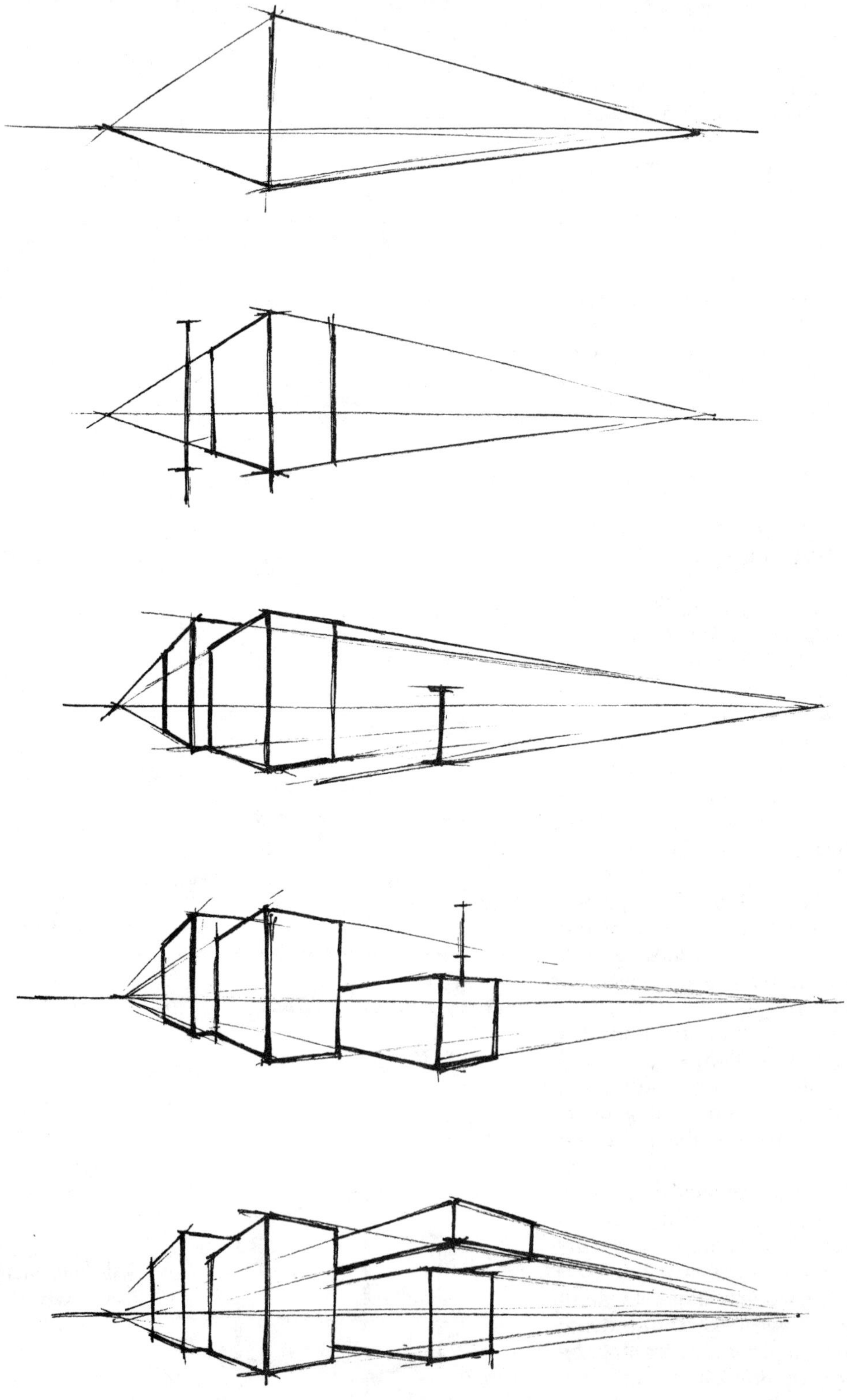

FIG. 48

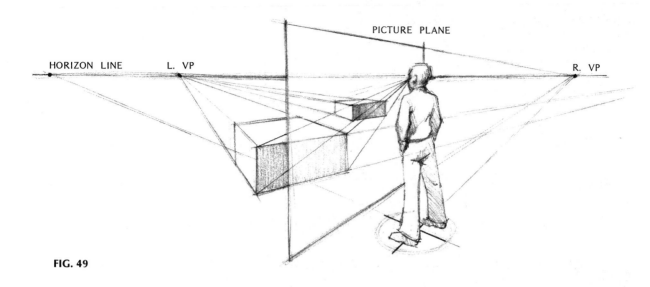

HORIZON LINE   L. VP   PICTURE PLANE   R. VP

FIG. 49

The viewer sees an image of the
object projected onto the picture plane.

17. SKETCHING OBJECTS IN PERSPECTIVE

The sketcher must transfer the image
on the picture plane to the drawing paper.

If you look directly ahead, the view recorded in your mind takes the form of a picture. It is framed by the limits of your vision. When making a perspective sketch, you are actually transferring the visual image or "picture" of the object from your mind to paper.

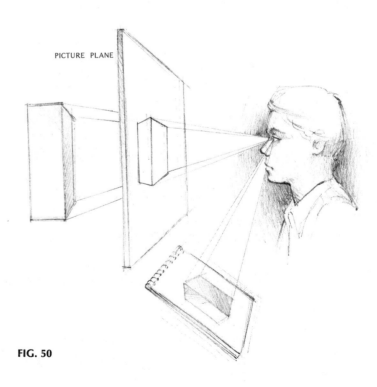

PICTURE PLANE

To assist you in picturing an object, assume that a transparent pane of glass has been placed on edge and extends upward in front of your face with its flat surface perpendicular to your line of sight. This forms a **picture plane** through which you can see. (This is sometimes referred to as a **viewing plane.**) The images of all objects visible to you are projected onto it [49]. If a camera were to be positioned where your eyes are located, the resulting photograph would record the same view that has been projected onto the picture plane.

Since drawing paper isn't as transparent as glass, it can't be positioned between your eyes and the object to receive the image directly. Instead, the paper must be placed to one side and the image transferred to it by a mental process rather than by a tracing operation [50].

Parallel and perpendicular lines

FIG. 50

**Rectangular patterns are
frequently seen
in our everyday activities.**

FIG. 51

and surfaces are very evident in most objects that we see in our daily lives. Buildings are generally designed with most of their surfaces perpendicular to each other. Streets and sidewalks are commonly laid out in rectangular patterns [51]. For this reason there usually are at least two sets of parallel lines to consider in sketching—those concerned with the width of the object and those concerned with its depth. In perspective sketching the parallel width lines vanish to one side of the object and the parallel depth lines vanish to the other side [52]. This condition is called *two-point perspective.*

**In two-point perspective . . .
the horizontal lines vanish to the left and to the right.**

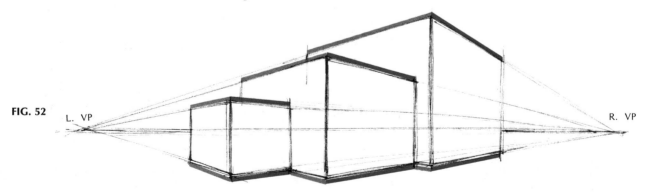

FIG. 52   L. VP   R. VP

As you walk around a building, your viewing direction relative to the building changes as you move from left to right [53]. This movement causes a continual change in the location of the width and depth vanishing points. As you approach the closest vertical edge of the building (the left corner of the front surface), the extensions of the horizontal top and bottom edges of the left side of the building converge more quickly. This forces the left vanishing point to move closer to the building. At the same time, the extensions of the top and bottom horizontal edges of the front surface of the building converge more gradually. This causes their vanishing point to move farther to the right. As you move closer to the center of the front of the building, the horizontal lines of the front surface converge less and less and their vanishing point moves off to infinity to the right [54]. At the same time, your view of the left side of the building is vanishing and its horizontal lines are converging rapidly to a point behind the building.

On arriving at the exact center of the front of the building, you will be looking directly at (perpendicular to) the front surface [55]. The top and bottom lines of the front surface will be parallel and the horizontal lines of the left side will have converged to a point centered behind the building. If you were to sketch the object from this viewing direction, you would produce what is known as **one-point perspective.** This is because the horizontal lines of both the left-side and right-side parallel surfaces converge to the same vanishing point.

As you walk to the right you will see part of the right side of the building [56]. Note that the horizontal lines of this surface converge very rapidly at first as their vanishing point moves out from behind the building. At the same time, the horizontal lines of the front surface are converging very slowly to a distant left vanishing point. As you continue walking to the right you will see that the vanishing point for the right side moves more to the right and the vanishing point for the front surface moves from the far left to a position closer to the building.

Your viewing direction changes as you walk around a building . . . the vanishing points appear to move on the horizon.

FIG. 53

FIG. 54

The left vanishing point is moving closer to the building . . . the right farther away.

FIG. 55

When you are looking directly at the front of the building . . . the vanishing points for the left and right sides are centered behind the building.

As the right side comes into view, the right vanishing point moves away from the building to the right . . . the left moves closer to the left side.

FIG. 56

18. EYE LEVEL AND PROPORTION RELATIONSHIPS

Exercise 7

Using a box or some other rectangular solid as a subject, make a series of five sketches. Begin the first sketch by establishing the horizon line. Add the closest vertical line of the object. Then locate the left and right vanishing points. Finally, establish the width and depth of the object. For the second and each following sketch rotate the object approximately 70° around a vertical axis. (Time limit of five minutes maximum for each sketch)

The appearance of an object drawn in perspective is always influenced by the height of the sketcher. If the base of the object that you are sketching is on the same ground level as you are, the height of your eyes determines the distance between the base of the object and the horizon line. When standing, your eyes are about 1.6 meters (m) (63 in) above the ground. On your sketch the distance from the base of the object to the horizon line must, therefore, represent 1.6 m (63 in) [57]. If you are kneeling down, your eyes will be about 1 m (39.4 in) above the ground. In this case the location of the horizon line above the base of the object

on your sketch will represent 1 m (39.4 in). The actual dimension that you select for this distance in your sketch may be any length. This selection is critical, however, because all other dimensions of the object will be established in proportion to it.

The first dimension on your sketch that the distance from the base of the object to the horizon line will influence is the height of the object. If your eyes are 1 m (39.4 in) above the ground as you look at a building, the total building height of 6 m (236.4 in) must be drawn six times as large as the distance from the base to the horizon [58]. The portion of the height between the horizon and the top of

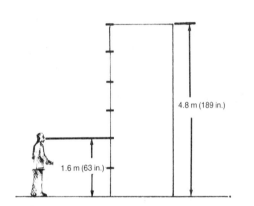
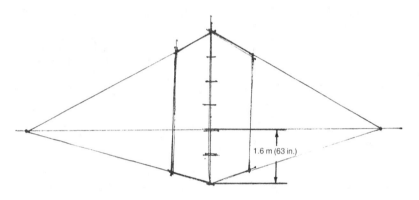

4.8 m (189 in.)

1.6 m (63 in.)

1.6 m (63 in.)

Vertical proportions can be estimated in relation to eye height.

FIG. 57

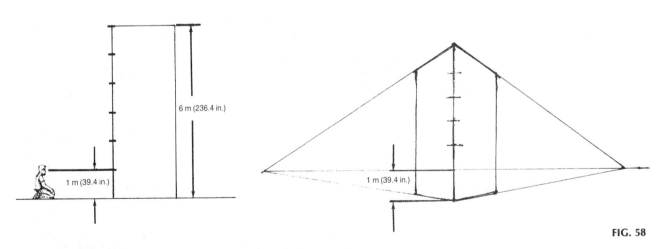

6 m (236.4 in.)

1 m (39.4 in.)

1 m (39.4 in.)

FIG. 58

Lowering eye height decreases the proportion of the building below the horizon.

the building represents 5 m (197 in). In sketching, the distance from the base of the object to the horizon line is usually visualized as one unit and **eye judgment** is used to decide how many of these units appear above the horizon line.

Eye judgments of distances and proportions are very important in sketching. One aid to accomplishing this is to sight over a marker held in line with the object. To estimate a vertical distance, hold your marker vertically at arm's length with your arm straight and elbow locked [59]. Sight past the marker with one eye closed and position the marker in line with the distance you wish to measure. Slide your thumb along the marker to adjust its length, matching the apparent distance on the object. This unit measurement can then be easily compared with other dimensions of the object to establish its basic proportions. Measurements in other directions can be estimated by aligning your marker in those directions [60]. Although this procedure

1 UNIT ESTABLISHED AS A STANDARD

1/2

Sight over a marker to estimate distances and proportions . . .
hold your arm straight with elbow locked.

FIG. 59

Distances can be estimated in any direction.

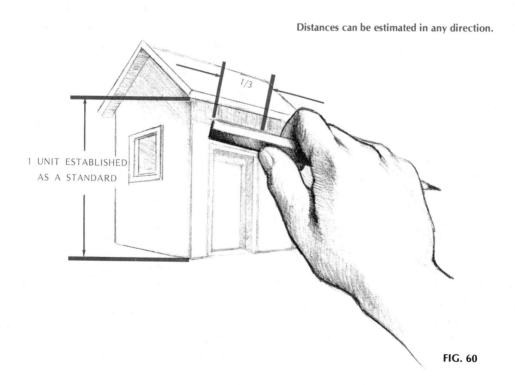

1/3

1 UNIT ESTABLISHED AS A STANDARD

FIG. 60

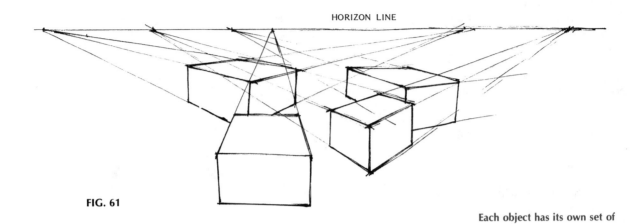

HORIZON LINE

FIG. 61

Each object has its own set of vanishing points on the horizon line.

FIG. 62

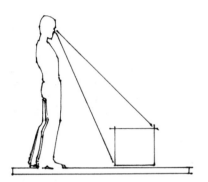

If you look down on an object . . .

. . . the horizon line may not appear on the drawing of the object.

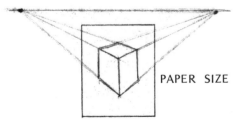

PAPER SIZE

FIG. 63

is a useful tool to help train your eye, don't become overly dependent on it. Make distance and proportion judgments directly with your eye as much as possible. This will greatly speed up your sketching.

19. PERSPECTIVE COMPLEXITIES

Occasionally a building is constructed, a street located, or a box set down so that it is not aligned in an orderly rectangular pattern with other nearby objects. This presents a new problem for the sketcher who is trying to portray accurately each object in the sketch. What must be realized is that while the group of objects has a common horizon line, each object has its own separate set of vanishing points on this horizon line [61].

Occasionally you will need to sketch an object from a high viewpoint [62]. This is often referred to as a "bird's eye view." It may be difficult or even impossible to include the horizon line in the sketch [63]. In this event, the lines representing the horizontal edges of the object must be extended to meet at vanishing points located some distance off the paper. Only a small portion of these construction lines will be used to

frame the object, but the longer these lines can be extended on the paper, the better. People's eyes are more adept at identifying directional trends of long lines [64]. It may be helpful to identify vanishing points that exist off the paper by marking them on the table with a thumb tack or a chalk mark. If you do this, be careful not to move your paper while making the sketch.

Exercise 8

Use the same or a similar object to that used in Exercise 7. Place the object on a table high enough so that the horizon line intersects the object. Sketch it in this location. Then move the object to a lower table or shelf and sketch that view of the object. Finally, sketch the object as it appears when placed on the floor. (None of these sketches should take longer than five minutes.)

Another problem occurs in perspective sketching as the sketcher moves from a distant to a closer view of the same object. Examination of a rectangular building at three different distances demonstrates that the horizon line and the vanishing points remain constant for the three views [65]. The problem arises in that the closer the viewer is to the object, the longer the edges appear.

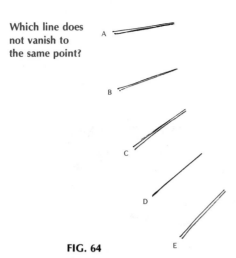

Which line does
not vanish to
the same point?

A

B

C

D

E

FIG. 64

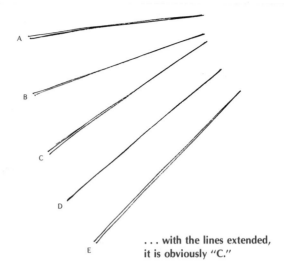

A

B

C

D

E

. . . with the lines extended,
it is obviously "C."

Also, the nearest vertical edge of the object appears to lengthen at a rate greater than the distant vertical edges. This causes the angle on the top corner to become more acute. A similar situation occurs when sketching objects of varying sizes. The best way to determine the various angles is to observe how they occur on real objects. As you become more skilled in sketching objects that exist only in your mind, you will be able to imply the size or nearness of an object by merely manipulating these angles.

Remember that your major objective is to improve your visual perception so that your sketches will ade-

quately portray the real world. Don't let anything deter the accomplishment of this objective. Too many sketchers become slaves to established guidelines hoping that in following them the need to make judgments will be eliminated. These guidelines only *aid* the development of perceptual and portrayal skills. Always strive to improve the quality of your *judgment.*

Exercise 9

(a) Find a small rectangular object. Place it on your desk as far away from your eye as possible. Position it high enough so that the horizon line intersects the object. Make a quick

sketch on paper large enough to include both vanishing points. Next, move the object as close as possible to you and sketch it on top of your previous sketch. Use the same vanishing points. It may help you to close one eye when sketching close objects. Compare the angles of the lines that converge to the vanishing points on the two sketches.

(b) Go outdoors. Quickly sketch several (at least five) large buildings. Avoid details such as windows, doors, and decorations. Pay attention to overall perspective and proportion. Repeat the exercise on another day. Compare your best sketches each day. (Time limit of ten minutes for each sketch)

Vanishing points remain constant when
you move from a distant to a closer view.

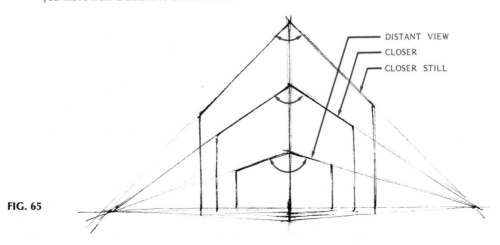

DISTANT VIEW
CLOSER
CLOSER STILL

FIG. 65

A circle drawn inside a square
shares its center and is tangent at the
midpoints of the sides.

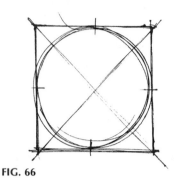

FIG. 66

When the square is drawn in perspective,
the circle becomes an ellipse.

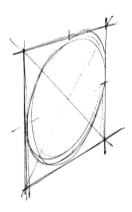

FIG. 67

A line perpendicular to the ellipse
at its center is the "axle."

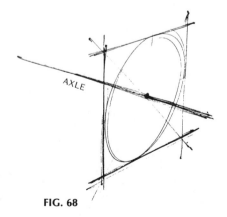

AXLE

FIG. 68

The perpendicular shaft at the center of
this satellite is like the axle of a wheel.

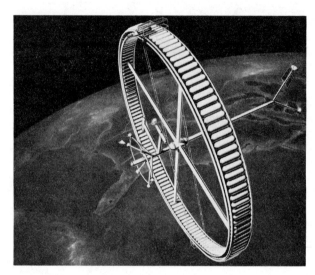

FIG. 69

The major axis is the widest dimension
of the ellipse . . . the minor axis is
perpendicular and in line with the axle.

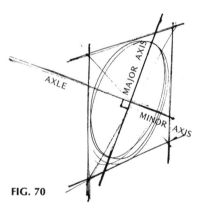

AXLE

MAJOR AXIS

MINOR AXIS

FIG. 70

20. CIRCLES IN PERSPECTIVE

Sooner or later those who sketch objects in perspective need to draw a circle in perspective. Much of our technological society is based on the use of wheels and gears. Fortunately, circles are not difficult to sketch if a few simple fundamentals are kept in mind.

In some ways a circle and a square are closely related. A circle can always be placed within a square so that it touches the mid-point of each side of the square and shares the square's center [66]. This basic relationship is preserved when the square and circle are viewed in perspective [67]. The circle now appears as an ellipse but is still tangent to the midpoints of the sides of the distorted square and shares its center. If a line runs through the center of the circle and is perpendicular to its surface, the line becomes an "axle" [68]. This axle has the same relationship to the circle as a true axle would have to a wheel [69].

A line drawn at 90° to the axle so that it runs across the ellipse at its widest point is known as its *major axis* [70]. The major axis crosses the axle close to, but not exactly at, the center of the circle. The shortest distance across the ellipse is known as its *minor axis.* The minor axis is also located at a right angle (90°) to the major axis and appears to lie over the axle. The relationship of these parts of the ellipse allows us to sketch them easily.

To sketch an ellipse, draw a line that is approximately 90° to the long direction that you expect the ellipse to take [71]. This will represent the axle. Next, draw a line at right angles to it, close to where you expect the center of the circle to be [72]. This will be the major axis. The direction of the minor axis was established automatically when the axle was drawn. The proportions of width and length of the ellipse are now defined by making small marks on opposite ends of the major and minor axes. These marks will serve as references as you sketch the actual lines of the ellipse [73].

To sketch an ellipse . . .
draw a line to represent the axle.

FIG. 71

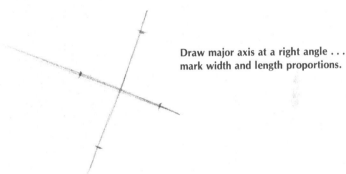

Draw major axis at a right angle . . .
mark width and length proportions.

FIG. 72

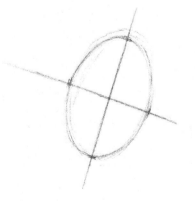

Sketch the ellipse through the marks on the axes.

FIG. 73

Let your arm move freely and rapidly as you sketch.

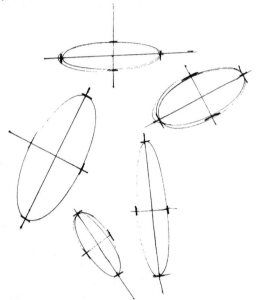

FIG. 74

Sketch a set of wheels on an axle that recedes into the distance.

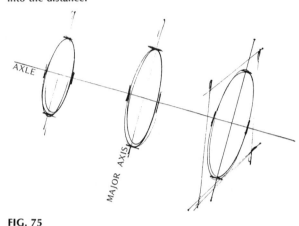

FIG. 75

The only successful way to sketch an ellipse is to let your arm do it for you—easily, naturally, and rapidly. Try it! Set up some construction lines as previously discussed, then loosen up and let your arm muscles work by themselves [74]. This will require some practice. As you sketch your ellipses, imagine that the marker is a racing car trying to get around the racetrack as fast as possible. Make a 'few imaginary passes with the point of the marker just above the paper. Let the point drop to the paper surface and make a few more passes. To save time, avoid turning the paper.

Exercise 10

First, practice sketching several ellipses of varying sizes and in various positions. Allow your arm to move easily, naturally, and rapidly. Next, sketch an axle that recedes into the distance to meet a horizon line. Mark six intervals along the axle. At each interval sketch an ellipse that would describe a wheel attached to the axle [75].

21. CYLINDERS IN PERSPECTIVE

When sketches are used to define the shape of objects, circles are frequently seen as the ends of cylinders. A cylinder may be hollow as in the case of a round tube, or it may be a solid shape. In the most common case of a cylinder, such as a beverage can, the circular end surfaces are perpendicular to the longitudinal centerline or *axis* of the cylinder. This axis, therefore, is the same as the "axle" of the end circles.

To sketch a solid cylinder lying on its side, establish as the first step the direction of the longitudinal edge lines as they converge toward a vanishing point on the horizon [76]. You can then sketch a centerline representing the axis of the cylinder and the axle for the end circles. Place it midway between the edge lines [77]. Mark on the axis the end points defining the length of the cylinder. Now you can sketch the long

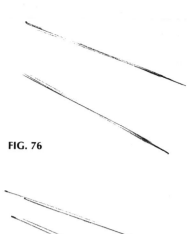

FIG. 76

Sketch the edge lines of the cylinder.

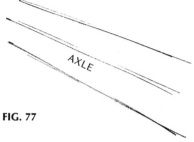

FIG. 77

The axis lies midway between the edge lines and forms the axle.

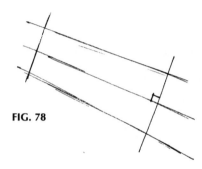

FIG. 78

Establish cylinder length and sketch the major axes perpendicular to the axle.

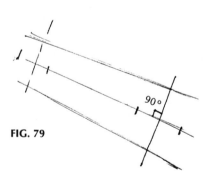

FIG. 79

Mark minor axis proportions.

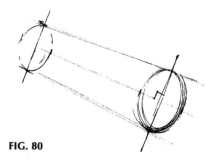

FIG. 80

Sketch end ellipses.

major axes of the end ellipses passing through the end points and perpendicular to the axis [78]. The minor axes coincide with the axle. Points are marked to establish their lengths relative to those of the major axes that are terminated by the cylinder's edge lines [79]. The proportions can be estimated by eye or by holding up a marker and sighting past it as described earlier. You are now ready to sketch the end ellipses tangent to the edge lines and passing through the major and minor axes points [80]. Darken in only the visible portion of the ellipse representing the far end of the cylinder.

Vertical cylinders have a vertical axis that also forms the axle for the end ellipses. If sketched in two-point perspective, the edge lines will be parallel, vertical lines. The major axes of the ellipses will be horizontal since they must be perpendicular to the vertical axle [81]. The minor ellipse axes are aligned with the axle.

Vertical cylinders with horizontal ends . . . the major axes of the ellipses are horizontal . . . the minor axes are vertical.

FIG. 81

As the far flap rises,
its right vanishing point rises . . .
the left does not change.

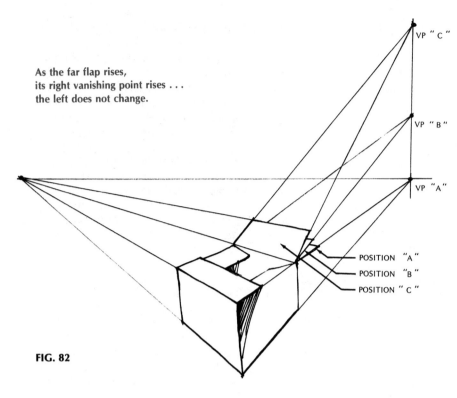

POSITION "A"
POSITION "B"
POSITION "C"

FIG. 82

22. INCLINED PLANES

Up to this time you have dealt with vanishing points that always lie on the horizon line. This is true for objects that are composed of vertical and horizontal surfaces. What happens in perspective when part of an object or a surface is positioned at an angle to the other elements of your sketch? Examples of this situation occur commonly—pitched roofs, cars parked on a hill, and so on.

Consider [82]. A common cardboard box rests on a flat surface with its two vanishing points located on the horizon line. The top flap farthest from you has been opened out flat. As this flap is lifted away from a horizontal position (parallel to the ground) into an angled position, the vanishing point to the right rises with it. The more erect the flap is, the **higher** the vanishing point is **above** the horizon line. These new vanishing points are directly **above** the original one. Note that the left vanishing point of the flap lines remains stationary.

In [83] the flap closest to you is raised from an open horizontal position. The right vanishing point will drop down **below** the original vanishing point. Again, the vanishing point to the left remains stationary.

Examine the sketch of a simple "houselike" structure [84]. The front

As the near flap rises,
its right vanishing point drops . . .
the left does not change.

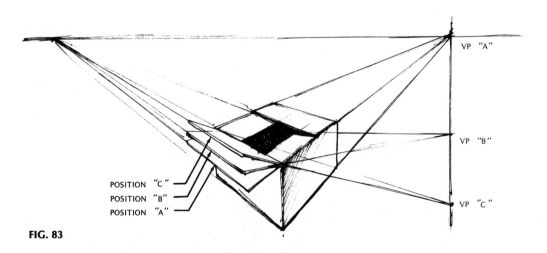

POSITION "C"
POSITION "B"
POSITION "A"

FIG. 83

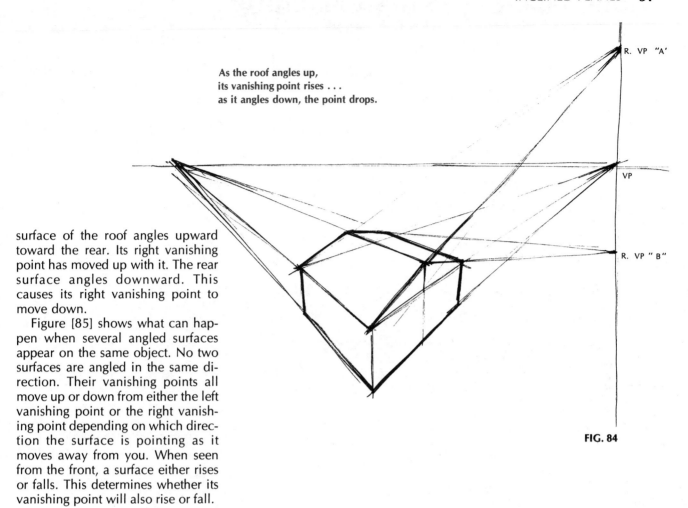

**As the roof angles up,
its vanishing point rises . . .
as it angles down, the point drops.**

R. VP "A'

VP

R. VP " B"

surface of the roof angles upward toward the rear. Its right vanishing point has moved up with it. The rear surface angles downward. This causes its right vanishing point to move down.

Figure [85] shows what can happen when several angled surfaces appear on the same object. No two surfaces are angled in the same direction. Their vanishing points all move up or down from either the left vanishing point or the right vanishing point depending on which direction the surface is pointing as it moves away from you. When seen from the front, a surface either rises or falls. This determines whether its vanishing point will also rise or fall.

FIG. 84

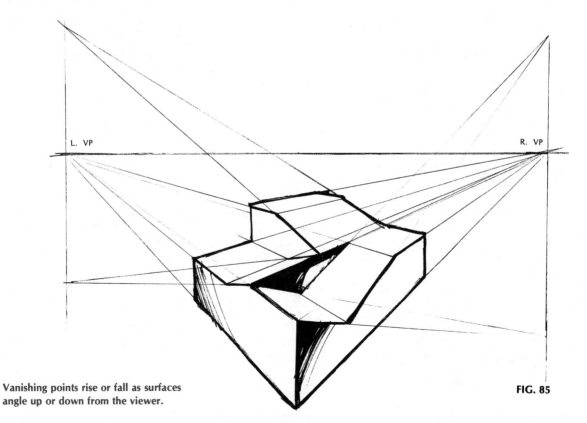

L. VP

R. VP

**Vanishing points rise or fall as surfaces
angle up or down from the viewer.**

FIG. 85

Additional Sketching Qualities

23. VALUE AND VALUE CONTRAST

There are several ways to imply space, depth, form, texture, and volume in sketching. Among these are the use of overlapping shapes, relative size, aerial positioning, atmospheric effects, and perspective. Another very effective illusion technique is the use of value. First, the term *value* must be understood. Value refers to how light or dark each surface of an object appears to a viewer. Surface colors have a relative lightness or darkness in relation to each other. Yellow, for example, appears much lighter than black, yet darker ("heavier" value) than white. On the other hand, the same tint of yellow may appear to be heavier or lighter under changing lighting conditions.

   Value contrast refers to the relation of two color areas to each other. A distinctly light color placed next to a very dark (heavy value) color produces **high** value contrast [86]. When two color areas similar in value are placed together, **low** value contrast is produced [87].

FIG. 86

High value contrasts . . .
light and heavy values adjacent.

Low value contrasts . . .
light values adjacent . . .

FIG. 87

. . . or heavy values adjacent.

Exercise 11

Make a ten-unit "value scale" study using a soft lead pencil or charcoal. First, lay out a rectangle 25 centimeters long and 3 centimeters (cm) wide. Subdivide this rectangle into ten smaller rectangles using very light lines. Each rectangle should measure approximately 2.5 × 3 cm. Leave the white of the paper in the top rectangle. Now make the bottom rectangle as dark as possible. Progressively darken each area in between by the same amount so that the value contrast between adjacent areas remains equal all along the scale [88]. Some people prefer to darken the rectangles separately, cut them out, correct where necessary, then paste them all together to make a total pattern. There is one caution: inserting visible lines to separate the areas will destroy the effectiveness of this exercise.

A value scale . . .
the value contrast
between each of the pairs
of shaded blocks is equal.

FIG. 88

24. LIGHT AND SHADE

In addition to representing color variations, value contrast is used to portray conditions of light and shade. These conditions are a part of life and daily experience. Looking at [89], you can easily see how adding value contrast to portray light and shade conditions improves the perception of the cylinder as a solid form.

In [89] you can see three basic value areas on the cylinder: (1) a lighted surface, (2) a shadow "core,"

Value contrast may portray light and shade to clarify forms.

REFLECTED LIGHT
SHADOW CORE
LIGHTED SURFACE

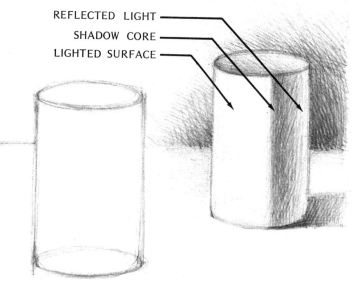

FIG. 89

and (3) a reflected light area. The lighted surface is always the lightest value tone, whereas the shadow core is always the darkest. The reflected light area lies somewhere in between. The shadow core is the area on an object where the lighted surface stops and the shaded area begins. It exists on both sides of the object. The shadow core is also the starting point for any shadow that is *cast* by the object onto an adjacent surface [90].

A great deal of what we see is lit by reflected light. Light can be compared to a ricocheting bullet [91]. Light that enables us to see an object has bounced off its surface. It will hit one surface, strike another, then be deflected again. This may occur several times. Each time, the light loses some intensity. Finally, it is absorbed almost completely in the last surface that it strikes.

The shaded areas of an object are visible only because of reflected light. A common error in sketching is the representation of shaded areas

and cast shadows as completely black, lightless areas. If this were true, everyone would continually be falling into holes they couldn't see or bumping into unseen walls. The surface lit directly by the light source is always the brightest area. In the reflected light area, light has bounced at least once or twice from the surfaces of other objects and has lost much of its illuminating quality.

Illuminating an object properly can create a good visual impression of the volume and space that an object occupies. The most descriptive lighting source is from above and to the side [92]. Light the object so that a distinct shadow core is visible on a side and some light is reflected onto the shaded surface from nearby objects or surfaces. The surfaces of a properly lighted cube are readily distinguishable. Notice that the top isn't lighter toward the front, as might be expected. The light that you see on this surface isn't received totally from the light source. It is partially reflected from a nearby surface.

The shadow cast on an adjacent surface starts at the shadow core.

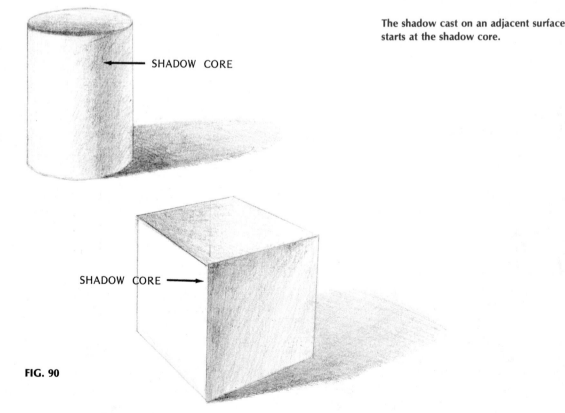

SHADOW CORE

SHADOW CORE

FIG. 90

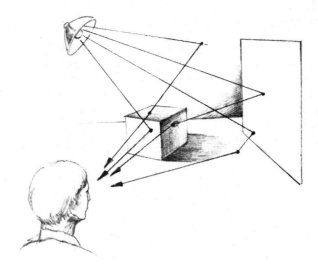

Reflecting light ricochets off surfaces like a bullet.

FIG. 91

Components of good lighting.

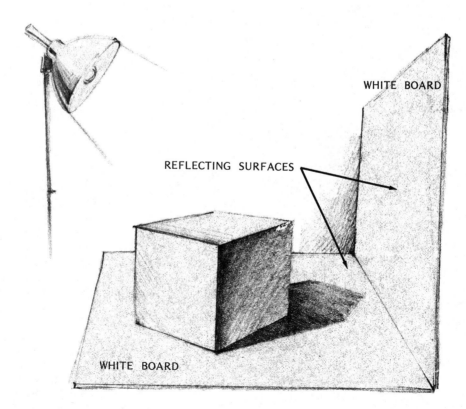

WHITE BOARD

REFLECTING SURFACES

WHITE BOARD

FIG. 92

Well-lighted shapes.

FIG. 93

Examples of geometric shapes and the way that they may be lighted effectively are shown in [93]. Figure [94] shows some examples of poor lighting of an object. Practice sketching directly from models in different real-life situations whenever you can. In [95] the various shapes are well defined by careful selection of the lighting direction.

Exercise 12

Obtain several objects such as a small 20 × 20 × 50 cm cardboard box, a beverage can, a paper cone, and a ball. Paint them flat white. Shine a light on each object as shown in [92]. Now sketch each object. To shade the darker areas with their full values, use charcoal as your marker. Use care to keep areas of contrast separate. Avoid smudging and an overall gray appearance. With experience you may switch to a soft pencil.

25. SHADOWS CAST BY OBJECTS

The sketching of shadows cast by objects needs understanding both in regard to value relationships and to perspective. A cast shadow indicated correctly adds immeasurably to the illusion of reality in a sketch and is well worth the effort required. An incorrectly drawn shadow, on the other hand, can do much to destroy the third dimension illusion that you are trying to establish. Remember that the objective of your sketch is to transfer your ideas to others by creating a sense of reality for them.

Poorly lighted shapes . . .
. . . lighting from the back.

. . . lighting from the front.

. . . side lighting with inadequate reflected light.

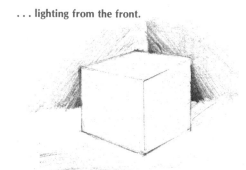

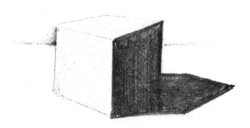

FIG. 94

Shapes are well defined by
carefully selecting
lighting direction.

FIG. 95

26. SHADOWS IN PERSPECTIVE CAST ON A HORIZONTAL SURFACE

The form of an object seems more complete with the addition of a cast shadow when sketching it. The shadow is formed because the object blocks direct light. Consider light rays approaching from a light source at the same level as the object, like sunlight in the early morning or late afternoon. When the light source is directly at the side of the object, the edges of the shadow are parallel to the picture plane and to the horizon. They do not vanish [96].

As the light source moves toward the front of the object, the edges of the shadow will vanish away from the light toward the horizon line [97]. Changing the light source to a point behind the object causes the edges of the shadow to vanish in the direction of the light toward the horizon line [98].

If the light source is raised over-head, the light will pass over the object and create an additional shadow edge line on the far side of the object. This shadow edge vanishes to the same vanishing point as the edge line of the object that produced it [99].

Combinations of several light sources and complexities in the shape of objects produce intricate shadow patterns. Experiment with sketching a variety of object shapes lighted by various light sources.

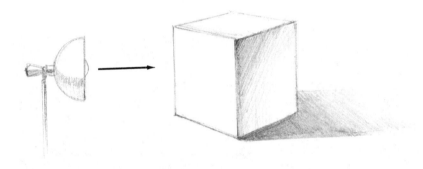

A light source on the same level as the object creates a shadow on the far side . . .
the shadow edges are parallel.

FIG. 96

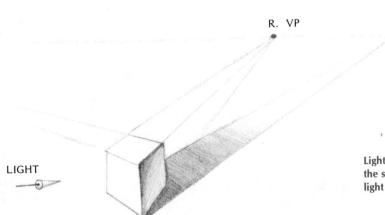

R. VP

LIGHT

Light source moved to the front . . .
the shadow edges converge away from the light to the horizon.

FIG. 97

Light source moved to the rear . . .
the shadow edges converge toward the
horizon in the direction of the light.

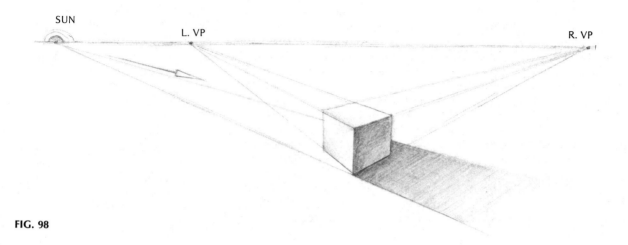

FIG. 98

Light source raised . . .
the shadow produced by a horizontal edge
vanishes to the same point as the edge itself.

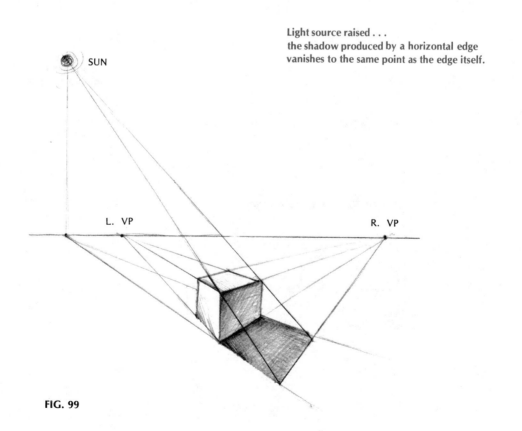

FIG. 99

27. VALUE RELATIONSHIPS FOR CAST SHADOWS

Value relationships are important within shadows as well as between the shadows and the surfaces on which they fall. Figure [100] illustrates typical cast shadows for a cube and a cylinder. Notice that the shadow is darker near the object and becomes lighter farther away. Although this is a simplification of what actually happens, it does illustrate the influence of reflected light on shadows. The lighter part of the shadow is caused by reflected light from nearby objects or surfaces bouncing back into it. More light is likely to be reflected into the more distant portion of the shadow because it is closer to the reflecting object. When a shadow changes its value from strong and dark close to

the object to lighter farther away, you may assume that there is a surface nearby that is reflecting light back into the shadow. The object itself also reflects light back into the shadow, causing areas of weakness in shadow intensity.

The sharpness of the shadow's edge lines varies with the quality of light that strikes the object. The softer the shadow's edges, the larger and more diffuse the light source [101]. The outer boundaries of the shadow also become less sharply defined as the shadow extends farther out from the object [102].

A large value contrast between a shadow and the lighted surface on which it falls indicates that the light source is very intense, such as might

occur on a bright summer day [103]. A small value contrast between the shadow and the surrounding lighted surface accompanied by a fuzzy shadow edge, suggests a subdued light, such as an overcast day [104]. Much can be inferred about an object and its surroundings by such seemingly subtle means. A sketch will be much more effective if the shadows are correctly drawn!

Exercise 13

Use the objects that were painted flat white in Exercise 12. Sketch each object, including shade and shadow, using a variety of light source types and placements to produce varying cast shadow patterns.

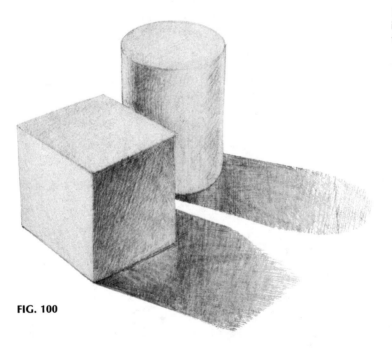

Reflected light is more evident in the portion of the shadow farthest from the object.

FIG. 100

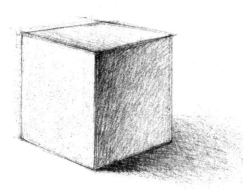

Soft shadows
are caused by large,
diffused light sources.

FIG. 101

Shadow boundaries
become less defined
as they extend farther
from the object.

FIG. 102

Strong light produces strong shadows.

FIG. 103

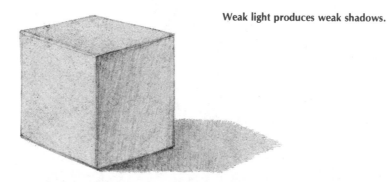

Weak light produces weak shadows.

FIG. 104

Space illusion is heightened by greater value contrast.

FIG. 105

28. SPACE ILLUSION USING VALUE CONTRAST

One of the most positive uses of value contrast is the creation of the illusion of depth, even of vast spaces. In nature your eye depends heavily on value contrast to identify depth. The more value contrast that is evident, the greater the illusion of space [105]. In sketching, value contrast is especially important in separating objects from other objects and their background. To achieve a visual perception of depth, it doesn't

Space illusion depends on value contrast . . .

FIG. 106

. . . not on the order of light and dark objects.

matter whether the closest or farthest object is darker or lighter [106].

The effects of atmospheric perspective can be used to provide the illlusion of deep space. Here the use of high value contrast will make the objects appear closer to the viewer. Low value contrast will push surfaces into the distance. Figure [107] illustrates this effect with a lightly shaded object nearby and a much darker object farther away. Beyond the second object several other objects appear to be posi-tioned farther and farther away. As they recede into the distance they grow closer together in value, ap-proaching a middle-tone value (that is, midway between white and black).

It may be difficult for you to mea-sure value. Try squinting your eyes when looking at an object. This temporarily blurs details and surface texture that tend to obscure the true values of the object and its surround-ings. Squinting helps you see con-trasts and patterns of values.

Exercise 14

(a) Select four simple objects of differing surface color. Sketch each object using a value of gray to represent the color.

(b) Arrange the objects in a pleasing group. Sketch the group controlling your perception of depth through the use of value contrast. Introduce background value and begin to use value changes instead of lines to de-fine edges.

Value contrast decreasing with distance provides the illusion of deep space.

FIG. 107

Developing Mental Images

29. RETENTION AND RECALL

Today's culture is vision based—over 80 percent of your knowledge is a direct result of your eyesight. The eye is an organ that transfers light rays reflected from objects into electric impulses to the brain [108]. There they are decoded into mental images. These impulses form images that are recognizable patterns of nature based strictly on what you can see. Real objects, however, possess many more properties that we cannot see. The eye does not discern odor, flavor, or temperature. The mind must rely on other sensory inputs for a more complete identification. Since your mind is so accustomed to *seeing* representations (images) of real objects sent to it by the eye, it can also be made to *see* representations of objects in your imagination—images that do not exist.

A physical phenomenon that can aid in development of visualization skill is the "after-image" effect. Stare at the center of the design in [109] for one minute. Close your eyes. The image will be retained by your eyes. This is an "after-image." It will soon disappear. Now try to recreate the image in your mind.

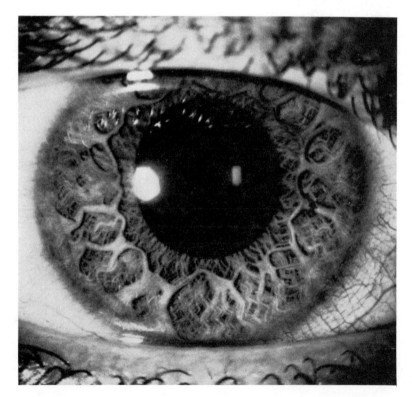

The eye is a masterful creation enabling you to perceive form, color, brightness, and motion.

FIG. 108

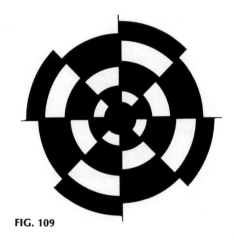

FIG. 109

Exercise 15

Go into a lighted room at night. Study the room arrangement. Turn out the lights. Your eyes will retain the image. Try to make your way to the other side of the room basing your movements on visual recall. Go to another room and try to picture in your mind the room you just left. Most people can recall the image of the first room. Some will recall color, others the number and type of objects. Some have difficulty in visualizing the exact spacing of objects.

30. IMAGINATION AND VISUALIZATION

Visualization is more than recall. It is also the ability to manufacture an image in your mind. It is the ability to develop an idea of what the other side of something looks like even though only one side is visible. Child psychologists point out that young children are not always aware that backs of objects exist. Through time and experience an adult learns that life is not like a movie set with false store fronts. Most things do possess the third dimension—depth.

Quite often an impression of the nonvisible side of an existing object is created in the mind. Surprise occurs when the actual appearance of that side is not the way you imagined it to be. The same phenomenon may occur when you ask directions to a desired location. As the instructions are given, your mind begins to wander down the described streets, finally arriving at a typical setting. You may be surprised later to find that the location is not at all like you envisioned it to be.

The ability to visualize, recall, or formulate an image is of extreme importance to you. The capability of

FIG. 110

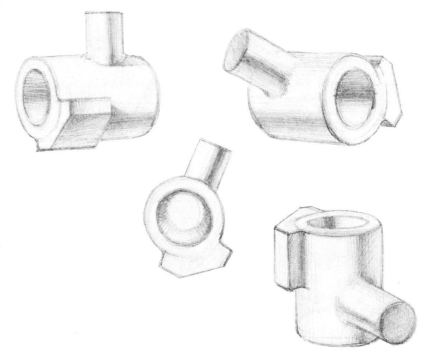

Visualize an object from several directions.

image development in your mind will help to solve many problems. You can develop a knack for image conception by studying everyday objects. Try to imagine what their hidden sides look like. Practice will rapidly develop this ability to "see through" an object. Also, it will increase your visual ability. The drawing process can be simplified by conceiving various views in one's mind before sketching an object or idea on paper [110].

Exercise 16

Try closing your eyes and remove all images from your mind. If this is difficult, try focusing on an imaginary black sheet. Concentrate on one of the sketching exercises that you have done. Try to make the image appear in your mind.

There is a direct correlation between the ability to visualize and the ability to sketch and draw quickly and effectively. Perceived images can be stored in your mind much like data are programmed into a computer. Based on the original collection and recording, your mind will interpret, coordinate, and respond with a visual image. More complete subject data will be transformed into more detailed mental pictures. Before television was developed, the mind necessarily formed visual images of radio drama characters. The ability to visualize was essential in order to empathize with the individuals in the story. Picture in your mind, for example, a sinister man carrying a cane. What image forms? What is his age? What kind of clothing is he wearing? Have you ever seen him before? What is the background setting? If you can answer any of these questions, your mind has recalled images from your reservoir of knowledge.

Retention and recall from the mind are not limited to experiences initiated by the visual sense. For example, you may already be able to recall the smell of lilacs, the sound of bacon sizzling, the pungent odor of sliced onion, or the feel of the smooth texture of velvet. It is only necessary that before recalling the sensation your mind must have been previously subjected to the real experience.

Input awareness can be strengthened by sketching a variety of objects. The sketching process requires careful attention to details. This eventually leads to a more complete understanding of the makeup of objects. Sketching leads to seeing, understanding, and recall of information concerning existing objects. In time, visualization of images that are created only in the imagination will come naturally.

Exercise 17

Close your eyes and try the following exercises:

(a)
1. Picture an object on a table.
2. Move away from the object.
3. Move toward the object.
4. Slowly walk around the object. Picture in your mind the back of the object.
5. Picture the back of the object differently from how you first imagined it to be.

6. Raise the object off the table.
7. Continue to raise the object until it is over your head.
8. Lower the object onto a turntable.
9. Rotate the object.
10. Increase the speed of rotation.
11. Make the object blur.
12. Imagine the object changing to a new and different object.
13. Stop. Go back through this exercise and sketch what you imagined at stages 1, 2, 3, 7, and 12.

(b) Picture yourself flying in a helicopter. It is speeding over a city, dodging the tops of tall buildings. What do you hear?

It begins to rain. The helicopter stops and hovers. The rain causes the helicopter to melt. You are suspended in space. You begin to fall in slow motion. You see a bird fly past.

The bird turns into a butterfly. You begin to tumble as you fall. Below you is a giant marshmallow sundae. The sundae cushions your fall. Now come back to reality.

Think back. Sketch some of the objects that you envisioned at the various stages of this exercise.

31. VISUALIZATION AIDS

One of the greatest challenges facing you is to understand completely the shape of the object that you want to sketch. If the real object is not available and you are unable to visualize it clearly in your mind, it may be necessary to construct a model. This may often be done very simply and quickly using clay, wood, or cardboard. Models are especially helpful in sketching complex features that are difficult to visualize. They are also helpful in clarifying the relationship between objects.

Sketching leads to increased visual sensitivity. This, in turn, will increase your ability to develop mental images. It will make all objects more understandable. The full development of this visualization skill can only be attained by continual practice, using written material and illustrations as guidelines.

Using a proven system based on understanding line, shape, form, and space illusions, you can communicate in a visual language and bring realism to a sketch. The illusion of realism will not only permit a better understanding of an idea by the sketcher but will also simplify the communication of that idea to others. The value of sketching as a communications tool will become apparent as the material is absorbed and practiced, and confidence is gained.

Technical illustrators must be accomplished in making freehand sketches. Mastering the fundamentals discussed in the next sections of this text will enable you to grasp quickly the specific techniques and procedures used by professional technical illustrators that are described in the later sections.

Technical Illustration

Technical illustrations became an important training aid in World War II.

FIG. 111

32. INTRODUCTION

Technical illustration became a large and complicated educational pursuit during World War II. For the first time, highly technical systems and machines were used by individuals who were not previously trained in their use and maintenance. In the air corps alone, the number of pilots, ground maintenance personnel, and planes of different types expanded to many times their prewar numbers [111]. The pilots and ground crews were made up largely of people who had demonstrated a measured aptitude for aviation but likely had never flown a plane or tuned an engine, let alone performed critical combat maintenance.

The aircraft used by the United States at that time were fairly complex pieces of machinery even by today's standards. Also, the engineering data and training manuals were too complicated and took too long to read. How could the number of technical personnel necessary to staff the U. S. Air Corps be rapidly trained?

The various armed services who were confronted with this "speeded-up" educational need conceived the idea of simplifying the complicated engineering and technical drawings and publishing them in a pictorial form in pilot's manuals and in overhaul and maintenance manuals. Each complicated operation was reduced to a series of simplified steps. Each step was profusely illustrated with drawings and photographs using much the same format as the comic books that were so widely popular at the time [112]. This idea was a resounding success! In fact, technical illustrations that show the proper use, maintenance, and care of almost anything imaginable exist today in both the armed services and the civilian marketplace.

Today technical illustrators work in hundreds of scientific and industrial applications such as aeronautics, astronautics, shipbuilding, automobiles, nucleonics, medicine,

Complicated operations were made simple with drawings.

FIG. 112

Modern manufactured products frequently require assembly instructions.

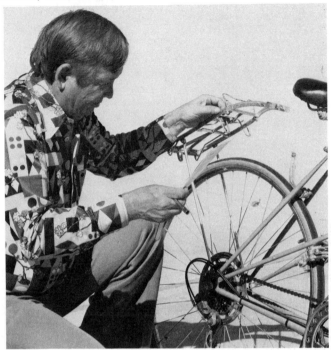

FIG. 113

and electronics. Although these illustrators work in widely separated fields of interest, their basic job remains the same—to reduce complicated technical data to a series of illustrations and notes that enables someone without much technical training to understand and perform complex operations as though they were routine.

Many manufactured products, from stereo components to tricycles, are delivered with some of the assembly work left for the buyer to do. How well or how badly that final assembly is done is usually a measure of how well or how badly the technical instructions were planned and illustrated [113]. Do-it-yourself books and manuals on every conceivable subject from bricklaying to weaving crowd the bookstore shelves. All are profusely illustrated in step-by-step increments.

Automobile maintenance manuals run to hundreds of pages with two or three illustrations per page [114]. Aircraft maintenance manuals are infinitely more complicated. The maintenance manuals for the Boeing 747 jetliner are said to occupy a 14 foot bookshelf and are revised every 90 days. Manufacturers of all types of equipment produce catalogs where parts in exploded assemblies are identified by "keyed" illustrations.

Automotive maintenance manuals require many illustrations.

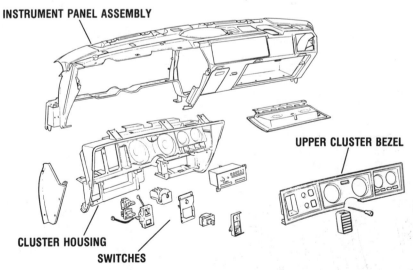

INSTRUMENT PANEL ASSEMBLY

UPPER CLUSTER BEZEL

CLUSTER HOUSING

SWITCHES

INSTRUMENT CLUSTER — INTERMEDIATE CAR

FIG. 114

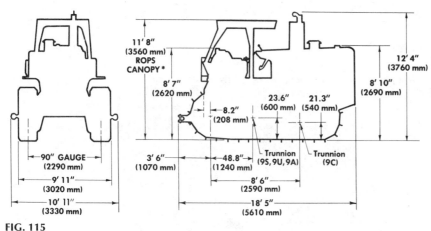

FIG. 115

Some technical illustrations are very simple line drawings providing only basic overall dimensions for a piece of machinery [115]. Others enlarge small details in a series of views to show maintenance and assembly information [116]. Still others get into very complicated detail to show the inner workings of a manufactured product [117].

The twentieth century technological explosion and the expanded everyday use of complicated equipment in every field has made technical illustration an important tool for the successful application of technology.

33. THE TECHNICAL ILLUSTRATOR

In order to become a technical illustrator, a drafter must know some related fields and techniques. Since a technical illustrator's main job is to translate technical data for nontechnical people, the illustrator must understand the technical language used in the original materials [118]. In most cases, this means that an illustrator's ability to read production drawings must be at least equal to the ability required to assemble the parts described. If, in addition, the illustrator understands the functions of the product, the illustrations will be much more effective.

Frequently, technical illustrators are asked to create one or more illustrations of a "design concept" when no specific information, let alone production drawings, exists. The success of this type of assignment depends entirely on how well the illustrator and the engineer/designer communicate and how complete the illustrator's knowledge and understanding of similar designs is.

Engineering drawings will frequently contain surface finish or other machining instructions in a series of notes. These instructions usually are not reflected in the drawing itself, but they will affect the appearance or shape of the finished article. The illustrator should have a good working knowledge of the various machining processes to interpret these notes on the drawing.

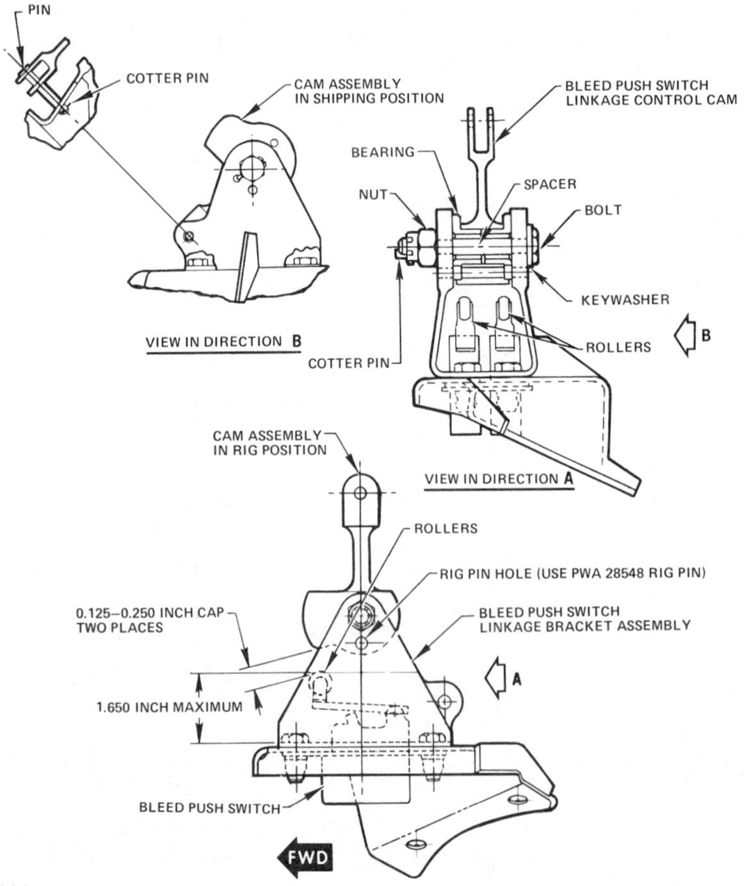

FIG. 116

FIG. 117

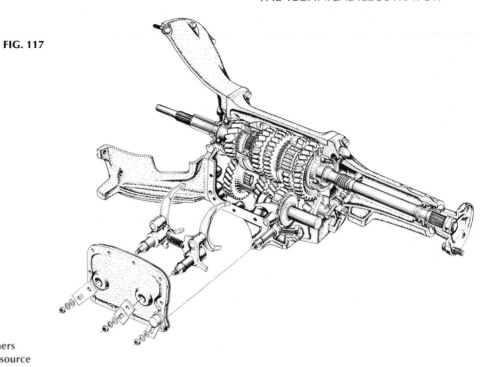

Simplifying technical data for others
requires an understanding of the source
material.

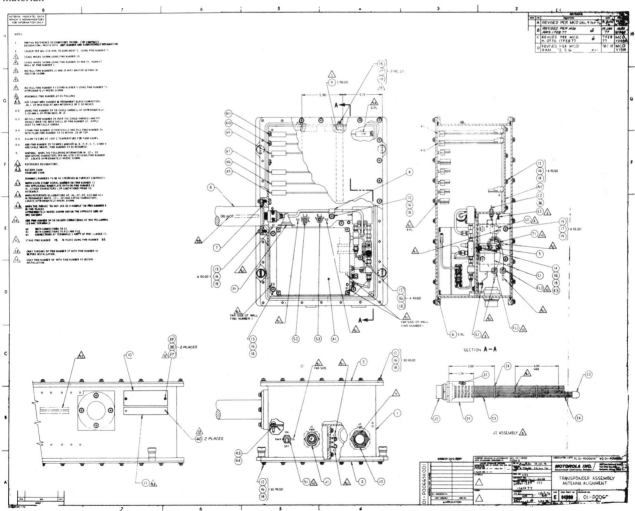

FIG. 118

Pictorial drawings clarify assembly instructions.

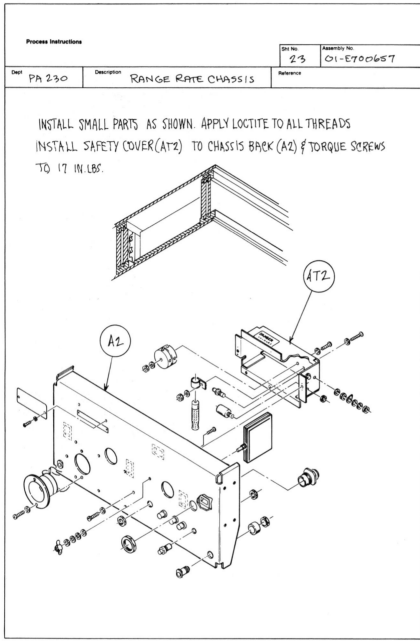

Process Instructions		Sht No.	Assembly No.
		23	01-E700657
Dept PA 230	Description RANGE RATE CHASSIS	Reference	

INSTALL SMALL PARTS AS SHOWN. APPLY LOCTITE TO ALL THREADS
INSTALL SAFETY COVER (AT2) TO CHASSIS BACK (A2) & TORQUE SCREWS
TO 17 IN. LBS.

AT2

A2

FIG. 119

appropriate scales.

In some advanced applications of technical illustration, abstract and near-abstract subjects such as antenna emission patterns, fluid disturbances, electronic signal characteristics, and geological profiles must be described [120]. The illustrator is usually given only a numerical listing of the parameters of the subject to make such a drawing. In this situation, the illustrator is not able to "visualize" the end result as is the case when starting with a set of production drawings. Instead, a good working knowledge of descriptive geometry techniques is required to plot the various contours of the subject.

Technical illustrations also clarify abstract scientific concepts.

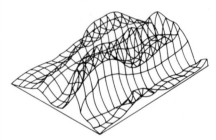

FIG. 120

In addition to technical knowledge, a technical illustrator should have a certain amount of artistic ability. The illustrator who has a sense of balance and proportion will be able to make layouts of parts or groups of parts that are pleasing to the eye. In addition, the functions and relationships of the parts will be better established so that they are easy to understand. Like the artist, the illustrator should be a good observer of real life. This will help in visualizing how light from different directions interacts with objects to emphasize certain features and produce shade and shadows. For some types of illustrations, the artist's knowledge of color and its effective use is also very valuable. The best technical illustrations use a blend of technical and artistic skills to transmit information quickly and clearly. For an illustration like [121] where an unknown

Nearly all technical illustrations are drawn to scale. This is especially true when the illustrations must guide the assembly of an object by workers or customers who cannot read engineering drawings. They must rely on three-dimensional pictorial drawings to understand where each part must be inserted and which piece matches which assembly [119]. Although an illustration need not be drawn as accurately as a production drawing, the scale of the illustration does indicate the relative size and fit of the various parts. In order to interpret technical drawings properly, illustrators must have sufficient mathematical understanding to work with all forms of dimensioning and tolerancing and be able to translate this information into

Some technical illustrations require an
artist's creative skills.

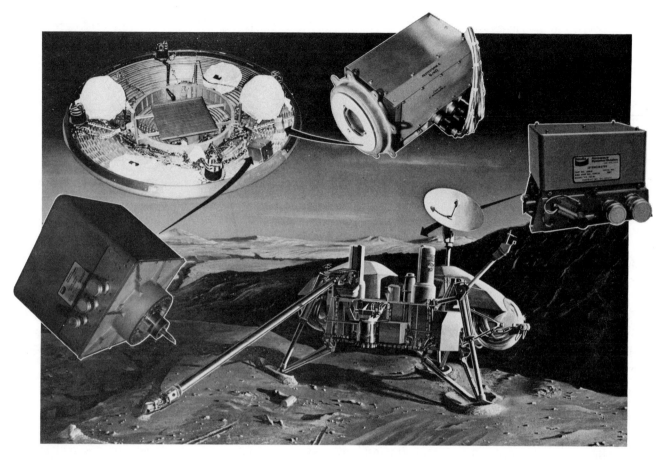

FIG. 121

environment must be portrayed, the
creative skills of an artist are a must.

Finally, a successful illustrator is
familiar with the graphic reproduction methods that are used to copy
drawings. The illustrator knows such
things as when a line is too thin to
remain intact after a camera reduction, when two lines are so close together that they will appear to merge
on a printing plate, and when pencil
lines are so light that a readable blue-
line print cannot be made.

Although practical, basic, and
useful, the information contained in
this book is only a beginning to developing proficiency in the field of
technical illustration. Reaching the
professional level requires a great deal

of training and practice beyond this
basic information. The total effort is
worthwhile, however, because technical illustration is a fascinating and
well-paid profession that is guaran-
teed to be in great demand as long as
technology continues to grow.

34. DRAWING SYSTEMS

Over the years several drawing
systems have evolved that are used
almost universally by technical illustrators. These are **axonometric, perspective,** and **oblique.** All of these
systems are designed to show the three
dimensions of space—width, height,
and depth—in one view [122]. Since
a single view of this type gives a rel-

Pictorial drawings are used for technical
illustration . . . they show all three
dimensions of space.

FIG. 122

atively complete picture of an object, the drawings produced are known as *pictorial* drawings. This is in contrast to the *multiview* drawing system that is commonly used for production drawings [123]. In the latter system, each view shows only two dimensions of space. A front view in a multiview drawing, for example, fails to show any depth; therefore, it is an incomplete description by itself. One or more additional views are needed to complete the description.

Pictorial drawing systems (as well as drawings made in the multiview system) are based on the assumption that the drawn image is a recording of what our eyes see when looking at an object in space. The image that is drawn is considered to be the one that is projected onto a transparent *viewing plane* by the *lines of sight* passing between the observer's eyes and the object. The various drawing systems differ in the theoretical relationship between the observer, the lines of sight, the viewing plane, and the object. Let us look at each of these systems.

(1) The Multiview System. In the *multiview* system, the lines of sight are parallel to each other and perpendicular to the viewing plane [124]. The viewing plane can be placed at any location relative to a stationary

Multiview drawings are used for production . . . each view shows only two dimensions of space.

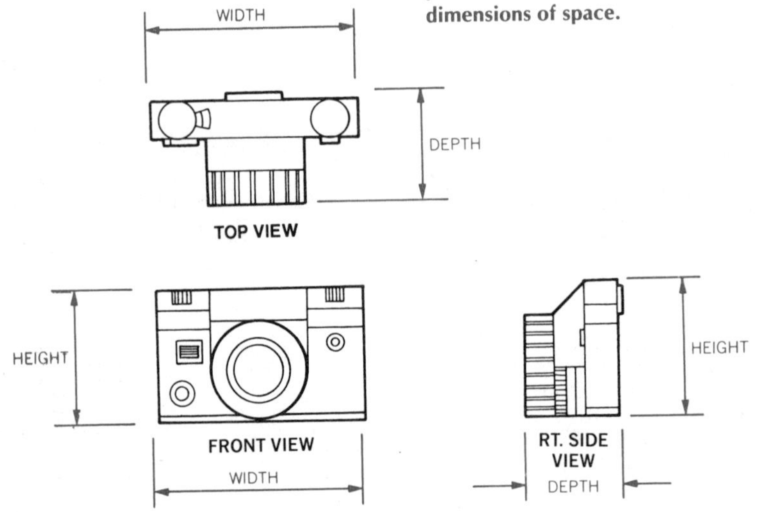

WIDTH

DEPTH

TOP VIEW

HEIGHT

FRONT VIEW
WIDTH

HEIGHT

RT. SIDE VIEW
DEPTH

FIG. 123

object so that a view from that direction can be projected onto the viewing plane and drawn. The most commonly drawn views in the multiview system are those known as *principal* views [125]. These views are obtained by placing viewing planes parallel to the six principal faces of the object—the front, top, right and left sides, back, and bottom. The resulting views are aligned in a standard pattern on the drawing so that a viewer will know immediately the relationship of the views to the object. In the multiview system, the viewing plane shows a true, undistorted image of the shape and size of the face to which it is parallel. This feature makes multiview drawings valuable in making design and production drawings.

(2) The Axonometric System. In *axonometric,* the first of the *pictorial* drawing systems that we will discuss, the lines of sight are parallel to each other and perpendicular to the viewing plane just as in the multiview system. The difference lies in the relationship between the viewing plane and the object. In the multiview system, the object was considered to be stationary, and the viewing plane was moved around the object to vary the viewing direction. In axonometric drawing the viewing plane is stationary in a "front" viewing position. The object is then rotated and tilted from its normal "use" position until three principal faces can be seen through the viewing plane [126]. Since each of these faces will be at an angle with the viewing plane, the object's shape and size will be distorted more or less depending on the size of the angle. Any disadvantages from the distortion are far out-

Multiview drawing . . . the lines of sight are parallel to each other and perpendicular to the viewing plane.

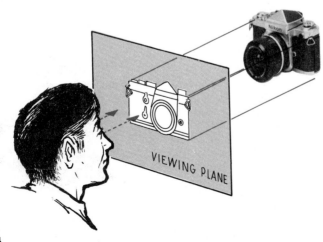

VIEWING PLANE

FIG. 124

Principal views . . . viewing planes are placed parallel to the principal faces of the object.

TOP VIEW

REAR VIEW   LEFT SIDE
                   VIEW   FRONT VIEW   RT. SIDE
                                                    VIEW

BOTTOM VIEW

FIG. 125

Axonometric drawing . . . the lines of sight are parallel to each other and perpendicular to the viewing plane . . . the object is at an angle with the viewing plane.

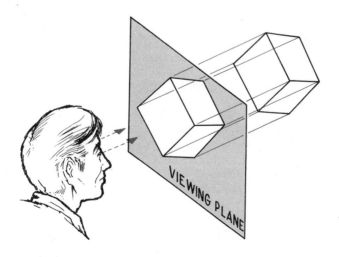

VIEWING PLANE

FIG. 126

Perspective drawing . . . the lines of sight
are not parallel . . . they converge in the
distance.

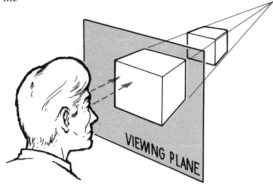

FIG. 127

weighed by the advantages of being able to "picture" the entire object in one three-dimensional view for general descriptive purposes.

(3) The Perspective System. In ***perspective,*** the second ***pictorial*** drawing system, the lines of sight are not parallel. Instead, they converge to a vanishing point or points in the distance in the same way that your eyes actually see an object [127]. In perspective, the object is usually fixed in its normal "use" position, and the observer's lines of sight are directed through a viewing plane placed at a specific angle with the object to see more than one face in a single view.

The converging lines of sight in perspective distort the shapes of the faces more than in the axonometric system, but the overall appearance of the object is more realistic because it closely approximates the way your eyes normally see the object. Axonometric and perspective views look very similar except for the convergence of the parallel object lines in perspective. Since an axonometric view is easier to draw than a perspective view, the axonometric system is more popular for technical illustrations unless exceptional realism is required.

(4) The Oblique System. The last of the three ***pictorial*** drawing systems is ***oblique.*** This is the least frequently used system for technical illustration because it provides the least amount of realism. In the oblique system, the viewing plane is stationary in a po-

sition parallel to one principal face of the object. The lines of sight are parallel to each other but are directed at an angle with the viewing plane [128]. This permits three principal faces of the object to be seen in one view. The face that is parallel to the viewing plane appears undistorted. The other two faces are distorted in shape and size depending on the angle between the lines of sight and the viewing plane. This lack of distortion of one face is the primary advantage of the oblique system. The true appearance of one face saves time in illustrating an object that has complex contours on one face.

As you look closely at each of the three pictorial drawing systems in the following sections, you will gain a better understanding of their differences and how this affects their suitability for technical illustration purposes. You will also find that there are several important subsystems within each drawing system. Axonometric drawings are classified as ***isometric, dimetric,*** or ***trimetric*** depending on the angles established between the object and the viewing plane. Perspective drawings are classified as ***one-point, two-point,*** or ***three-point*** perspective according to the number of vanishing points to which the lines of sight converge.

35. STANDARDIZED DRAWING PROCEDURES

Since technical illustration basically involves making a one-view

Oblique drawing . . . the lines of sight are parallel to each other . . . but at an angle with the viewing plane.

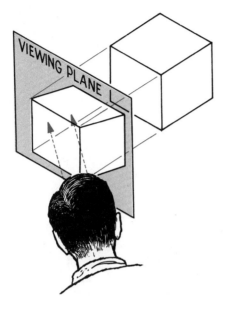

FIG. 128

"picture" of an object showing all three dimensions of space, it would seem that any picture-making procedure, such as an artist might use, would do the job. There are very sound reasons, however, why standard drawing systems are regularly used by technical illustrators. For one thing, if the industrial community had to depend only on that relatively small group of people who have a natural artistic ability for sketching and drawing objects accurately by just looking at them, the demand for illustrators would always far exceed the supply. By using a standard drawing system, such as axonometric, that has simple, methodical procedures, a much larger segment of the work force can be taught to produce high quality illustrations that are both technically accurate and attractive.

Another advantage in using standardized drawing procedures for technical illustration occurs when an entire group of illustrators works on a large project. In this situation, it is not always possible to have a drawing revised or even finished by the individual who started it. When a drawing is made according to one of the standard systems, any other competent illustrator can pick it up and add, modify, or delete areas without having to match another person's unique artistic style or technique.

36. TECHNICAL ILLUSTRATION PRACTICE

In pictorial drawing, there is a significant body of theoretical knowledge and practice that has been accumulated over the years on how to make drawings in any of the systems. Originally many of the pictorial drawing systems depended on first making an accurate multiview drawing of the object. The technical illustrator then used special techniques to transform these views into the required pictorial view. For industry, these classic methods are too cumbersome and time consuming to be cost effective. Time is usually the most prominent factor in controlling illustration costs. The method of transforming multiview drawings also increases the possibility for errors and inaccuracies.

In place of the slower transformation methods, most technical illustrations are now drawn directly [129]. To speed up this process and to make pictorial drawing easier, a large number of drawing aids are also commercially available or are easily constructed. These aids include specialized templates, scales, grids, charts, and even customized drawing boards. Some of these will be pointed out in the sections describing the various drawing systems. Others will be described in Section 68—Special Drawing Tools.

The following sections describe principally the modern, time-saving methods most used in professional practice. Only enough theory is provided to understand the principles of the various drawing systems. In cases where there is a choice of illustration method or drawing equipment, the simpler and less expensive method will be fully explained. The more complicated alternative will be described less extensively.

A technical illustrator at work.

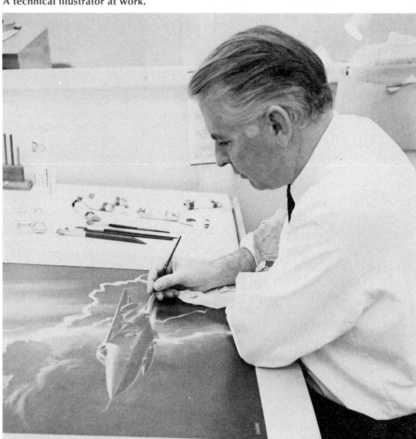

FIG. 129

Axonometric Drawing

37. BASIC PRINCIPLES OF AXONOMETRIC DRAWING

Axonometric drawing is a method of **directly** producing a three-dimensional pictorial view of an object. This contrasts with multiview drawing where one or more auxiliary or revolved views are needed to produce this type of view. The finished view is exactly the same in both systems— only the location and orientation on the drawing sheet is changed. By creating the desired three-dimensional view directly, you can orient and locate the view in the exact position desired.

In both multiview and axonometric drawing sytems, the lines of sight are parallel to each other and perpendicular to the viewing plane. The view location and orientation differ in the two systems because, in multiview drawing, the object is held sta-

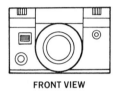
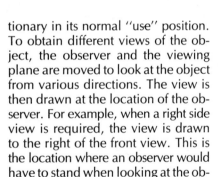

FRONT VIEW

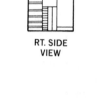

RT. SIDE VIEW

FIG. 130

tionary in its normal "use" position. To obtain different views of the object, the observer and the viewing plane are moved to look at the object from various directions. The view is then drawn at the location of the observer. For example, when a right side view is required, the view is drawn to the right of the front view. This is the location where an observer would have to stand when looking at the object from the right. Similarly, when a

view is required looking at the object from an angle other than directly from the right, the view is drawn at the angle and location where an observer would have to stand to see this view.

Figure [130] shows the front view of a 35mm camera and a right side view that has been drawn to the right of the front view. To see more than one face of the camera in a single view, select an angled viewing direc-

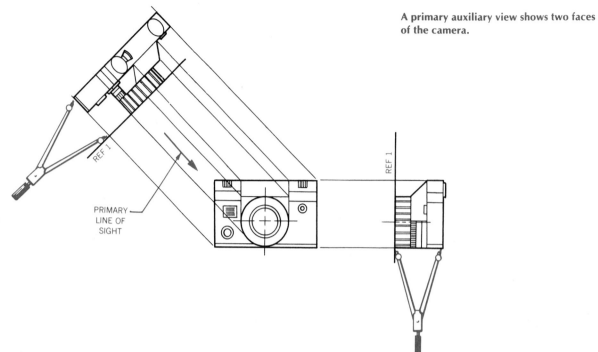

A primary auxiliary view shows two faces of the camera.

FIG. 131

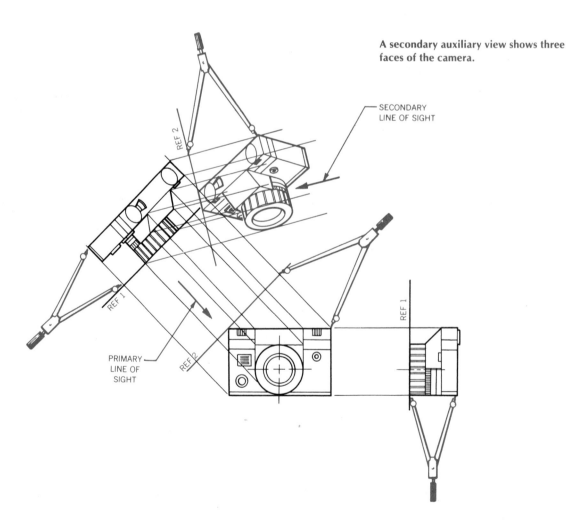

A secondary auxiliary view shows three faces of the camera.

FIG. 132

tion and project an *auxiliary* view into this location. Figure [131] shows a primary auxiliary view looking at the camera from the upper left. The top and left sides of the camera are visible in this view.

In [132] a secondary auxiliary view has been projected from the primary auxiliary to show the front, top, and right faces. This view is positioned in the location where an observer would have to stand to see these faces. Although these auxiliary views provide good "pictorial" descriptions of the camera, their locations are not convenient and their orientations are not realistic if used by themselves. Establishing the correct viewing directions to obtain the exact auxiliary view required may also prove difficult and time consuming.

The same three-dimensional view of the camera as seen in the secondary auxiliary view can be drawn directly using the axonometric drawing system. To do this, hold the viewing plane stationary in the "front" viewing position and rotate and tilt the camera from its normal "use" position in space. If you want to see the front, top, and right faces, first rotate the camera about a vertical axis to show the front and right side [133].

Tilt the camera forward to see the top surface also.

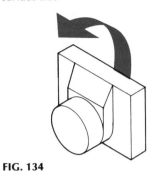

FIG. 134

38. AXONOMETRIC DRAWING PROCEDURES

To understand how the axonometric drawing system can be used to lay out a pictorial view of an object directly, first observe what happens to the basic width, height, and depth measurements as the pictorial view is formed. As the camera is rotated about a vertical axis from its front view position, the true height is retained but the width is visually shortened [135]. This phenomenon, called *foreshortening,* occurs because the lines of the object along which width might be measured are no longer parallel to the viewing plane.

The more the front face is rotated away from the viewing plane, the shorter the width will appear. The result is that in axonometric drawing only those lines of the object that are parallel to the viewing plane can be drawn in their true size. All other dimensions must be reduced in size by using an appropriate scale. Note that the depth measurement of the camera did not show at all in the true front view [130]. As the camera is rotated to show both the front and right faces, the depth becomes visible [135]. This depth measurement, however, is foreshortened because it is at an angle with the viewing plane. If the front face and the right face are at the same angle with the viewing plane, the same reducing scale can be used for both width and depth directions. When the front face is at a smaller angle with the viewing plane, it will have less distortion than the right face, and the width scale will not be reduced as much as the depth scale, or vice versa.

In the simple single-axis rotation just described, the height measurement remained true because it stayed parallel to the viewing plane. If the rotated object is tilted forward about a horizontal axis so that the top surface is visible, the visual height is

To obtain an axonometric view . . . rotate the camera about a vertical axis to see the front and right side.

FIG. 133

Then tilt the camera forward about a horizontal axis so that you can also see the top surface [134]. Since this view is exactly the same as the auxiliary view previously drawn, it is apparent that axonometric drawing correctly retains all of the basic geometric characteristics of the object. Parallel lines, for example, always appear parallel in both multiview and axonometric drawing systems.

When rotating, true height is retained . . . width is foreshortened . . . the foreshortened depth comes into view.

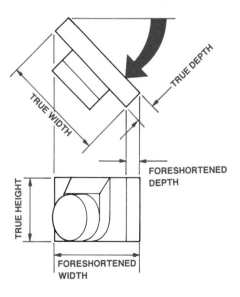

FIG. 135

foreshortened since it is no longer parallel to the viewing plane [136]. To see more of the top, the camera would have to be tilted at a greater angle with the horizontal. This increases the angle of the height measurement with the viewing plane and causes additional foreshortening. Note that tilting the camera also changes the angles between the width and depth measurements and the viewing plane, thereby requiring new scales for these values.

39. TYPES OF AXONOMETRIC DRAWINGS

From the foregoing discussion, you should have learned that reducing scales required in the width, height, and depth directions are dependent upon the angle between each of these directions and the viewing plane. If the three angles are equal, then the reducing scales for each direction will be identical. The type of axonometric view produced in this situation is called an *isometric* view [137]. The prefix "iso," meaning equal, indicates that equal measurements are made in all three basic directions.

A second type of axonometric drawing is called *dimetric.* The prefix "di" indicates that two of the basic measuring directions are at the same angle with the viewing plane [138]. Two reducing scales are required—one scale for two of the directions and a separate scale for the third. In [138] the width and depth measuring directions are at the same angle with the viewing plane and use the same scale. The height direction is at a different angle and, therefore, requires a different scale.

Trimetric is the third type of axonometric drawing [139]. The "tri" prefix indicates that three different reducing scales are required because the angles with the viewing plane are different for each of the three basic measuring directions.

In the following sections, you will find out how to lay out the three types of axonometric drawings. In each case, you must first establish the direction of the width, height, and depth. Then you must select or construct corresponding reducing scales.

When tilted forward, height is also foreshortened.

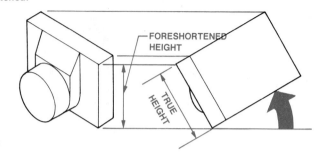

FIG. 136

Isometric . . . width, height, and depth are foreshortened equally . . . only one scale is required.

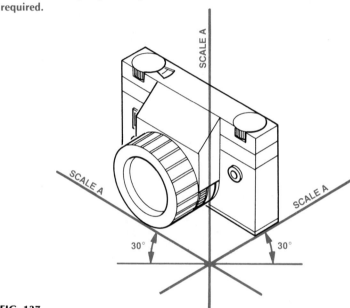

FIG. 137

Dimetric . . . width and depth are foreshortened equally . . . height is different . . . two scales are required.

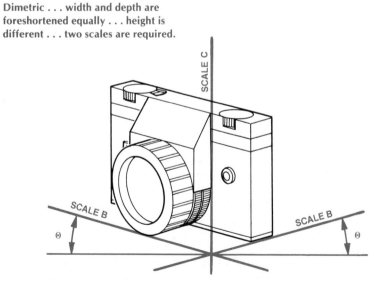

FIG. 138

Trimetric . . . width, height, and depth are foreshortened different amounts . . . three scales are required.

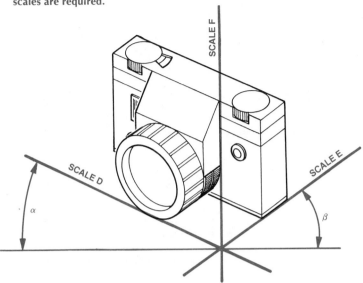

FIG. 139

The actual drawing procedures for all three types are basically the same. The more angles and reducing scales you work with, the more difficult the work becomes.

Isometric is the simplest type of axonometric drawing to use and is very satisfactory for many technical illustrations. The only drawback in using it is that one face cannot be emphasized more than another. Since the three principal faces of an object are positioned at the same angle with the viewing plane, they are all equally visible. Trimetric is the most versatile type of axonometric drawing since there is nearly complete freedom of viewing direction. The object may be rotated and tilted at almost any angle. This also makes trimetric the most difficult to draw. Dimetric represents a very popular compromise between isometric and trimetric for most illustrators. Viewing direction is sufficiently versatile, while layout is still relatively easy.

Probably the most important skill an illustrator can have is the ability to visualize how an object will look as it is viewed from different directions. In most cases, the actual object will not be available to look at while drawing. Production drawings will usually be available. The illustrator must, therefore, understand multiview drawing to be able to read the production drawings used to manufacture the object. With this skill, the technical illustrator can more easily and correctly visualize the object in space. Some knowledge of the various types of manufacturing processes and the shapes that they produce is also very helpful.

40. ISOMETRIC DRAWING

Isometric drawing is the simplest form of axonometric drawing because measurements along all three basic measuring directions are foreshortened equally. To determine the amount of foreshortening, you must find out how much rotation and tilt is needed to make equal angles between the measuring directions and the viewing plane. This is best done by studying a cube where width, height, and depth are all equal.

Looking directly down the diagonal of a cube will provide you with a view showing all three basic measurements equally shortened. To arrive at this position, first rotate the cube 45° about a vertical axis so that

the width and depth measurements are visually shortened the same amount [140]. Then tilt the cube forward about a horizontal axis, exposing its top surface, until the diagonal appears as a point [141]. The three axes of the cube appear at equal angles with each other, and all three axes are at the same angle with the viewing plane. You can check that all three basic measurements are equal in this position by using dividers to compare the length of the edges of the cube.

To form an isometric view . . . rotate cube 45° about a vertical axis   . . . width and depth are foreshortened equally.

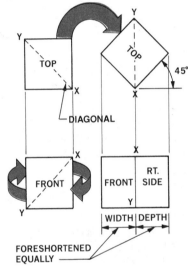

FIG. 140

Tilt cube forward about a horizontal axis until diagonal appears as a point . . . width, height, and depth are foreshortened equally.

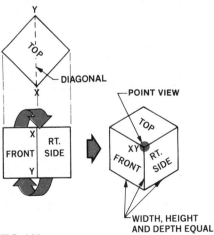

FIG. 141

With the cube in the isometric position, you can now measure the angle at which the width and depth directions will appear in an isometric drawing. This turns out to be a very convenient 30° angle [142]. The angle through which the cube has been tilted is 35° 16'. This is also the angle between the height-measuring direction and the viewing plane. You can use a foreshortened scale made for this direction for the other two basic measuring directions as well, since all three directions are distorted equally.

angle. The length of the isometric scale is about 82 percent of the true length since the cosine of 35° 16' is approximately 0.82.

In constructing any scale, be sure to make accurate projections from your regular scale, keeping all projection lines perfectly parallel. Any inaccuracies will multiply and create distortions in your drawings. Many illustrators scribe isometric scales onto the three edges of a plastic 30°–60° triangle [144]. Usually the finer subdivisions are marked only on the end units of each scale. The divisions must

Isometric scales may be scribed on a 30°–60° triangle for convenience.

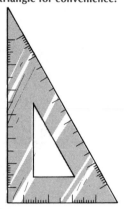

FIG. 144

Width and depth axes appear at 30° with the horizontal in isometric . . . the cube has been tilted 35° 16'.

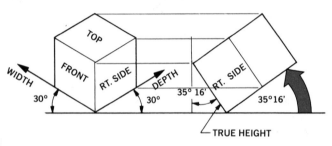

FIG. 142

A simple method of constructing a foreshortened scale is shown in [143]. The graduations are transferred by a series of parallel projection lines from a regular scale positioned at a 35° 16'

be carefully scribed into the triangle with a sharp pointed tool. Then they can be filled in with black drawing ink and the excess ink wiped away.

What units and subdivisions you

use on your scales depends on how the production drawings you will be using have been dimensioned. Isometric scales can also be purchased. The majority of production drawings in the United States are made using decimally divided engineering scales that have principal division marks at every inch or every 10 millimeters. Dimensions on production drawings are normally stated in decimals with decimal tolerances so that accurate relationships can be established between mating parts.

41. DRAWING AN ISOMETRIC VIEW

The first step in making any axonometric drawing is to lay out the width, height, and depth measuring directions through a common point. These three lines are referred to as *axis lines.* The point where they intersect is called the *origin* of the axis system. The axis lines are also commonly referred to as the *X-, Y-, and Z-axes.* For isometric drawing, use either a drafting machine set at 30° or a 30°–60° triangle placed on a parallel rule or a T-square. Draw a 30° line upward to the left and another one 30° upward to the right [145]. Now draw a vertical line through the point where the first two lines intersect. These width, depth, and height axis lines will form the basis for plotting the contours of whatever object you choose.

As an example, let us make an isometric drawing showing the front, top, and right side of a simple rectangular

Project parallel lines from a regular scale to create an isometric scale.

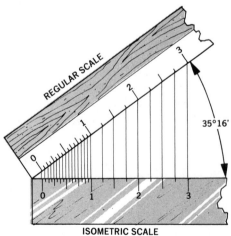

FIG. 143

Starting an isometric view . . . draw 30° lines for width and depth axes . . . draw a vertical line for the height axis.

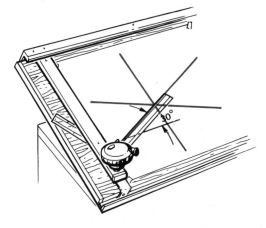

FIG. 145

block. The front, bottom, right corner of the block is chosen as the origin of the axis system. The dimensions of the block are 4 units wide, 2 units high, and 3 units deep [146]. Draw the front face first. Using your isometric scale, lay out the width and height of the block along the X- and Y-axis lines [147]. Draw light construction lines parallel to these axes to outline the front face. Now mark the depth on the Z-axis and lightly draw the outlines of the side and top surfaces using lines parallel to the axes [148]. Complete the drawing by darkening the visible lines [149]. Remove excess construction and axis lines with an eraser and an erasing shield.

Hidden lines are rarely shown in a

pictorial drawing because the object is usually well enough described without them. Any additional lines tend to detract from the overall "picture" of the object. If an important feature is hidden as a result of the viewing direction that has been selected, the object should be repositioned. If our block [149] has a rectangular recess on its bottom surface, the view drawn would not show this feature. By reversing the direction of the width and depth axis lines, you can redraw the block to make its front, bottom, and right side surfaces visible [150]. The recess can now be clearly seen. A view of this type is often referred to as a ***worm's eye*** view in contrast to the previous view that is a ***bird's eye*** view.

Multiview drawing of a rectangular block.

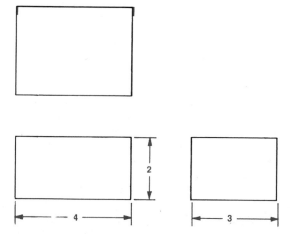

FIG. 146

Draw front face first using width and height measurements.

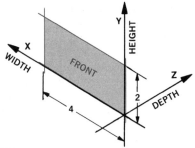

FIG. 147

Mark depth measurement and draw right side and top surfaces.

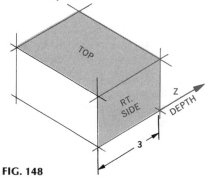

FIG. 148

Darken visible lines . . . erase excess lines using an erasing shield . . . do not draw hidden lines.

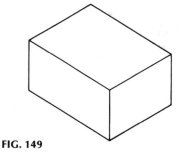

FIG. 149

Reverse width and depth axes to show hidden contours on bottom surface.

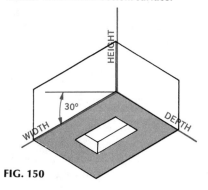

FIG. 150

If it is not important to keep the block in its normal "use" position, you could turn it around so that the bottom surface is in the "front" position [151]. Only rarely will hidden lines be necessary if you use good judgment in orienting an object in a pictorial view. The selection of viewing directions for all types of axonometric drawings will be discussed further in Section 53—Selecting Axonometric Viewing Directions.

Rotating block from its normal use position also shows the hidden contours.

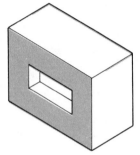

FIG. 151

The rectangular block you just drew is bounded by six planes. Each of these planes is parallel to two of the isometric axes and perpendicular to the third. Planes of this type are known as **principal planes** [152]. The orientation of a principal plane is more specifically described by referring to it as a horizontal, frontal, or profile plane, depending on the axes to which it is parallel. A **horizontal plane** is parallel to the width and depth axes. A **frontal plane** is parallel to the width and height axes. A **profile plane** is parallel to the height and depth axes. You will see these terms used frequently when describing many of the surfaces that form the contours of an object. For now, we will refer to any plane that is at an angle with any or all of the principal planes as an **angled plane.** In Section 43—Angled Surfaces in Isometric, angled planes will be subdivided into two classifications—**inclined planes** and **oblique planes.**

Before going on to drawing more complex objects, note that although your first isometric drawing was laid

Principal planes . . . horizontal, frontal, and profile.

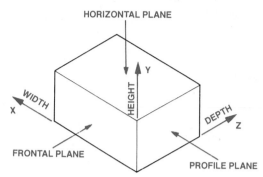

FIG. 152

out with a foreshortened isometric scale, this is not always necessary or desirable. In isometric, any scale can be used as long as the same scale is used on all three axes. Drawing an object with a regular full size scale only results in a slightly larger view than if an isometric scale is used. [153].

An isometric view made with a foreshortened isometric scale is usually referred to as an **isometric projection.** A view made with a regular scale is called an **isometric drawing.**

The increased size produced by using a regular scale is no problem in technical illustration because the finished drawing is very often enlarged

Drawing an isometric view with a regular scale is more convenient . . . the view is just larger.

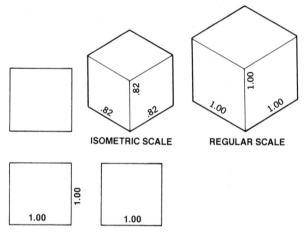

FIG. 153

In the drawing made with a regular scale, all dimensions that are parallel to the isometric axes are about 1¼ times larger since the 0.82 dimension of the foreshortened isometric scale corresponds to the 1.00 dimension of the regular scale. The actual size increase is 1.22474. This is the secant of the 35° 16' angle between the axes lines and the viewing plane.

or reduced to fit specific printing requirements. Changing size is very easy with modern photographic or xerographic copying machines. Freedom of scale choice is one of the big advantages of isometric drawing. In dimetric and trimetric drawing, the proper foreshortened scales **must** be used because of different scale requirements for the different axes.

To aid in centering an isometric view on your drawing sheet, use the following procedure. Locate the center of the available drawing area by drawing light diagonal lines from opposite corners [154]. From the center point established by the crossing of these two lines, draw a line vertically down for a distance equal to one-half of the overall height of the object to be drawn [155]. Continue from this point by drawing a line to the left at a 30° angle down from the horizontal. The length of this line should be one-half of the overall depth of the object. Now, draw a line to the right at a 30° angle down from the horizontal. Its length should be one-half of the overall width of the object.

The end of the last line drawn locates the origin 0 of the isometric axis system. The axes lines are drawn through this point [156]. Now lightly draw on the axes lines a rectangular box with dimensions equal to the overall width, height, and depth of the object to provide a starting frame of reference for the isometric view that will be drawn. In the following paragraphs, this box will be referred to as the **enclosing box,** and its use in drawing the complete object will be described.

lightly draw the outline of the enclosing box with its front, bottom, right corner at the origin of the isometric axes lines [159].

Top, front, and right side views of a typesetting machine bracket.

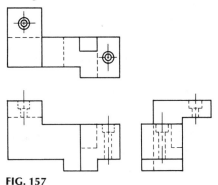

FIG. 157

Start isometric view by enclosing bracket in the smallest possible rectangular box.

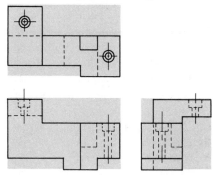

FIG. 158

Draw outline of enclosing box on the isometric axes.

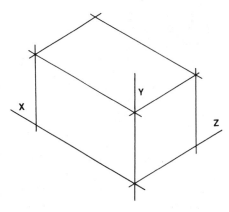

FIG. 159

Centering an isometric view . . . draw diagonals from the corners of the drawing area.

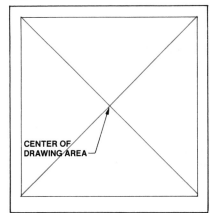

FIG. 154

To locate origin, draw lines from the center representing half of the height, depth, and width.

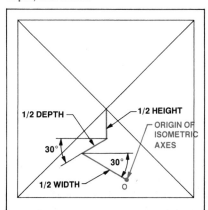

FIG. 155

Draw isometric axes through origin . . . draw light outline of a rectangular box at full height, depth, and width.

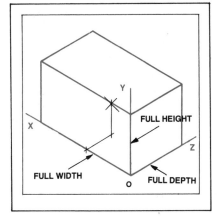

FIG. 156

Knowing how to draw a rectangular box in isometric is an important step toward successfully drawing more complex objects in any form of axonometric drawing. As an example, let us make an isometric drawing of a bracket for a type-setting machine [157]. Like the rectangular block, the surfaces of this object are all horizontal, frontal, and profile planes with boundary lines parallel to the isometric axes. The first step in making the isometric drawing is to imagine the smallest possible rectangular box that would just enclose the bracket [158]. The outermost features of the bracket will be in contact with the faces of this **enclosing box.** The width, height, and depth of the box represent the overall dimensions of the bracket. To show the front, top, and right side surfaces of the bracket,

The enclosing box method of constructing an isometric drawing is of great help in visualizing objects in the three dimensions of space. After drawing the box on the isometric axes, the illustrator simply marks the locations of the object's features on its surfaces and then "cuts" away everything that is not part of the final object. This process is very similar to using a knife to carve the object out of a solid block of wood or clay.

After drawing the enclosing box of the type-setting machine bracket, the second step is to transfer all points, lines, and planes of the object that touch its visible faces [160]. The bracket has an L-shaped plane on the front, a rectangular plane on the top, and an almost square plane on the right side. Read the sizes and locations of these surfaces on the multiview drawing of the bracket and lay them out with the chosen scale. If the multiview drawing is accurate, you can transfer dimensions parallel to the isometric axes directly with dividers. *In isometric drawing remember that any measurement laid out with a scale or transferred with dividers must be parallel to one of the isometric axes.*

Transfer the features of the bracket that lie inside the box next. Any interior line can be drawn by locating the X-, Y-, and Z (width, height, and depth)-coordinates of its two end points. For an object, like this bracket, where all of the surfaces are principal planes (horizontal, frontal, or profile), it is usually quicker to lay out the boundary lines on planes set back from the surfaces of the enclosing box. The outside features previously drawn provide convenient starting points to lay out the interior planes.

Lay out the Z-shaped plane seen in the front view on a frontal plane set back from the front of the enclosing box [161]. The front edge of the top plane previously drawn is a common boundary line and establishes the set back distance. Only two new measurements are required to draw the contours of the Z-shaped plane. The top left point is a corner of the top surface. Locate the top and bottom points on the right edge by drawing projection lines parallel to the Z (depth)-axis from corners of the front surface.

Lay out the Z-shaped plane on a frontal plane set back from the front of the box.

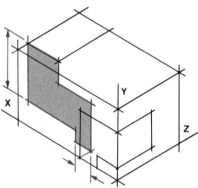

FIG. 161

Lay out the interior planes visible in the top and right side views that are set back from the top and right side of the box in a similar manner [162]. Start at the lines on the outside surfaces. One new measurement is required. In drawing any plane of the object, be sure that all lines that are parallel to the width, height, and depth axis lines are drawn parallel to these lines in the isometric view.

Lay out the interior planes that are set back from the top and right side.

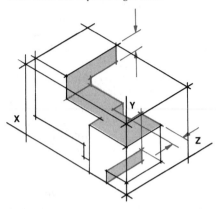

FIG. 162

The final step is to darken the visible lines of all features of the object and to erase any unused construction lines [163]. Note that some portions of an interior plane may be hidden behind another feature. Since hidden lines are seldom drawn in pictorial views, these portions will not appear in your isometric drawing. The only two features of the bracket that have not been shown are the counterbored holes. Before drawing these holes, you must understand how circles appear in an isometric drawing.

Darken visible lines . . . erase unused construction lines . . . do not draw hidden lines.

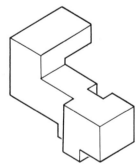

FIG. 163

Exercise 18

The objects listed below and illustrated in Section 90—Problems for Assignment are suitable examples to use in practicing the principles learned in the preceding section. Enlarge the ob-

Lay out all planes that touch the visible faces of the enclosing box.

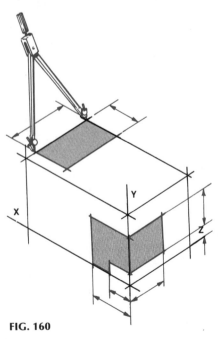

FIG. 160

jects as necessary to suit the available or assigned drawing sheet size. Maintain the proportions shown as closely as possible. Use either the viewing direction that provides the best description of the object or the viewing direction assigned by your instructor. Make a quick sketch of each object first to obtain a clear understanding of the object and to be sure that the given views are correct. The sketch will help you visualize the finished illustration and aid you in positioning it on your drawing sheet. Use a grid underlay sheet from Appendix C as an aid in sketching.

(a) The following objects have only principal planes and principal lines. Probs. 1, 2, 3, 4, 5, 6, 7.

42. CIRCLES IN ISOMETRIC

Circles of various sizes appear frequently in all kinds of illustrations. They occur in views of drilled holes, circular bosses, rounded corners, threaded holes and shafts, and various other types of cylindrical features. Depending on the viewing direction, a circle may appear as perfectly round or as a straight line. You see the true round shape when your line of sight is perpendicular to the plane of the circle. You see the straight line when you look at the edge view of the circle. When rotated anywhere between these two extremes, a circle assumes a true geometric shape known as an **ellipse** [164]. Hold a coin first so that you look squarely at its edge and then move it up above your line of sight and then down be-

Circular openings appear as ellipses on the surface of this satellite.

FIG. 164

low. The coin will assume an elliptical shape until it is so far above or below your eye that it appears as nearly a full circle [165].

A coin held above and below your eye appears elliptical.

FIG. 165

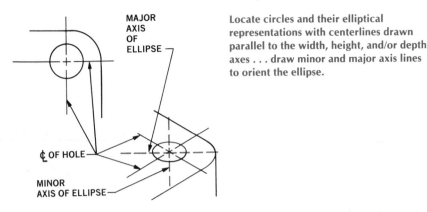

FIG. 166

Locate circles and their elliptical representations with centerlines drawn parallel to the width, height, and/or depth axes . . . draw minor and major axis lines to orient the ellipse.

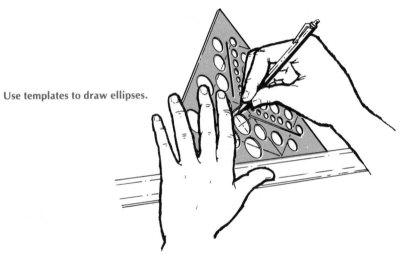

Use templates to draw ellipses.

FIG. 167

On isometric drawings, most of the surfaces of an object are positioned at some angle other than 90° with the observer's line of sight. Any circles occurring on these surfaces will, therefore, appear as ellipses. An ellipse is drawn in isometric in much the same way as a circle is drawn in a multiview drawing. The centers of both are first located by drawing centerlines parallel to the width, height, and/or depth axes [166]. In multiview drawing, the circle is then drawn with a compass or with a circle template whose printed centerlines are carefully aligned with the drawn centerlines.

In an isometric drawing, an ellipse template is normally used to draw an ellipse. First, a second set of centerlines is drawn to establish the orientation of the major and minor axes of the ellipse. The **major axis** is the longest dimension of an ellipse; the **minor axis** is the shortest. Technical illustrators almost always use templates to draw ellipses (and also circles) because they save time [167]. The only exception is for large or unusual-size ellipses. These may be approximated by one of the construction methods shown in Appendix A.

When drawing a circle on a multiview drawing, a template opening is chosen to match the specified size (diameter) of the circle. When drawing the elliptical representation of a circle in isometric, the ellipse template opening must be chosen for both size and angle. Recall from looking at a coin that the shape of an ellipse is governed by the angle at which the circle it represents is viewed. If your line of sight is perpendicular (90°) to the plane of the circle, you see a true circle [168]. If your line of sight is parallel (0°) to the plane of the circle, you only see a straight line (the edge view). Between these extreme angles, you see ellipses of different shapes.

When the plane of the circle is tilted slightly to form a 15° angle with a horizontal line of sight, the circle appears as a narrow ellipse with a very short minor axis [168]. As the angle with the line of sight increases, the ellipse becomes fatter and the minor axis increases in length. Beyond 60° the ellipse very quickly approaches the shape of a true circle. Note that although the shape of the ellipse changes, the length of the major axis remains constant and equal to the circle's diameter. The angle with the line of sight is the angle that is marked on an ellipse template. The most popular ellipse templates cover a range of 15° to 60° in 5° increments. If a required ellipse angle falls between these increments, most technical illustrators choose the closest

The ellipse angle is the angle between the plane of the circle and the line of sight . . . the major axis remains constant as the circle is rotated.

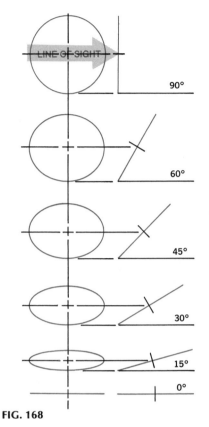

FIG. 168

5° template because the amount of error is so small.

There are two basic types of ellipse templates used by technical illustrators. **Standard ellipse templates** are made for the most commonly used ellipse angles [169]. This type of template is also sometimes referred to as an **angle-size ellipse template.** On some standard templates, the ellipses are all the same angle. On others, several popular ellipse angles are grouped together. The size markings adjacent to each ellipse refer to the diameters of the circles that the ellipses represent. If you were to measure one of the ellipse openings on a standard template, you would find that the length of the major axis equals the marked size. This is because the major axis of an ellipse that represents a circle always appears true length. No matter how you tip the plane of a circle, one of the circle's diameters will always be perpendic-

Standard ellipse templates . . . available for many different ellipse angles.

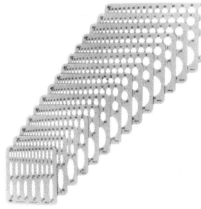

FIG. 169

ular to the line of sight and, therefore, be true length. It is this diameter that forms the major axis of the ellipse.

The second type of ellipse template is the **isometric ellipse template** [170]. This template has only 35° 16′ ellipse openings to draw cir-

cles that occur on principal planes in an isometric drawing. An isometric ellipse template differs from a standard 35° ellipse template in that the size markings refer to the diameters of the circles that the ellipses represent *only if the isometric view is laid out with a regular scale*—not a foreshortened isometric scale. Measuring one of the openings on an isometric ellipse template, you would find that the major axis measures about 1¼ times the marked size. This is to compensate for the increased drawing size that results from using a regular scale [153].

The isometric ellipse template has 30° isometric axes lines marked on each opening in addition to the customary major and minor axis centerlines. This aids in aligning the template on the principal planes of an object. Some isometric templates have sides cut at 30° with the base to align the ellipses quickly when positioning the template on the scale of a drafting machine or on a parallel rule or T-square. The convenience of an isometric ellipse template is limited by the fact that it has only the 35° 16′ ellipses that are required for circles that occur on principal surfaces. Circles on angled surfaces are at a different angle with the line of sight. They must be drawn with a standard el-

An isometric ellipse template . . . has only 35° 16′ ellipses for use on principal planes.

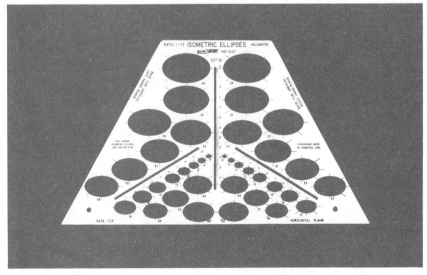

FIG. 170

lipse template using an ellipse angle that matches the plane's angle with the line of sight.

When making an isometric drawing using a regular scale, as is commonly done, a 1.00″ diameter circle can be drawn with an isometric ellipse template opening marked 1.00″ if the circle is on a principal plane. If the circle is on an angled plane, a standard ellipse template of the appropriate angle size must be used. A 1¼ times size adjustment must be made with the standard template to compensate for the increased view size produced by using a regular scale for the drawing. An opening marked 1.25″ will have to be used for the 1.00″ diameter circle. If an isometric view is drawn with a foreshortened isometric scale, illustrators use a standard ellipse template for all surfaces. The marked template opening sizes will match exactly the specified circle diameters.

The correct orientation of an ellipse is just as important as the correct size and angle. In all types of axonometric drawing (isometric, dimetric, and trimetric), ***the minor axis of an ellipse that represents a circle must follow the direction of a line that is perpendicular to the plane on which the circle occurs*** [171]. If the circle is on a principal plane (horizontal, frontal, or profile), the minor axis of the ellipse that represents it in an isometric view follows the direction of the height, depth, or width axis that is perpendicular to that plane. The minor axis on a horizontal plane is always parallel to the height axis [172]. On a frontal plane, the minor axis is always parallel to the depth axis. On a profile plane, the minor axis is always parallel to the width axis.

To understand the drawing of isometric ellipses, let us draw circles at the middle of the top, front, and right side surfaces of a rectangular block. The first step is to locate the center of each ellipse by drawing centerlines parallel to the width, height, and depth axes [173]. These are the same centerlines that you see in the multiview drawing. Next, establish the orientation of the minor axis of each ellipse by drawing a line through each

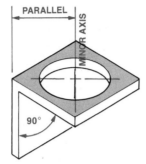

FIG. 171

The minor axis of an ellipse follows the direction of a line that is perpendicular to the plane of the circle.

Circles on principal planes . . . the minor axes follow the height, depth, and width directions.

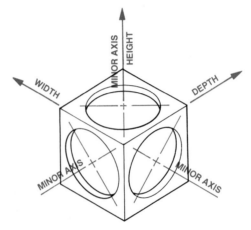

FIG. 172

center parallel to the axis line that is perpendicular to the surface [174]. Draw a second line perpendicular to the minor axis at each center to align the major axis.

If desired, you can mark the true diameter of the circle being repre-

sented on the major axis, since this is always a true length line. If the drawing is laid out with a regular scale, the size will have to be multiplied by 1¼. It is not really necessary to mark the length of the major axis unless the correct size ellipse template is not

Draw ellipses representing circles on the three faces of the block . . . first locate centers by drawing centerlines.

Orient the ellipses by drawing minor axes parallel to the isometric axes . . . draw major axes perpendicular.

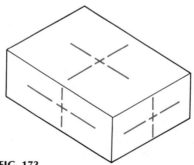

FIG. 173

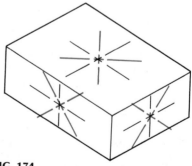

FIG. 174

available and you must make some approximation. The final step is to align carefully the centerlines of a 35° ellipse template opening of the specified size with the axis lines and draw the ellipses [175]. The 35° ellipse is required because the circles are on principal planes, which in isometric are at a 35° 16′ angle with the viewing plane. Draw the three ellipses to complete the drawing [176].

Carefully align 35° ellipse template centerlines with minor and major axis lines . . .

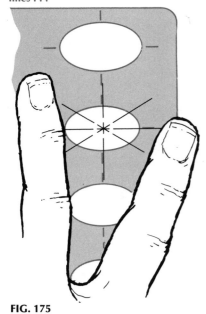

FIG. 175

. . . draw the three ellipses.

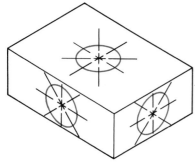

FIG. 176

Now let us look at another example of drawing circles on principal planes by completing the counterbored holes on the type-setting ma-chine bracket [163]. Draw the locating and ellipse-orienting centerlines on the two horizontal surfaces [177]. You may also have to draw a second set of centerlines for each hole at a lower level. These will be used for the ellipses representing the bottom of the counterbore and the top of the drilled hole if they are visible. The 35° ellipses at each location are then drawn with ellipse template openings of the specified sizes [178].

Remember that if you lay out an isometric drawing with a regular scale and use a standard 35° ellipse template, you must choose an ellipse size that is about 1¼ times the specified size. Note that the minor axis of each ellipse on the type-setting machine bracket is also the axial centerline of the holes that have been drilled and counterbored perpendicular to the surfaces.

So far we have only considered ellipses representing circles that occur on principal planes. These are all 35° 16′ ellipses because principal planes in isometric are positioned at a 35° 16′ angle with the line of sight. Angled surfaces are positioned at various angles with the line of sight. Circles occurring on these surfaces are represented by ellipses whose angles equal the angles of the surfaces with the line of sight. Methods of determining these angles are described in Section 44—Circles on Angled Surfaces.

Although the ellipse angle varies for different angled surfaces, the basic ellipse orientation rule for axonometric drawings holds true. *The minor axis of an ellipse that represents a circle must follow the direction of a line that is perpendicular to the plane on which the circle occurs.* In later sections you will see the use of this rule in dimetric and trimetric drawings.

Exercise 19

The objects listed below and illustrated in Section 90—Problems for Assignment are suitable examples to use in practicing the principles learned in the preceding section. Enlarge the objects as necessary to suit the available or assigned drawing sheet size. Maintain the proportions shown as closely as

Draw counterbored holes on the type-setting machine bracket . . . locate hole centers . . . draw minor and major axis lines.

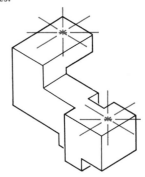

FIG. 177

Draw visible portions of the holes with a 35° ellipse template.

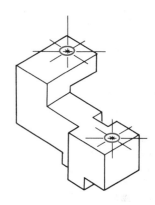

FIG. 178

possible. Use either the viewing direction that provides the best description of the object or the viewing direction assigned by your instructor. Make a quick sketch of each object first to obtain a clear understanding of the object and to be sure that the given views are correct. The sketch will help you visualize the finished illustration and aid you in positioning it on your drawing sheet. Use a grid underlay sheet from Appendix C as an aid in sketching.

(a) The following objects have one or more circular arcs on principal planes.
   Probs. 36, 37, 38, 39, 40, 41.
(b) The following objects have one or more circles and circular arcs on principal planes.
   Probs. 42, 43, 45, 46, 47, 48, 49, 50, 51.

(c) The following objects are basically cylindrical.
Probs. 52, 53, 54, 55, 56.
Note: More complex objects having circles and circular arcs on principal planes are listed in Exercise 22.

43. ANGLED SURFACES IN ISOMETRIC

The rectangular block and the typesetting machine bracket in Section 42 were relatively simple to draw because all of the surfaces were horizontal, frontal, or profile planes. The boundary lines were all parallel to the isometric axes. Since all measurements in an isometric drawing must be made parallel to one of the isometric axes, the length of each boundary line could be measured directly with a scale as it was laid out on an outside plane of the enclosing box or on a parallel interior plane.

If an object has surfaces that are at an angle with the principal planes, some or all of their boundary lines will lie at an angle with the isometric axes. The lengths of these angled lines cannot be laid out directly with a regular scale or with a foreshortened isometric scale because they are at an angle other than 35° 16' with the line of sight. Their lengths will be foreshortened by different amounts depending on the angle. The normal procedure in drawing angled lines is to locate their end points using dimensions parallel to the isometric axes. Some special direct measuring devices for angled lines are available from Graphic-Standard Instruments Company, Troy, Michigan.

Principal planes (horizontal, frontal, and profile) in an isometric drawing are referred to as **true isometric planes** or just simply as **isometric planes.** Planes that lie at an angle with the principal planes are referred to as **off-axis** or **nonisometric planes.** These planes fall into two categories—**inclined** and **oblique.** Figures [179] and [180] show examples of **inclined** planes. These are planes that lie at an angle with two of the principal planes and are perpendicular to the third. In [179] the two inclined planes *ABCD* and *BEFC* are perpendicular to the horizontal plane and at an angle with

Inclined planes . . . planes that lie at an angle with two principal planes and are perpendicular to the third.

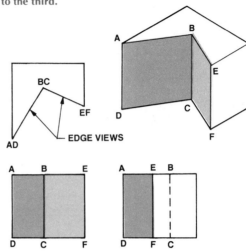

FIG. 179

More inclined planes . . .

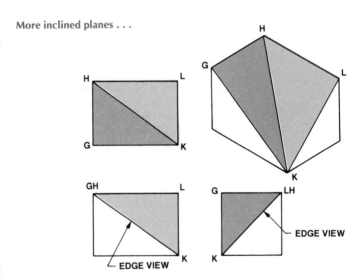

FIG. 180

the frontal and profile planes. The top view in the multiview drawing of the object shows each of the planes as single lines—their **edge views.**

Both inclined planes in [180] are at an angle with the horizontal. Plane *GHK* is also at an angle with the profile plane and perpendicular to the frontal plane. Its edge view is seen in the front view of the multiview drawing. The other inclined plane *HLK* is at an angle with the horizontal and frontal planes and perpendicular to the profile plane. Its edge view is seen in the right side view of the multiview drawing.

Oblique planes are planes that lie at an angle with all three principal planes [181]. Plane *MNO* is at an angle with the horizontal, frontal, and profile planes. Its edge view cannot be seen in any principal view of a multiview drawing.

The lines of an object in an isometric view that are parallel to an isometric axis line are referred to as **true isometric lines** or just simply as **isometric lines.** Lines that are not parallel to an isometric axis line are referred to as **off-axis** or **nonisometric lines.** These angled lines fall into two categories—**inclined** and **oblique.**

An oblique plane . . . a plane that lies at an angle with all three principal planes.

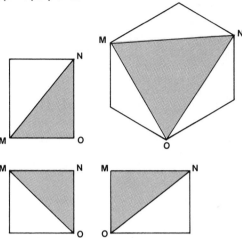

FIG. 181

Inclined lines are angled lines that lie in principal planes . . . oblique lines are angled lines that are not parallel to any principal plane.

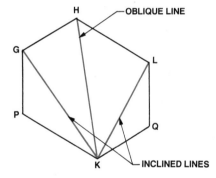

FIG. 182

Inclined lines are angled lines that lie in principal planes. In [182] lines *GK* and *LK* are inclined lines. Line *GK* in the frontal plane is at an angle with the horizontal and profile planes. Line *LK* in the profile plane is at an angle with the horizontal and frontal planes. If an imaginary line were drawn connecting points *G* and *L*, it would also be classified as an inclined line. It would lie in a horizontal plane and be at an angle with the frontal and profile planes.

Inclined lines as well as isometric lines may also be described as *horizontal, frontal,* or *profile* lines depending on whether they are parallel to the horizontal, frontal, or profile planes. In [182] lines *GH, HL, PK,* and *KQ* are horizontal lines. A line drawn from *G* to *L* would also be a horizontal line. Lines *GP, GK, PK, HL,* and *LQ* are frontal lines. Lines *GH, LK, LQ,* and *KQ* are profile lines.

Oblique lines are angled lines that are not parallel to any principal plane. Line *HK* in [182] is an oblique line. It is at an angle with the horizontal, frontal, and profile planes.

When drawing the isometric view of an object that has angled surfaces, you will find that some or all of the boundary lines of these surfaces are inclined or oblique lines. These lines can be laid out by plotting the *X-, Y-,* and *Z* (width, height, and depth)-coordinates of their end points [183].

Lay out inclined and oblique plane boundaries by plotting the *X-, Y-,* and *Z*-coordinates of their end points.

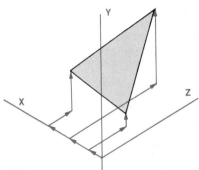

FIG. 183

The dimensions are obtained from a multiview drawing of the object. If the direction of a line is specified by an angular dimension, the angle can be laid out on an isometric drawing with a special isometric ellipse protractor.

When a boundary line of an angled plane is an inclined line, its end points can be located quite easily on a principal plane using dimensions parallel to the isometric axes. In [184] the inclined plane ABCD has been drawn by first laying out the inclined boundary line BC on the right side of the enclosing box. Once line BC has been drawn in the isometric view, the rest of the plane can be completed easily by drawing parallel horizontal lines from B to A and from C to D on the top and front surfaces of the enclosing box. Line AD can then be drawn on the left side parallel to line BC.

Draw an isometric view of an inclined plane . . . lay out the inclined boundary line BC on the right side of the enclosing box . . . draw horizontal lines AB and CD . . . draw line AD parallel to BC.

An inclined line can also be drawn by laying out its angle. On a multiview drawing, the angle is measured with a *circular protractor* [185]. On an isometric drawing, the angle has to be measured with an *isometric ellipse protractor* [186]. This protractor is a 35° 16' ellipse with 360° graduations around its edge that correspond to the graduations seen on a circular protractor.

When using an ellipse protractor to make an angular measurement on an isometric drawing, the protractor must be positioned in the plane of the angle. This is done by aligning the protractor's minor axis with a line that is known to be perpendicular to the plane. In [187] the inclined line BC lies in the right side plane of the object and is positioned at a 30° angle with the vertical. To determine the direction of BC in the isometric drawing [188], the minor axis of the pro-

tractor is aligned with the width axis since this is perpendicular to the right side plane. The center of the protractor is positioned at point C. The 30° angle of line BC is read between the 90° vertical mark and the 60° mark on the protractor. Line BC can now be drawn from C to its intersection at B with the horizontal top edge of the right side plane.

This procedure used to determine the direction of line BC also establishes the angle of the inclined plane ABCD with the frontal plane. The true angle between two planes is measured in a plane that is perpendicular to both of them. The right side view in the multiview drawing [187] shows the edge views of both the inclined plane and the frontal plane. It also shows the true size of the right side plane that is perpendicular to both of them. Therefore, the 30° angle that is established by positioning the ellipse protractor on the right side plane is the same true angle for both the line BC and the plane ABCD.

The isometric view of an oblique plane is also drawn by laying out its boundary lines. Inclined boundary lines are drawn by locating their end points on a principal plane [189] or by establishing their angular directions with an ellipse protractor. Boundary lines that are oblique lines are usually drawn by laying out the X-, Y-, and Z-coordinates of their end points. Oblique lines can be laid out with an ellipse protractor, but the procedure involves several steps and is usually more time consuming than locating the end points of the lines.

The procedure for laying out oblique lines with an ellipse protractor is described in Section 44—Circles on Angled Surfaces. Here, an ellipse protractor is used to lay out an oblique plane and to establish the direction of a perpendicular line to orient an ellipse drawn on the plane [201]. Section 45—Cylindrical Surfaces in Isometric describes the procedure for laying out the centerline of a tube that is bent at an oblique angle [220].

The guide block for a dispensing machine shown in [190] has several angled surfaces. You would start an isometric drawing of an object like

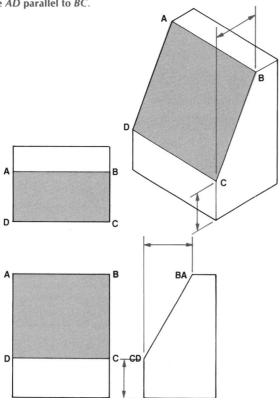

FIG. 184

Use a circular protractor to lay out angles on multiview drawings.

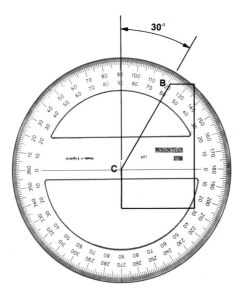

FIG. 185

Use an isometric ellipse protractor to lay out angles on isometric drawings.

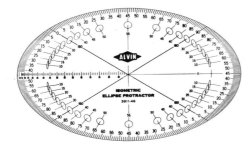

FIG. 186

Inclined line *BC* lies at a 30° angle with the vertical.

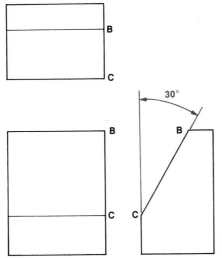

FIG. 187

Lay out the angle of line *BC* . . . position ellipse protractor in the plane of the angle by aligning its minor axis with the perpendicular width axis.

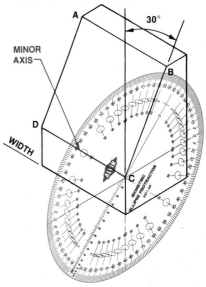

FIG. 188

Draw the isometric view of an oblique plane . . . draw the inclined boundary lines by locating their end points on the principal planes.

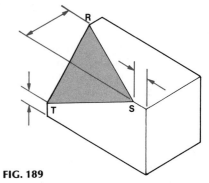

FIG. 189

This guide block for a dispensing machine has several angled surfaces.

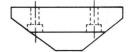

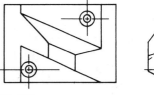

FIG. 190

this in the same way as the type-setting machine bracket. Draw an enclosing box that touches the outermost points, lines, and surfaces of the block [191]. After transferring the box to the isometric axes, first draw the surfaces that touch the surfaces of the enclosing box [192]. It is often helpful to label critical points on the object to avoid confusion when transferring lines to the isometric view.

Draw enclosing box . . . label critical points on the object.

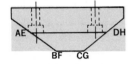

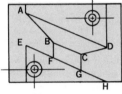

FIG. 191

Draw enclosing box on the isometric axes . . . draw lines of plane *BCGF* by laying out the coordinates of their end points . . . draw lines for top and bottom planes.

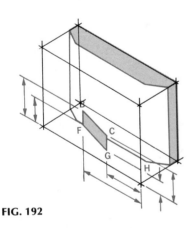

FIG. 192

Draw parallelogram *BCGF* on the front of the box by laying out the *X*- and *Y*-coordinates of each of the corner points. Draw rectangular planes on the right and left sides of the box. Draw the six-sided plane on the top surface. Also, draw the visible lines

of a duplicate plane on the bottom surface. Remember that you can only lay out dimensions parallel to the isometric axes in an isometric drawing.

The next surfaces to draw are the principal planes that are not on the surface of the enclosing box. The two surfaces of this type on the block are really parts of the same frontal plane that has been set back from the front of the box. Starting from the top surface, draw vertical lines down to points *A* and *D* [193]. From the bottom surface, draw a vertical line up to point *E*. Since these are true isometric lines, transfer their lengths directly from the multiview drawing to locate points *A*, *D*, and *E*. Draw inclined lines from *A* to *D* and from *E* to *H* to complete the two surfaces. Note that lines *AD*, *BC*, *FG*, and *EH* are all parallel and must be drawn parallel in the isometric view. In isometric drawing, as in multiview drawing, parallel lines must always be parallel.

Draw frontal planes set back from the front of the box . . . start at the lines already drawn on the outside surfaces of the box . . . keep parallel lines parallel.

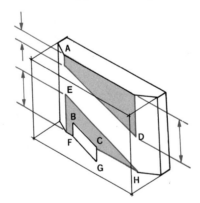

FIG. 193

The oblique plane *ABCD* can now be completed by drawing oblique lines *AB* and *CD* [194]. The two vertical, inclined planes are completed by drawing lines *EF* of one and *GH* of the other. The line *EH* is not needed since it turns out to be completely hidden. The inclined plane *EFGH* seen on edge in the front view of the multiview drawing is also hidden in the isometric drawing.

Complete oblique plane *ABCD* by drawing lines *AB* and *CD* . . . complete the vertical inclined planes by drawing lines *EF* and *GH*.

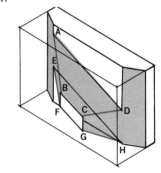

FIG. 194

The last step in drawing the guide block is to draw the one counter-bored hole that will be visible. Its centerlines are located on the frontal plane containing line *AD* [195]. Obtain the orientation of the ellipse on this surface by drawing a line parallel to the depth axis through the center point. The minor axis of the ellipse will lie on this line since the depth axis is perpendicular to the plane on which the ellipse appears. Use a 35° ellipse template to draw the visible portion of the counterbored hole.

Draw the visible counterbored hole . . . locate its center and draw minor axis parallel to the depth direction . . . use 35° template to draw the ellipse.

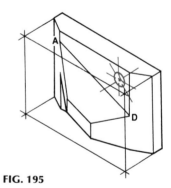

FIG. 195

Exercise 20

The objects listed below and illustrated in Section 90—Problems for Assignment are suitable examples to use in practicing the principles learned in the preceding section. Enlarge the objects as necessary to suit the available or assigned drawing sheet size. Maintain the proportions shown as closely as possible. Use either the viewing direction that provides the best description of the object or the viewing direction assigned by your instructor. Make a quick sketch of each object first to obtain a clear understanding of the object and to be sure that the given views are correct. The sketch will help you visualize the finished illustration and aid you in positioning it on your drawing sheet. Use a grid underlay sheet from Appendix C as an aid in sketching.

(a) The following objects have principal and inclined planes. The lines are all principal or inclined. Probs. 7, 8, 9, 10, 11, 13, 14, 15, 16, 22, 23, 24.
(b) The following objects have principal and inclined planes. The lines are principal, inclined, and oblique. Probs. 12, 17, 18, 19, 20, 21, 25, 26, 27, 28, 29, 30, 31.
(c) The following objects have principal, inclined, and oblique planes. The lines are principal, inclined, and oblique. Probs. 32, 33, 34, 35.

44. CIRCLES ON ANGLED SURFACES

A problem frequently encountered in isometric drawing is how to draw a circle that occurs on an inclined plane or on an oblique plane. You know that the circle will appear as an ellipse and that its center can be located using X-, Y-, and Z-coordinates. The ellipse size will equal the specified diameter of the circle. The main problem arises from having to determine the orientation of the ellipse and its angle.

The same basic rule applies for orienting an ellipse on an angled plane as on a principal plane. *The minor axis of an ellipse that represents a circle must follow the direction of a line that is perpendicular to the plane on which the circle occurs.* In the case of an inclined plane, you can determine this direction by using the same setting of the isometric ellipse protractor that was used to lay out the

angle of an inclined line and an inclined plane [188]. In [196] find the direction of a line perpendicular to line *BC* by reading 90° away from the mark establishing its 30° angle with the vertical. A perpendicular line starting at line C passes through the

Draw an ellipse on the inclined plane . . . minor axis follows a line perpendicular to the plane . . . read line direction on the protractor 90° away from line *BC* . . . also read ellipse angle at this mark.

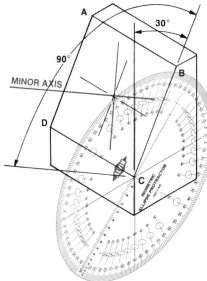

FIG. 196

30° mark on the protractor. This line is also perpendicular to the inclined plane *ABCD* because this plane is perpendicular to the right side plane in which the true angles have been established. The minor axis of an ellipse on plane *ABCD* follows the direction of the perpendicular line. Draw the major axis perpendicular.

The ellipse angle to use on an angled surface depends on the angle of the plane with the line of sight. This angle also appears on most ellipse protractors. A ring of varying angle ellipses and their associated angular values lies just inside the regular protractor markings. These show the shape and angle of ellipse that will be seen on a plane that is perpendicular to a line drawn at that particular protractor reading. The ellipse angle is also the angle of the perpendicular plane with the line of sight.

Determine the ellipse angle to use on the inclined plane of [196] by reading adjacent to the 30° mark that specifies the direction of the perpendicular line. This shows the angle to be approximately 51°. The closest standard ellipse template angle is seen from the pictured ellipses to be 50°. Use this angle template to draw an ellipse of the specified size at the previously determined orientation [197].

Draw the ellipse with a 50° template.

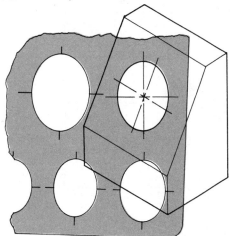

FIG. 197

If an ellipse protractor is not available, you can establish the orientation and angle for the ellipse in other ways. The right side view in the multiview drawing shows an edge view of the inclined plane on which the circle appears [198]. Draw a line perpendicular to this edge view line starting at the circle's center point *A* and intersecting the back surface of the object at point *B*. Draw the top and front views of line *AB* parallel to the profile plane to make the line truly perpendicular to the inclined plane. Locate point *B* in the isometric view by transferring its *X*- and *Y*-coordinates. Draw a line from *A* to *B*. This line is perpendicular to the inclined plane and establishes the direction of the minor axis of an ellipse on its sur-face. Draw the major axis perpendicular. Note that line *AB* would also be the axial centerline of a hole drilled perpendicular to the inclined surface.

You can determine the ellipse angle for the inclined plane by locating in the multiview drawing two points such as *R* and *S* at the left and right extremes of the horizontal centerline and transferring them to the isometric drawing [199]. Then try various angle ellipse template openings of the specified size on the major and minor axis lines until you find one that is closest to passing through points *R* and *S*. In this example, a 50° ellipse fits best.

Professional illustrators often use a quicker way of drawing an ellipse on an angled surface. They approximate the orientation and angle of the ellipse by constructing a tangent square around the circle in the multiview drawing [200]. In this example, the square appears as a rectangle in the top and front views. The square is transferred to the isometric view using dimensions parallel to the isometric axes. The resulting rhomboid is then used as a guide to draw the required ellipse. Various angle ellipse template openings of the specified size are tried until one is found that is closest to being *tangent* to the rhomboid at the *midpoints* of its sides.

You can find the orientation and angle of an ellipse that represents a circle on an oblique plane by using an ellipse protractor. Again you must determine the direction of a line that

To find the direction of the minor axis . . . draw line *AB* perpendicular to the edge view . . . transfer *AB* to the isometric view . . . the minor axis follows this direction.

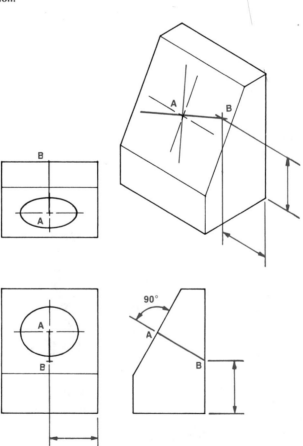

FIG. 198

To find the ellipse angle . . . locate points
R and *S* in the isometric view . . . try
various angle ellipses of the specified size
on the axis lines . . . select an ellipse that is
closest to passing through *R* and *S*.

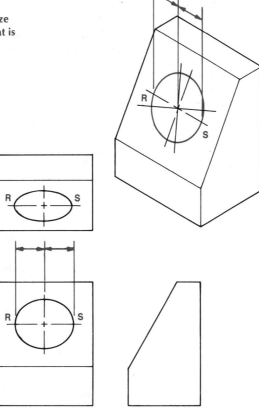

FIG. 199

To approximate ellipse orientation and
angle . . . draw tangent square around the
circle and transfer it to the isometric view
. . . try various angle ellipses of the
specified size . . . select an ellipse that is
closest to being tangent at the midpoints
of the sides.

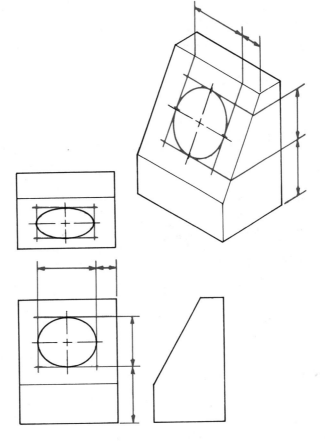

FIG. 200

is perpendicular to the plane to position the minor axis of the ellipse. In [201] the oblique plane lies at a 45° angle with the frontal plane and at a 50° angle with the horizontal plane. Before laying out the ellipse, use an ellipse protractor to draw the isometric view of the oblique plane. The first step will be to lay out the oblique boundary line XY that has the same compound angle as the plane.

sition an isometric ellipse protractor in a profile plane passing through point X [202]. Locate the center of the protractor at point X and align its minor axis with the width axis. Trace the outline of the protractor and mark point A on the outline at a point 50° down from the 0° horizontal mark. Line XA is the isometric view of a profile line that is inclined 50° with the horizontal. Now rotate point A 45°

horizontally to establish the 45° angle of line XA with the frontal plane.

Establish a horizontal plane on which to rotate point A by drawing a line AX' parallel to the depth axis [203]. This locates the elevation of a point X' directly below point X. X' is the center of the horizontal plane on which you can position your ellipse protractor with its minor axis parallel to the height axis. Trace the outline of the protractor again, and mark a point B where the line X'A extended meets the outline. This is at the 90° reading on the protractor.

Now rotate point B 45° on the protractor's outline to a point B' at the 45° reading [204]. Draw lines X'B' and BB'. Also draw a line parallel to BB' starting at point A to establish point A' on the X'B' line. Point A has now been rotated to A' through the same 45° angle that B was rotated to become B'. Line XA' is the direction of line XY for which you have been looking.

Locate point Y by drawing a horizontal line from point V at a 45° angle with the frontal plane. To do this, reposition the ellipse protractor in the plane of the bottom of the object with its center at V [205]. Read the 45° angle from the 0° mark to the 45° mark and draw line VY. Complete the oblique plane by drawing line WZ parallel to XY and line YZ parallel to XW.

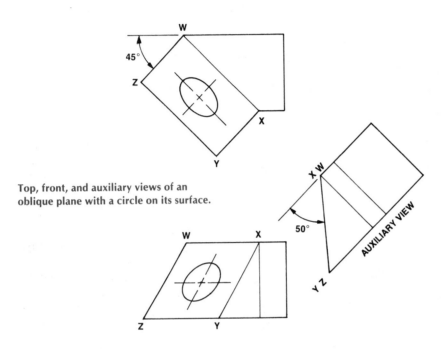

Top, front, and auxiliary views of an oblique plane with a circle on its surface.

FIG. 201

Before going any further, note that the procedure that will be described for using an ellipse protractor to determine the direction of an oblique line depends on knowing the values of the two angles with principal planes that produce the oblique angle. In this example, you know the 45° angle with the frontal plane and the 50° angle with the horizontal plane. Even with this knowledge, the procedure is fairly lengthy and time consuming. In later paragraphs, some shorter methods will be described [211, 212].

To obtain the direction of line XY in the isometric view, first establish the 50° angle with the horizontal. Po-

Lay out the 50° angle of line XY with the horizontal . . . position protractor in a profile plane by aligning its minor axis with the perpendicular width axis . . . trace protractor outline and mark point A at 50° with the horizontal.

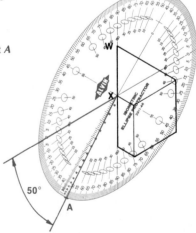

FIG. 202

Establish a horizontal plane on which to rotate point *A* . . . draw line *AX'* parallel to the depth axis to locate the plane's center below point *X* at *X'* . . . position protractor in the horizontal plane by aligning its minor axis with the perpendicular height axis . . . trace protractor outline and mark point *B* where line *XA* meets the outline.

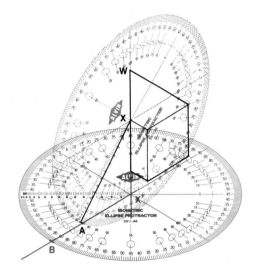

FIG. 203

Rotate point *B* through a 45° angle to *B'* . . . draw lines *X'B'* and *BB'* . . . draw line *AA'* parallel to *BB'* . . . line *XA'* is the direction of the oblique line *XY*.

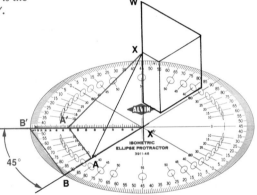

FIG. 204

Reposition the protractor in a horizontal plane through *V* . . . draw line *VY* at 45° with the frontal plane . . . point *Y* is at the intersection with line *XA'* . . . complete the oblique plane by drawing line *WZ* parallel to *XY* and line *YZ* parallel to *XW*.

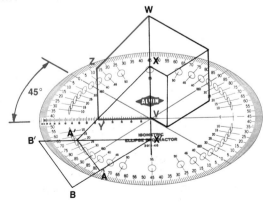

FIG. 205

To draw the elliptical representation of the circle on the oblique plane *WXYZ*, find the orientation and angle of the ellipse. Determine the orientation by the direction of a line perpendicular to the plane. Return to the position of the ellipse protractor where the 50° angle of line *XA* with the horizontal was laid out [202]. Find the direction of a line *XC* that is perpendicular to line *XA* by locating point *C* on the protractor's outline at a point 90° away from point *A* [206]. *C* is at the 40° reading in this example.

Draw a line perpendicular to line *XA* . . . reposition protractor in a profile plane through point *X* . . . draw line *XC* 90° away from line *XA*.

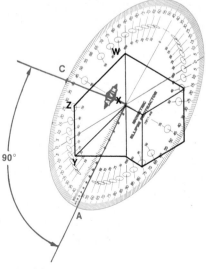

FIG. 206

Establish a horizontal plane on which to rotate point C . . . draw line CX″ parallel to the depth axis to locate plane's center above point X . . . position protractor in the horizontal plane by aligning its minor axis with the height axis . . . trace protractor outline and mark point D where line X″C meets the outline.

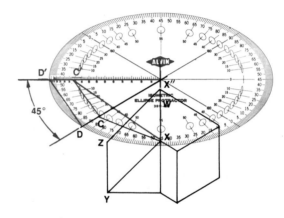

FIG. 207

Rotate point D through a 45° angle to D′ . . . draw lines X″D′ and DD′ . . . draw line CC′ parallel to DD′ . . . line XC′ is the direction of a line perpendicular to oblique plane WXYZ.

FIG. 208

Establish a horizontal plane on which to rotate point C by drawing line CX″ parallel to the depth axis [207]. This locates the elevation of a point X″ directly above point X. X″ is the center of the horizontal plane on which you can position your ellipse protractor with its minor axis parallel to the height axis. Trace the outline of the protractor, and mark a point D where the line X″C extended meets the outline. This is at the 90° reading on the protractor.

Now rotate point D 45° on the protractor's outline to a point D′ at the 45° reading [208]. Draw lines X″D′ and DD′. Also draw a line parallel to DD′ starting at point C to establish point C′ on the X″D′ line. Point C has now been rotated to C′ through the same 45° angle that D was rotated to become D′. Line XC′ is the direction of a line perpendicular to the oblique plane WXYZ for which you have been looking.

Now draw the locating centerlines for the ellipse on the oblique plane [209]. Draw the minor axis line parallel to line XC′ and passing through the center point. Draw the major axis perpendicular. Obtain the angle of the ellipse by positioning the ellipse protractor with its center at point X and the major axis scale reading along line XC′ [209]. At point C′ the 20° scale reading indicates that you should use a 20° ellipse. This also indicates that plane WXYZ is at a 20° angle with the line of sight.

If the object that you are drawing is a bent plate instead of a solid block, the 90° edge lines of plane WXYZ can be drawn using the perpendicular line direction XC′ that was established for the minor axis of the ellipse. In [210] the edge line YU has been drawn parallel to the minor axis line. The ellipse on plane WXYZ is one end of a cylindrical hole that is perpendicular to the plate. The lower end of the hole

Draw an ellipse on the oblique plane . . . draw locating centerlines for the ellipse . . . draw minor axis parallel to line XC′ and major axis perpendicular . . . position protractor's center at X with the major axis scale along XC′ . . . read the perpendicular ellipse angle (20°) on the scale at C′ and draw the ellipse.

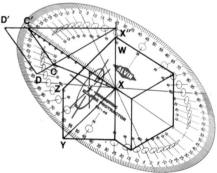

FIG. 209

showing through the plate is a parallel ellipse oriented on the same minor axis line.

Note that when using an ellipse protractor to measure an angle, the protractor must always be positioned in the plane of the angle. This is easy to do when the plane of the angle is a horizontal, frontal, or profile plane. Since the direction of lines perpendicular to these planes is known, it is easy to orient the minor axis of the protractor. A standard isometric ellipse protractor can also be used on these planes because principal planes in isometric are positioned at 35° 16′ with the line of sight.

In the last example, you laid out an oblique line XY where the plane of the angle was an inclined plane. It was necessary to lay out the angle in two steps—an angle with the horizontal and an angle with the frontal. By doing this, you were able to use a standard isometric ellipse protractor positioned in the profile and horizontal planes of the two angles. In order to position an ellipse protractor directly in the inclined plane of the 50° angle, you would have had to know the direction of a line perpendicular to the plane of the angle to orient the protractor. You would also need to know the angle of this plane with the line of sight to choose the proper angle ellipse protractor to use.

In [201] line XW is seen to be perpendicular to the plane of the 50° angle of line XY with the horizontal. This would enable you to position an ellipse protractor directly in the plane of the angle by aligning its minor axis with line XW. However, you would not know what angle ellipse protractor to use. Even if you took the time to find the angle, it is very likely that it would turn out to be an odd angle for which no commercial ellipse protractor is made.

If an ellipse protractor is not available, or if you want to save time, you can make a reasonably accurate approximation of the ellipse angle. Construct a tangent square around the

A bent plate with a cylindrical hole perpendicular to plane *WXYZ* . . . perpendicular edge line *YU* is parallel to the minor axis of the ellipse . . . parallel ellipse on the lower surface follows the same minor axis line.

FIG. 210

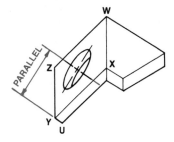

circle as was done in the case of a circle drawn on an inclined plane [200]. In [211] the square appears as a rectangle in the top view of the multiview drawing and as a rhomboid in the front view. Transfer the parallel tangent lines to the isometric view using dimensions parallel to the iso- metric axes. You can use the result- ing rhomboid in the isometric view as a guide to draw the required el- lipse. Try various angle ellipse tem- plate openings of the specified size until you find one that is closest to being *tangent* to the rhomboid at the *midpoints* of its sides.

Approximate the ellipse orientation and angle . . . draw a tangent square around the circle and transfer it to the isometric view . . . try various angle ellipses of the specified size . . . select an ellipse that is closest to being tangent at the midpoints of the sides.

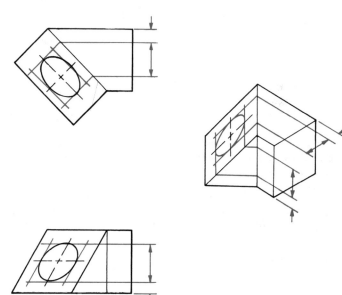

FIG. 211

If you want to determine more positively the direction of the minor axis of the ellipse just drawn, construct a line perpendicular to the oblique plane. Draw this line perpendicular to plane *WXYZ* starting at the circle's center point in the multiview drawing [212]. Find the direction of the line by drawing it perpendicular to two nonparallel lines in the plane. A line is perpendicular to another line if it is drawn perpendicular to a true length view of the other line.

Obtain one true length line by drawing a frontal line *CD* through point *A* in the top view of the multiview drawing. Points *C* and *D* are projected to the front view where line *CD* will be true length. Line *WX* is true length in the top view because the front view shows it to be a horizontal line. A line drawn through point *A* perpendicular to line *CD* in the front view and perpendicular to line *WX* in the top view will be perpendicular to plane *WXYZ*. Extend this perpendicular line until it intersects the bottom plane of the object at point *B*. Transfer the width and depth coordinates of *B* to the isometric view, and draw line *AB*. The minor axis of the ellipse will be along line *AB*.

The procedure for orienting the elliptical representation of a circle in an isometric drawing applies to multiview drawings as well. A good example of this is seen in the top and front views of the object just drawn [212]. In both of these views, the circle on the oblique plane appears as an ellipse. The minor axis follows the direction of line *AB* that you constructed perpendicular to the plane by drawing its top view perpendicular to true length line *WX* and its front view perpendicular to true length line *CD*.

Isometric, dimetric, and trimetric are all forms of axonometric drawing which, in turn, is a special application of multiview drawing. All of these drawing systems follow the same fundamental rules of orthographic projection. A professional illustrator will greatly benefit from a thorough understanding of all facets of orthographic projection. This can best be gained from a study of descriptive geometry.

Exercise 21

The objects listed below and illustrated in Section 90—Problems for Assignment are suitable examples to use in practicing the principles learned in the preceding section. Enlarge the objects as necessary to suit the available or assigned drawing sheet size. Maintain the proportions shown as closely as possible. Use either the viewing direction that provides the best description of the object or the viewing direction assigned by your instructor. Make a quick sketch of each object first to obtain a clear understanding of the object and to be sure that the given views are correct. The sketch will help you visualize the finished illustration and aid you in positioning it on your drawing sheet. Use a grid underlay sheet from Appendix C as an aid in sketching.

(a) The following objects have one or more circles on inclined planes as well as principal planes.
Probs. 71, 72, 73, 74, 77, 78, 79, 80, 81, 82.
(b) The following objects have one or more circles on oblique planes as well as principal planes.
Probs. 83, 85, 87.
Note: At this time when drawing 77, 78, 79, 80, 81, 82, 83, 85, 87, it is more important to concentrate on drawing the circles on the visible inclined and oblique planes. In Exercise 22, more attention will be given to the complete holes.

45. CYLINDRICAL SURFACES IN ISOMETRIC

In Sections 42 and 44 you studied how circles on principal and angled planes are represented by ellipses in an isometric view. Circles are usually produced by the intersection of a solid cylinder or a cylindrical hole with a plane. It is important to know how to

Find the direction of the minor axis . . . draw line *AB* perpendicular to true length lines *CD* in the front view and *WX* in the top view . . . line *AB* transferred to the isometric view is the minor axis direction . . . line *AB* is also the direction of the minor axes of the ellipses in the top and front views.

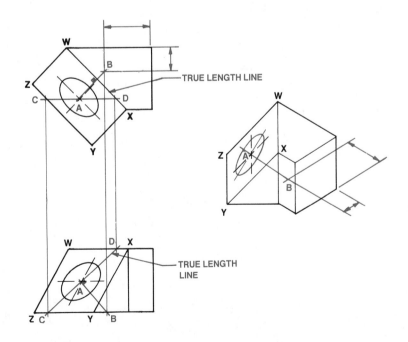

FIG. 212

Perpendicular planes on the ends of solid cylinders or cylindrical holes produce circles.

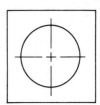

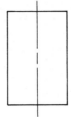

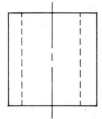

FIG. 213

Circular ends of cylinders and holes appear as ellipses in isometric views.

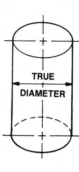

TRUE
DIAMETER

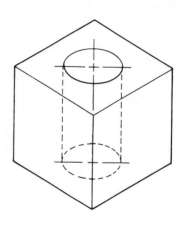

FIG. 214

Top and front views of a tube with a 30° bend.

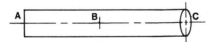

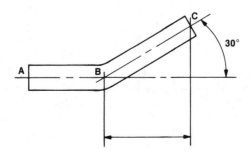

30°

FIG. 215

draw cylindrical surfaces in isometric because they occur so frequently.

When the end of a solid cylinder or a cylindrical hole is cut off by a **perpendicular** plane, the result is a circle [213]. Isometric views of these objects show the circles as ellipses [214]. Note that the outside lines of a cylinder always terminate at the ends of the major axis of the ellipse. Since the length of the major axis equals the true diameter of the circle that it represents, the distance between the outside lines of a cylinder is always equal to its true diameter. Also note that the minor axis of the ellipse is in line with the longitudinal axis of the cylinder when its plane is perpendicular to the axis.

One of the most common cylindrical objects drawn in isometric is a piece of bent tubing. The ends are normally cut off at 90° to permit joining the tubes with standard tube fittings. In [215] a length of tubing is bent at 30° with the horizontal. To draw an isometric view of this tube, first lay out the centerline of the horizontal segment *AB* along the isometric width axis [216]. Center an isometric ellipse protractor on point *B* and align its minor axis with the isometric depth axis. This will position the protractor in the plane of the required 30° bend angle because the depth axis is a line perpendicular to the frontal plane that contains the bend angle.

the end ellipse. Draw the ellipse using a 50° template opening equal in size to the specified diameter of the tube. Be sure that the size used is 1¼ times the specified size if you laid out the drawing with a regular scale.

At the *A* end of the tube, draw a line perpendicular to the width axis to establish the major axis of the end ellipse [218]. Use a 35° template to draw the ellipse at point *A* since this end of the tube is a principal plane. Now you can draw the outside lines

the tube (adjusted by the 1¼ size factor if a regular scale is used) will be seen because its outside lines are tangent at the end points of the true length major axes. The curved lines blending together the outside lines of the cylindrical segments at their intersection are approximated with the aid of an irregular curve.

If an ellipse protractor is not available, you can draw an isometric view of the bent tube's centerline by laying out the width and height coordinates

Draw an isometric view of the tube . . . position protractor in the frontal plane by aligning its minor axis with the perpendicular depth axis . . . draw tube centerline *BX* at 30° with the horizontal . . . read angle (50°) of perpendicular end ellipse on scale adjacent to point *X*.

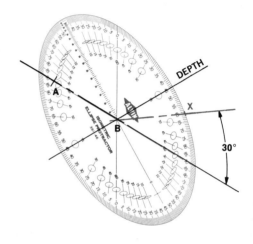

FIG. 216

Mark a point *X* on the outline of the protractor at a point 30° from the horizontal. This is at the 60° mark on the protractor. You can now draw the centerline of the inclined axis segment *BC* from *B* through *X*. Since the centerline is perpendicular to the circular end of the tube, the angle of ellipse to represent this circle can be read on the inner scale of the protractor adjacent to point *X*. The closest ellipse angle is seen to be 50° in this example. The centerline *BX* also establishes the orientation of the end ellipse. Its minor axis must follow the direction of the tube's centerline since this is a line that is perpendicular to its plane.

To complete the isometric view of the bent tube, locate point *C* on the inclined centerline *BX* by laying out the *X*-coordinate of *C* along the width axis [217]. A vertical line drawn from this point will locate point *C* at its intersection with line *BX*. A line drawn perpendicular to the inclined centerline at *C* establishes the major axis of

Draw ellipse at *C* end of the tube . . . locate point *C* on line *BX* by transferring its *X*-coordinate from the multiview drawing . . . minor axis of ellipse at *C* follows the perpendicular centerline *BX* . . . draw major axis perpendicular . . . use 50° template equal in size to tube's diameter to draw the ellipse.

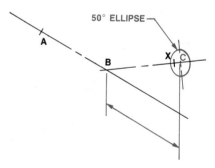

FIG. 217

Complete the isometric view of the tube . . . minor axis of ellipse at *A* end follows perpendicular centerline *AB* . . . draw major axis perpendicular . . . use 35° template equal in size to tube's diameter to draw the ellipse . . . draw outside lines of the tube tangent to the end ellipses and parallel to centerlines . . . draw curved intersection lines with an irregular curve.

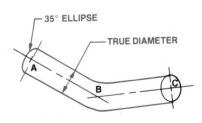

FIG. 218

of the tube tangent to the end ellipses and parallel to the centerlines of the two segments. The true diameter of

of point *C* [219]. Line *BC* determines the direction of the minor axis of the ellipse at *C*. Draw a line perpendic-

Draw an isometric view of the tube without a protractor . . . locate C end of the tube by transferring its X- and Y-coordinates from the multiview drawing . . . minor axis of the end ellipse follows the perpendicular centerline BC . . . draw major axis perpendicular . . . transfer points R and S to the isometric view . . . try various angle ellipses equal in size to tube's diameter on the axes lines . . . select an ellipse that is closest to passing through R and S.

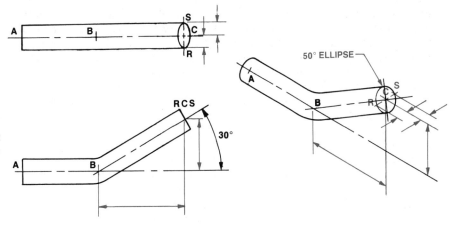

FIG. 219

ular at C to establish the major axis. Mark points R and S at the ends of the horizontal major axis line of the ellipse in the top view of the multiview drawing. Project them to the front view. After transferring these points to the isometric view, try various angle ellipse template openings equal in size to the tube's diameter on the major and minor axis lines un-

til you find one that is closest to passing through points R and S. In this case a 50° ellipse was found to fit best.

Some tubes are bent at an angle with both the horizontal and frontal planes [220]. The oblique segment of the tube requires two settings of an ellipse protractor to establish its direction in an isometric view. First lay out the 30° angle with the horizontal

[221]. Trace around the protractor's outline, and mark a point X at the location on the outline where the 30° angle is read. X is at the 60° mark on the protractor in this example.

Now rotate line BX through the specified 45° angle with the frontal plane. Draw a line XB' parallel to the width axis to locate point B' directly above point B and on the same ele-

Top, front, and auxiliary views of a tube bent at an oblique angle.

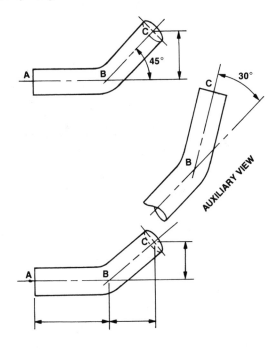

FIG. 220

Draw an isometric view of the tube . . . position protractor in the frontal plane by aligning its minor axis with the perpendicular depth axis . . . trace protractor outline and mark point X at 30° with the horizontal.

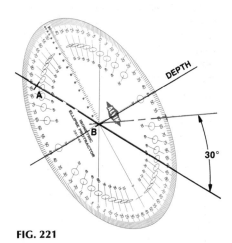

FIG. 221

vation as point X [222]. Point B' will be the center point of a horizontal plane on which the ellipse protractor can be positioned with its minor axis in the direction of a line perpendicular to the horizontal plane. Trace the outline of the protractor again and mark a point Y where the line B'X extended meets the outline. This is at the 0° mark on the protractor.

The next step is to rotate point Y' through a 45° angle on the protractor's outline to a point Y' at the 45° mark [223]. Draw lines from B' to Y' and from Y to Y'. Also draw a line parallel to YY' starting at X to estab-

lish a point X' on the B'Y' line. Point X has now been rotated to X' through the same 45° angle that Y was rotated to become Y'. Draw a line from B to X'. This is the centerline of the oblique segment of the bent tube and also the direction of the minor axis of the perpendicular end ellipse.

Read the angle of the ellipse by positioning the ellipse protractor with its center at point B and the major axis scale reading along line BX' [224]. At point X' the 15° scale reading indicates that you should use a 15° ellipse template to draw this end of the tube.

To complete the isometric view of the bent tube, locate point C on the BX' centerline by transferring its X-, Y-, and Z-coordinates from the multiview drawing [225]. Draw a line perpendicular to the centerline at C to establish the major axis of the end ellipse. Use a 15° ellipse template opening equal in size to the tube's diameter to draw the ellipse. The A end of the tube is completed by drawing a 35° ellipse as in the previous example. The last step is to draw the outside lines of the tube tangent to the end ellipses and parallel to the centerlines of the two segments.

Establish a horizontal plane on which to rotate point X . . . draw line XB' parallel to the width axis to locate plane's center above point B . . . position protractor in the horizontal plane by aligning its minor axis with the height axis . . . trace protractor outline and mark point Y where line B'X meets the outline.

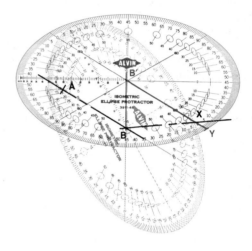

FIG. 222

Rotate point Y through a 45° angle to Y' . . . draw lines B'Y' and YY' . . . draw line XX' parallel to YY' . . . line BX' is the direction of the oblique centerline of the tube and the direction of the minor axis of the perpendicular end ellipse.

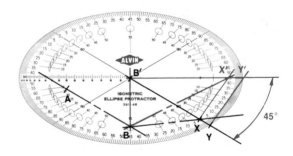

FIG. 223

Find angle of end ellipse . . . position protractor's center at point B with the major axis scale along BX' . . . read the perpendicular ellipse angle (15°) on the scale at X'.

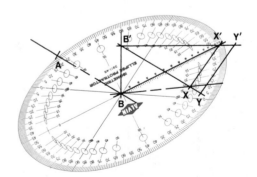

FIG. 224

Complete the isometric view of the tube
. . . locate point *C* on line *BX'* by
transferring its *X-*, *Y-*, and *Z*-coordinates
from the multiview drawing . . . minor axis
of ellipse at *C* follows the perpendicular
centerline *BX'*. . . draw major axis
perpendicular . . . use 15° template equal
in size to tube's diameter to draw ellipse
. . . draw 35° ellipse at *A* and tangent to
outside lines of the tube.

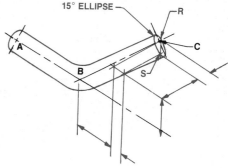

FIG. 225

Again, note that the true diameter of the tube will be seen. This diameter, of course, will be 1¼ times the specified size if you have laid out the drawing with a regular scale. The curved lines at the bend are approximated with an irregular curve.

The oblique angle tube that you have just drawn can also be drawn without the aid of an ellipse protractor. In [225] you located point *C* with dimensions parallel to the isometric axes taken from the multiview draw-

ing. In so doing, you determined the direction of centerline *BC* without the aid of the ellipse protractor. To find the proper ellipse angle to use at *C* mark two points *R* and *S* on the ends of the true length major axis of the ellipse in the top view of the multiview drawing [226]. When projected to the front view, *R* and *S* lie on the ends of a horizontal line because the top view of line *RS* is true length.

Now locate points *R* and *S* in the isometric view by transferring their

X-, *Y-*, and *Z*-coordinates [227]. The minor axis of the end ellipse will be aligned with the *BC* centerline. Draw a line perpendicular to the centerline at *C* to establish the major axis. Then try various angle ellipse template openings equal in size to the tube's diameter on the axes lines until you find one that is closest to passing through points *R* and *S*. In this case a 15° ellipse fits best. Draw the ellipse, and complete the isometric view as before.

Draw an isometric view of the tube without a protractor . . . mark points *R* and *S* on the true length major axis in the top view and on the horizontal front view.

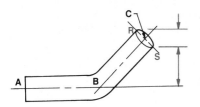
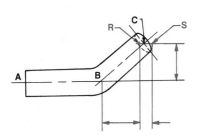

FIG. 226

Lay out isometric view of the tube . . . locate *C* end of the tube by transferring its *X-*, *Y-*, and *Z*-coordinates from the multiview drawing . . . locate points *R* and *S* by transferring their coordinates . . . minor axis of ellipse at *C* follows the perpendicular centerline *BC* . . . draw major axis perpendicular . . . try various angle ellipses equal in size to tube's diameter on the axes lines . . . select an ellipse that is closest to passing through *R* and *S*.

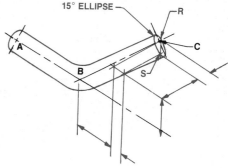

FIG. 227

When a solid cylinder or a cylindrical hole is perpendicular to a plane, the intersection is a **circle.** In an isometric view, this circle appears as an **ellipse** and you can draw it as described in Section 42—Circles in Isometric and in Section 44—Circles on Angled Surfaces. Figure [228] shows an example of perpendicular intersections. The perpendicular ends of the cylinder and of the cylindrical hole are circles in the multiview drawing. These circles appear as ellipses in the isometric view.

When a cylindrical surface meets a plane at some angle other than 90°, the intersection is an **ellipse** instead of a circle [229]. Since the isometric view of this ellipse also has an elliptical appearance, there is always a temptation to use the same procedure to draw the ellipse as was used to draw an ellipse that represented a circle. The minor axis of an ellipse that represents an ellipse **does not** follow the direction of a line perpendicular to its plane. You can also see in [229] that the length of the major axis is not equal to the diameter of the cylinder that has produced the elliptical intersection.

When drawing the isometric representation of an ellipse, there is no general rule for the direction of the minor axis. You can use an ellipse protractor to lay out the direction of a cylinder's centerline if it lies at an

The intersection of a solid cylinder or a cylindrical hole with a perpendicular plane is a circle . . . the isometric view of the circle is an ellipse.

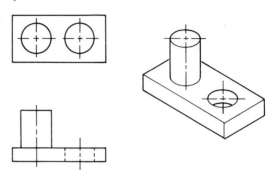

FIG. 228

angle with the principal planes. It is of no use, however, in determining the direction of the minor axis and the angle of the ellipse when the ellipse does not represent a circle. The most accurate procedure in drawing the isometric view of the ellipse is to plot the locations of a number of points on the ellipse. Then draw a smooth curve through the points with an irregular curve or with portions of an ellipse template.

To save time, you can usually make a reasonable approximation of an elliptical intersection by enclosing the ellipse in a tangent rectangle. In [229] the intersections of the solid cylinder and the cylindrical hole with the in-

clined plane are ellipses. An enclosing tangent rectangle drawn around each ellipse is transferred to the isometric view. Use the resulting rhomboids as guides to draw the required ellipses. Try various angles and sizes of ellipse template openings until you find one that is closest to being **tangent** to the rhomboids at the **midpoints** of their sides. Note that the ellipse you select will also be tangent to the outside lines of the cylinder which is seen at its true diameter (adjusted by 1¼ if you have used a regular scale).

In [230] a horizontal hole has been drilled through a rectangular block at an angle with the frontal and profile

The intersection of a solid cylinder or a cylindrical hole with an angled plane is an ellipse . . . the isometric view of the ellipse is also an ellipse.
To draw the isometric view . . . draw a tangent rectangle around the ellipse and transfer it to the isometric view . . . try various angle and size ellipses . . . select an ellipse that is closest to being tangent at the midpoints and also tangent to the outside lines of the cylinder.

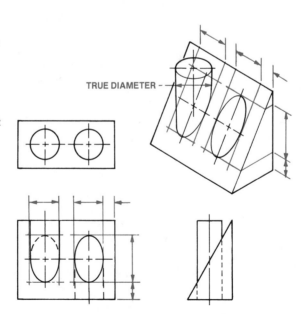

TRUE DIAMETER –

FIG. 229

Top, front, and right side views of a rectangular block . . . the horizontal hole is at an angle with the front and side surfaces of the block . . . draw tangent rectangles around the ellipses.

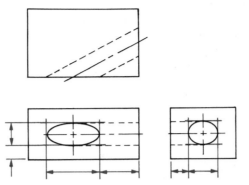

FIG. 230

planes. The intersections with these planes are ellipses in the multiview drawing. For the isometric view, draw two sets of parallel lines tangent to each ellipse and parallel to their centerlines in the multiview drawing. The tangent lines form enclosing rectangles with tangency points at the midpoints of their sides. Transfer the lines and tangency points to the isometric view of the block using dimensions parallel to the isometric axes [231]. Then try various angles and sizes of ellipse template openings for each ellipse until you find one that is closest to passing through the tangency points.

Another aid in selecting appropriate ellipse angles is the fact that the ellipses must be tangent to the outside lines of the cylindrical hole. Draw these lines parallel to the axis of the hole at a spacing equal to the true

Draw an isometric view of the ellipses . . . transfer tangent rectangles to the front and side surfaces . . . try various angle and size ellipses . . . select ellipses that are closest to being tangent at the midpoints of the sides . . . outside lines of the hole spaced at their true diameter are tangent to the ellipses.

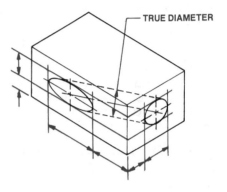

— TRUE DIAMETER

FIG. 231

diameter of the hole which you can always see. This diameter must be adjusted, of course, by the 1¼ ratio if the isometric drawing is laid out with a regular scale. In [231] note that the ellipses selected are tangent to the hidden outside lines of the hole.

Another example of a nonperpen-

dicular cylindrical intersection is [232] where a hole has been drilled through a block at an oblique angle. You can draw an approximation of the elliptical intersections in an isometric view by using the same technique used in the previous example where the axis of the hole was an inclined line.

Top, front, and right side views of a rectangular block . . . the oblique centerline of the hole is at an angle with all three principal planes . . . draw tangent rectangles around the ellipses.

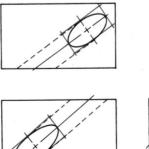

FIG. 232

Enclose the ellipses in tangent rectangles by drawing two sets of parallel lines tangent to each ellipse and parallel to their centerlines in the multiview drawing. Transfer the lines and their tangency points to the isometric view of the block [233]. Also draw the axis and the parallel outside lines of the hole at the true diameter spacing. Try various angles and sizes of ellipse template openings for each ellipse until you find one that is closest to passing through the tangency points of the ellipse and is also tangent to the outside lines of the hole. Sometimes it is helpful to first sketch an approximation of each ellipse to aid in selecting the best template opening.

Draw an isometric view of the ellipses . . . transfer tangent rectangles to the front and top surfaces . . . draw outside lines of the hole parallel to the centerline and spaced at their true diameter . . . try various angle and size ellipses . . . select ellipses that are closest to being tangent at the midpoints of the sides and also tangent to the outside lines of the hole.

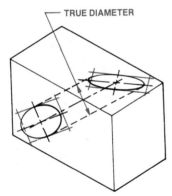

FIG. 233

Exercise 22

The objects listed below and illustrated in Section 90—Problems for Assignment are suitable examples to use in practicing the principles learned in the preceding section. Enlarge the objects as necessary to suit the available or assigned drawing sheet size. Maintain the proportions shown as closely as possible. Use either the viewing direction that provides the best description of the object or the viewing direction assigned by your instructor. Make a quick sketch of each object first to obtain a

clear understanding of the object and to be sure that the given views are correct. The sketch will help you visualize the finished illustration and aid you in positioning it on your drawing sheet. Use a grid underlay sheet from Appendix C as an aid in sketching.

(a) The following objects have one or more round holes or solid cylinders producing circles on principal planes.
Probs. 42, 43, 45, 46, 47, 48, 49, 50, 51, 61, 62, 63, 64, 65, 66, 67, 68, 69, 70.

(b) The following objects are basically cylindrical. The circles are all on principal planes.
Probs. 52, 53, 54, 55, 56, 57, 58, 59, 60.

(c) The following objects have round holes whose axes are perpendicular to an inclined plane.
Probs. 71, 72, 73, 74.

(d) The following objects have round holes whose axes are perpendicular to an inclined plane and at an angle with a principal plane. Draw the hidden as well as visible lines for the holes.
Probs. 77, 79, 81.

(e) The following objects have round holes whose axes are at an angle with an inclined plane and perpendicular to a principal plane. Draw the hidden as well as visible lines for the holes. Compare the results with (d).
Probs. 78, 80, 82.

(f) The following objects have round holes whose axes are perpendicular to an oblique plane and at an angle with a principal plane. Draw the hidden as well as visible lines for the holes.
Probs. 83, 85, 87.

(g) The following objects have round holes whose axes are at an angle with an oblique plane and perpendicular to a principal plane. Draw the hidden as well as visible lines for the holes. Compare the results with (f).
Probs. 84, 86, 88.

(h) The following objects have round holes whose axes are at an angle with two principal planes. Draw the hidden as well as visible lines for the holes.
Probs. 75, 76.

(i) The following object has a variety of fillets and rounds. Fillets and rounds may also be added to other objects in the problem set.
Prob. 44.

Note: In the multiview drawings for 72, 73, 74, 75, 76, 77, 79, 81, 83, 84,

85, 86, 87, 88, note how the ellipses shown follow the same basic rules as in isometric and other forms of axonometric drawing.

46. CURVED LINES AND SURFACES IN ISOMETRIC

The most difficult objects to draw in isometric or in any of the axonometric systems are those having plane surfaces whose boundaries are curved lines. Curved boundary lines are transferred from multiview drawings to isometric and other types of pictorial drawings in basically the same way as straight lines. The difference lies in having to locate and transfer the width, height, and depth coordinates of not only the end points of the lines but also the coordinates of as many intermediate points as necessary to describe the curvature of the line [234]. To accomplish this as quickly and orderly as possible, pass a series of parallel horizontal or vertical planes through the object. These planes, referred to as **cutting** or **section planes,** cut the object into sections that pass through the irregular contours. The number and location of these planes depends on the nature of the contours. The more complex the contour, the more planes that are required.

Two end points determine a straight line . . . curved lines require many points.

FIG. 234

In the simplest situation, the curved lines appear on or parallel to a principal plane of the object. In [235] the vertical end surfaces of a retaining clip have curved boundary lines. Pass uniformly spaced horizontal cutting planes through the view of the multiview drawing that shows the contour [236]. These planes intersect the

The vertical end planes of this retaining clip have curved boundary lines.

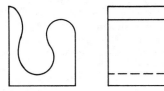

FIG. 235

Pass horizontal cutting planes through the contour line.

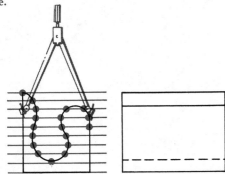

FIG. 236

Transfer cutting plane intersection lines to an isometric enclosing box . . . plot points by transferring measurements along the lines.

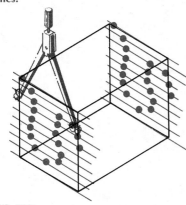

FIG. 237

end surfaces in a series of parallel horizontal lines and locate representative points on the contour lines. You can transfer the horizontal lines to the isometric drawing readily by plotting their end points on the surfaces of an enclosing box [237]. Since the intersection lines are parallel to an isometric axis, transfer measurements directly along the lines to locate the contour points. When all of

the points are plotted, lightly sketch a smooth curve through them [238]. Darken the curve by using an irregular curve. Note that vertical cutting planes could have been used instead of horizontal planes. Horizontal planes are, however, a little more efficient in this example because each one intersects at least two points on the curve.

You can use the same procedure for contour lines on inclined or oblique surfaces. In [239] the end of a piece of railroad rail has been cut off as an inclined plane. Horizontal cutting planes create a series of parallel lines intersecting the contoured surface [240]. Lay out the enclosing box and the inclined plane on the isometric axes [241]. Then transfer the vertical spacing of the cutting planes to the height axis. Project this spacing horizontally to meet the inclined plane, and draw the intersection lines of the cutting planes with the inclined plane. Since the rail is symmetrical, you can draw its cen-

Lightly sketch a smooth curve through the points . . . darken with an irregular curve.

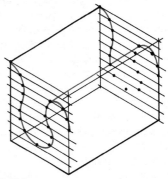

FIG. 238

The end of this railroad rail has been cut off by an inclined plane.

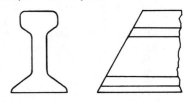

FIG. 239

Create an enclosing box and draw horizontal cutting planes.

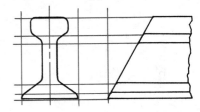

FIG. 240

Lay out enclosing box and inclined plane . . . project the vertical spacing of the cutting planes from the end of the enclosing box to the inclined plane and draw intersection lines.

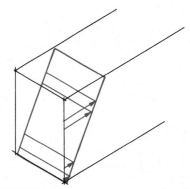

FIG. 241

terline on the inclined surface to aid in plotting points on the irregular boundary line. Transfer equal distances of the points on each side of the centerline directly from the multiview drawing since the intersection lines are parallel to an isometric axis [242]. Now you can sketch the irregular boundary lines lightly and then darken them with a triangle and an irregular curve [243]. Project horizontal edge lines from the contour to complete the view. In cases involving regular geometric shapes, uniform spacing of the cutting planes is not always necessary or desirable. The planes should be located to intersect important points such as intersections, tangencies, and points where the contour changes direction. Where the rate of curvature changes quickly, you need more cutting planes to obtain sufficient points to plot a smooth curve.

In [244] a circular hole has been drilled perpendicular to an oblique surface of the object. In the multiview drawing the intersection of the hole with the oblique surface appears as an ellipse in the top, front, and right side views. The true circular contour of the hole would only be visible in an auxiliary view showing the true size of the oblique surface. To draw an isometric view of this object, pass horizontal cutting planes through the object in the same way as in the preceding examples [245]. Project the parallel intersection lines to the top view. Lay out the general outline of the object on the isometric axes. Then transfer the vertical spacing of the cutting planes to the height axis and project it to the oblique sur-

face where the intersection lines are drawn [246].

Draw basic isometric outline of the object . . . project vertical spacing of the cutting planes to the oblique surface and draw intersection lines.

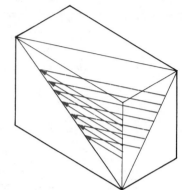

FIG. 246

Transfer equal distance measurements on each side of a centerline drawn on the inclined plane.

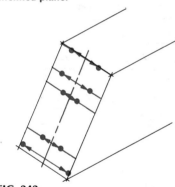

FIG. 242

Lightly sketch boundary lines . . . darken with a triangle and an irregular curve.

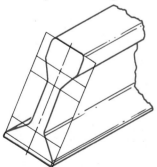

FIG. 243

A round hole has been drilled perpendicular to the oblique surface.

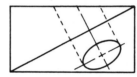

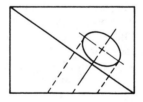

FIG. 244

Pass horizontal cutting planes through the object.

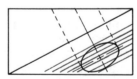

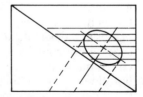

FIG. 245

Since the cutting plane intersection lines are not true isometric lines, you must locate the contour points on the lines by transferring the width coordinate of each point from the front view of the multiview drawing to the cutting plane intersections on the front surface of the enclosing box [247]. You can then project each point inwardly parallel to the depth axis until it meets the intersection line on the oblique surface. Sketch a smooth curve through the points and darken it with an irregular curve or an ellipse template [248].

Note that since the curved line in this example is known to be a circle, the procedures described in Section 44—Circles on Angled Surfaces would undoubtedly be quicker and easier to use. The curve is an ellipse in the isometric view and can be drawn with an ellipse template. The visible portion of the curved intersection of the drilled hole with the back surface of the object has been omitted but can be drawn using the procedures described in Section 45—Cylindrical Surfaces in Isometric. This curve in the isometric view is an ellipse that represents an ellipse.

You can use these plotting techniques just described in all forms of pictorial drawing to lay out irregular shapes of all kinds. Modern aircraft, for example, have few if any straight lines or regular geometric shapes. Aircraft are usually sectioned on design drawings by a series of planes parallel and perpendicular to the ground creating **fuselage stations, water lines, wing lines, butt lines,** and so forth [250]. Contours are seldom if ever used for exact dimensioning because of their compound curved nature.

The aircraft canopy shown in [249] has surfaces that curve in all three dimensions of space. In order to plot points describing the curving outlines of these surfaces in an isometric drawing, you must use a series of uniformly spaced vertical cutting planes that intersect the contours [250]. Place these parallel planes perpendicular to the longitudinal axis of the object to take advantage of symmetry in plotting the contour points. They cor-

Transfer width coordinates to intersection lines on front surface . . . project inwardly, parallel to the depth axis, to intersection lines on oblique surface.

Sketch a smooth curve through points . . . darken with instruments.

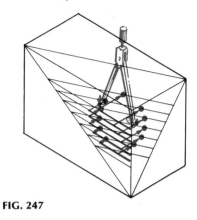

FIG. 247

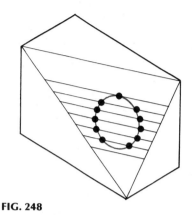

FIG. 248

An aircraft canopy has many curved surfaces with curved boundary lines.

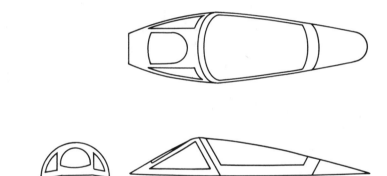

FIG. 249

Draw enclosing box . . . establish vertical cutting planes perpendicular to the longitudinal axis.

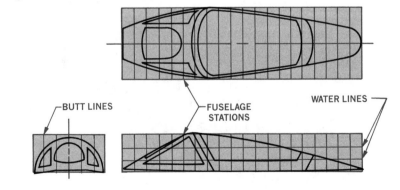

BUTT LINES   FUSELAGE STATIONS   WATER LINES

FIG. 250

Make rough sketch of likely appearance of the canopy to help plan visible contour lines to be plotted.

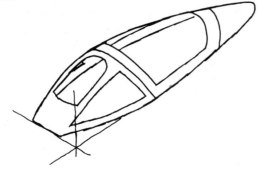

FIG. 251

Draw enclosing isometric box with a vertical plane passing through the longitudinal axis . . . space vertical cutting plane intersection lines along the plane.

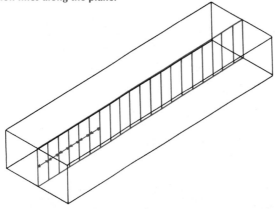

FIG. 252

Plot the visible bottom edge line . . . lay out height of each point on vertical plane intersection lines . . . lay out horizontal spacing of each point on one side of the plane . . . sketch the contour while plotting.

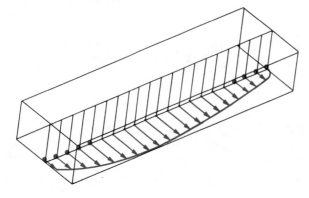

FIG. 253

respond to the fuselage stations on the multiview drawing.

Before starting to plot the contour points, it is often very helpful to make a rough sketch of how the object is likely to appear in the pictorial view [251]. This will provide an insight into which contour lines are likely to be visible and thus help avoid unnecessary plotting of hidden contours. The sketch may also be helpful in determining the best locations for cutting planes. Presketching of this type is valuable in all types of pictorial drawings.

Start the isometric drawing of the canopy by laying out an enclosing box on the isometric axes [252]. Draw a vertical plane passing through the longitudinal axis, and space the vertical lines of the cutting planes along it. Plot the boundary lines of the curved surfaces by transferring the points where each line is intersected by a cutting plane. Obtain the height of each point and its symmetrically opposite point from the view of the multiview drawing that shows the side of the canopy. Get the spacing on each side of the longitudinal centerline from the view showing the top of the canopy.

The first contour line plotted is the visible bottom edge of the canopy [253]. Lay out the height of each point on the vertical cutting plane intersections. Lay out the horizontal spacing to one side of the center plane on lines parallel to the isometric axis. As soon as you plot each series of points on a contour line, lightly sketch the curve to build up an understanding of the entire object's appearance gradually and to see if enough points are being plotted to define the object properly.

Following the bottom edge line, plot the boundary lines of the windshield and the visible side window [254]. Lay out the windshield points symmetrically on each side of the center plane after establishing their heights on the vertical cutting plane intersection lines. Plot the points for the side window in one direction only.

Next lay out the boundary lines of the large curved window in the rear half of the canopy. Plot symmetrical points on each side of the center plane at the proper height, and lightly sketch the curves [255]. Also plot the line defining where the two halves of the canopy join. In some cases it may be necessary to add special additional cutting planes to pick up critical contour points. Now you can join the sketched contours with a curving tangent line describing the top boundary of the canopy [256].

If you want to show the portions of the windows on the far side that can be seen through the visible windows, you should plot these contours now. Then you can complete the drawing

Plot points on each side of the center plane to define the windshield contour . . . plot visible side window boundary lines.

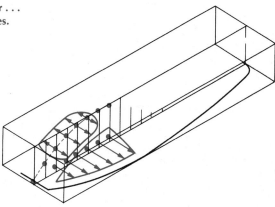

FIG. 254

Plot boundary lines of curved rear window . . . also line separating the two halves of the canopy.

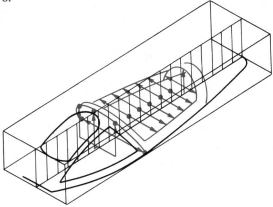

FIG. 255

Join sketch contours with tangent top boundary line.

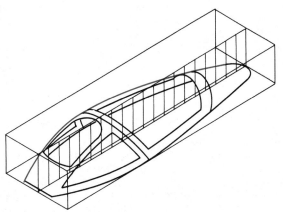

FIG. 256

by darkening the sketched lines with an irregular curve [257]. Erase all construction lines with the aid of an erasing shield.

When plotting curves that are not regular geometric shapes or where a large number of points are involved, it is always wise to use some labeling system to keep track of the points. This helps avoid confusion, reduces the possibility of error, and saves time in the long run. You can lightly mark small letters or numbers on the drawing as each point is plotted. After you draw the contour lines, erase the labels.

Any irregularly shaped surface may be plotted in the isometric drawing system using this method. The same basic plotting procedure is used in all forms of axonometric and also in perspective and oblique drawing. As you gain experience, you will need fewer cutting planes to determine the shape of a surface. From the examples shown in [258], you can see that this method can be used to define the shapes of intersecting cylinders, holes cut into cylindrical surfaces, off-axis ellipses, and many other irregular shapes.

One object that does not cause any shape description problems from a viewing direction in any drawing system is the true sphere. No matter how you look at it, a sphere always appears as a true circle. An example of this can be seen in the drawing of a *torus* [259]. This geometric shape is formed by a sphere rolling around a circular track. In the isometric view shown, the successive positions of the sphere as it rolls around all appear as circles. A partial sphere in the form of a spherical radius is often seen on the ends of rods and on the rectangular corners of castings. The true circle appearance of a sphere is also retained in these cases in all drawing systems. This is discussed further in Section 51—Drawing a Dimetric View [288].

Exercise 23

The objects listed below and illustrated in Section 90—Problems for Assignment are suitable examples to use in practicing the principles learned in the preceding section. Enlarge the objects as necessary to suit the available

Darken sketched lines with an irregular curve . . . clean up construction lines.

FIG. 257

Many types of contours can be plotted with the aid of cutting planes.

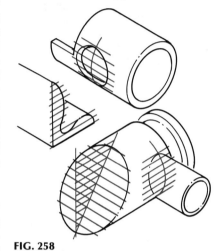

FIG. 258

A torus is formed when a sphere rolls around a circular track . . . a sphere seen in any position always appears as a true circle.

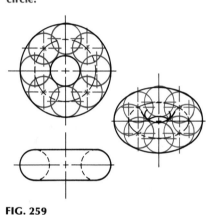

FIG. 259

An isometric viewing position may obscure details.

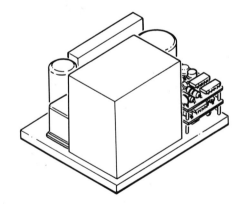

FIG. 260

or assigned drawing sheet size. Maintain the proportions shown as closely as possible. Use either the viewing direction that provides the best description of the object or the viewing direction assigned by your instructor. Make a quick

sketch of each object first to obtain a clear understanding of the object and to be sure that the given views are correct. The sketch will help you visualize the finished illustration and aid you in positioning it on your drawing sheet. Use a grid underlay sheet from Appendix C as an aid in sketching.

(a) The following objects have one or more circular or noncircular curved lines.
Probs. 89, 90, 91, 92, 93, 94, 95, 96, 97, 98.

47. DISADVANTAGES OF ISOMETRIC

Isometric drawings are widely used for technical illustrations, but they have certain inherent disadvantages. When a cube is rotated and tilted into an isometric viewing position, the corner closest to your eye and the corner farthest away appear superimposed. This is not a natural appearance and may be confusing in some instances. In an interior arrangement type of technical illustration where a group of components are pictured inside a box, a number of the components may be obscured in an isometric drawing if they are arranged one behind another [260].

In isometric, the larger the physical size of an object (unless it is symmetrical), the more apparent will be the distortion caused by the fact that the edges are drawn parallel, rather than converging as the eye normally sees them. This distortion is most apparent in long objects such as aircraft or ships. Although this is a problem common to all types of axonometric drawing, it is less noticeable in dimetric or trimetric drawing [261].

Axonometric drawings are generally limited in their use to technical literature because of the distorted appearance of parallel edge lines. This distortion is especially a problem in advertising or sales literature where an object must be pictured so that it will appear as realistic as possible. With the rising cost of labor and materials, most buyers of illustrations want the drawings to be made suitable for as many different applications as possible without limiting their effectiveness. In this situation the drawings may have to be made using the perspective drawing system or at least in dimetric or trimetric.

Distortion is most apparent in large and long objects drawn in isometric . . . this is less noticeable in dimetric and trimetric drawings.

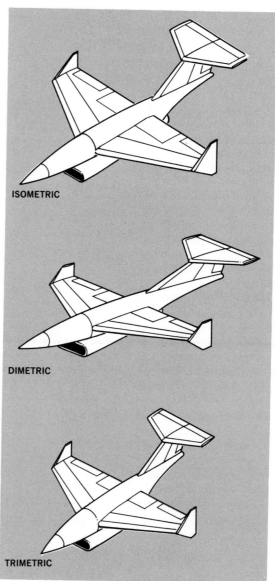

ISOMETRIC

DIMETRIC

TRIMETRIC

FIG. 261

48. DIMETRIC DRAWING

In *isometric drawing,* the width, height, and depth axes are drawn at 120° between each other [262]. This is the result of rotating the object 45° about a vertical axis and tilting it forward 35° 16′ about a horizontal axis so that all three of its principal faces are at the same angle with the viewing plane. The axes are distorted the same amount so that the same foreshortened scale can be used on each axis.

In *dimetric drawing,* the axes are drawn such that any two angles between axes are equal [263]. The third angle is equal to the difference between the sum of the first two and 360°. This is the result of rotating the object 45° about a vertical axis and tilting it forward a selected number of degrees about a horizontal axis so that two principal faces will be at the same angle with the viewing plane and the third will be at a different angle. Two of the axes are distorted the same amount because they are at the same angle with the viewing plane. The third axis is distorted a different amount because it is at a different angle.

In [263] the 110° equal angles and the 140° third angle are the result of a 21° tilt. The width and depth axes appear at 20° angles with the horizontal. The front and side faces are at equal angles with the viewing plane. The top face is at a different angle. The top face in this case is less visible than in the isometric view where the tilt angle was 35° 16′. This loss is offset by the gain in visibility of the front and side faces.

As implied by the prefix *di* in the word "dimetric," two foreshortened measuring scales are required in dimetric because of the two different angles between the axes and the viewing plane. If the width and depth axes are at the same angle with the viewing plane, measurements along these axes are made with the same foreshortened scale [263]. The height axis requires a different scale since it is at a different angle with the viewing plane.

Selecting other tilt angles will increase or decrease the visibility of the

Isometric . . . the 45° rotation and 35° 16′ tilt positions the axes at equal angles with each other and with the viewing plane . . . the same scale is used on each axis.

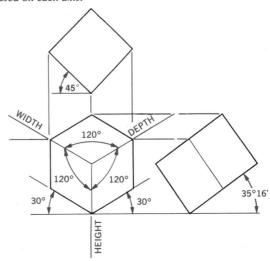

FIG. 262

Dimetric . . . the 45° rotation positions two axes at equal angles with each other and with the viewing plane . . . the tilt angle positions the third axis at a different angle with the viewing plane . . . the sum of the angles between axes must be 360°.

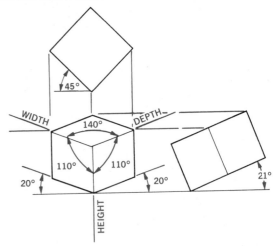

FIG. 263

top surface. The two scales required vary with the tilt angle used [264]. The visibility of the other faces can also be increased or decreased in dimetric by selecting a rotation angle other than 45° [265]. In this case the height and either the width or depth axis is usually held at the same angle

with the viewing plane so that their scales will be the same. Many tilt and rotation combinations can be used [266]. Just be certain that two axes have the same angle with the viewing plane.

Dimetric drawing produces a picture that has a more natural appear-

Dimetric tilt angles can be selected to vary visibility of the top surface . . . the width and depth axes use the same scale.

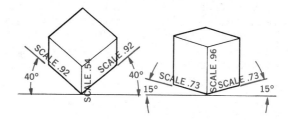

FIG. 264

Dimetric rotation angles can also be selected to vary the visibility of other faces . . . the height and either the width or depth scales are the same.

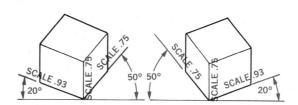

FIG. 265

ance than isometric without having to spend the extra time required for a perspective drawing. The use of only two rather than three equal angles relieves some of the "boxy" appearance of isometric. In addition, dimetric provides the illustrator with a larger selection of viewing directions for the object than is possible with isometric.

Many tilt and rotation combinations can be used . . . two scales always remain the same.

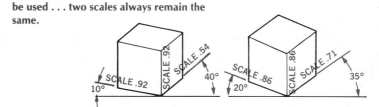

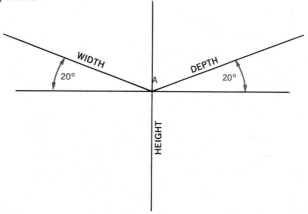

FIG. 266

49. CONSTRUCTING DIMETRIC SCALES

Two foreshortened scales are always required in laying out a dimetric drawing. In trimetric drawing three foreshortened scales are required. The basic procedure outlined in the following steps for dimetric will also be used later for constructing trimetric scales.

(1) Select angles with the horizontal for the width and depth axes to suit the object being drawn (20° in this case) [267]. Draw a vertical height axis through the intersection point A of the width and depth axes.

To construct dimetric scales . . . draw width and depth axes at desired angles . . . draw vertical height axis through their intersection point A.

FIG. 267

(2) Choose point *X* at a convenient distance along the width axis and draw line *XZ* perpendicular to the height axis [268].

(3) Draw lines *XY* and *ZY* perpendic-ular to the width and depth axes and intersecting the height axis at *Y* [269].

(4) Using a circle template or a com-pass, draw semicircles based on diameters *XY* and *XZ* [270].

(5) Extend lines *ZA* and *YA* to inter-sect the semicircles at *Z'* and *Y'* [270].

(6) Mark off full size scales along *Y'X*

Draw line *XZ* perpendicular to the height axis at a convenient location.

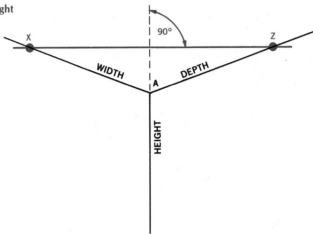

FIG. 268

Draw line *XY* perpendicular to the depth axis . . . draw line *ZY* perpendicular to the width axis.

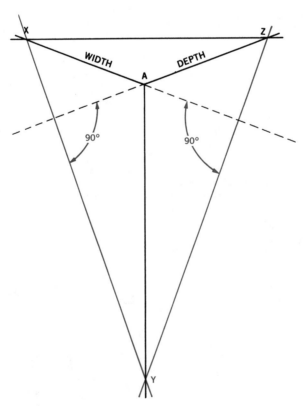

FIG. 269

Draw semicircles based on lines *XY* and
XZ . . . extend lines *ZA* and *YA* to intersect
the semicircles at *Z'* and *Y'*.

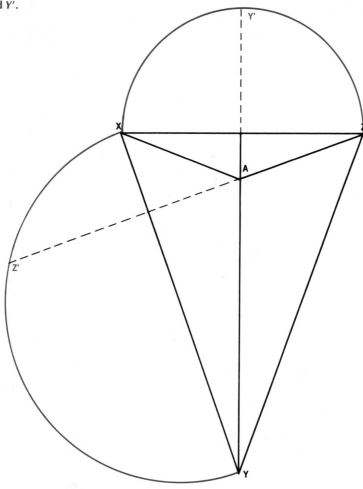

FIG. 270

Mark full size scales on Y'X and Y'Z . . .
project scale marks parallel to the height
axis onto the width and depth axes . . .
mark full size scale on Z'Y . . . project
scale marks onto height axis.

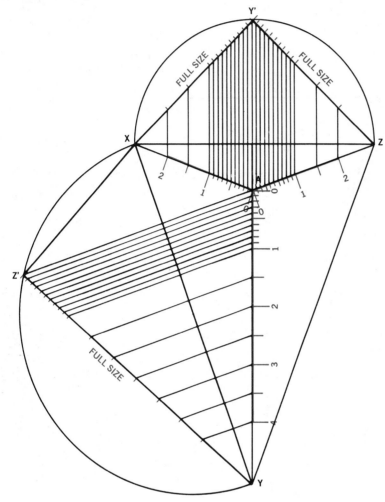

FIG. 271

and Y'Z [271]. Using a series of
lines parallel to the height axis
Y'Y, project foreshortened scale
marks onto the width and depth
axes.

(7) Mark off a full size scale along
Z'Y [271]. Using a series of lines
parallel to the depth axis Z'Z,
project foreshortened scale marks
onto the height axis.

(8) Transfer the foreshortened scales
to a template of plastic or illustration board [272].

Note that the two foreshortened scales
AX and AZ are identical. When you
use this construction procedure in

Transfer foreshortened scales to a
template.

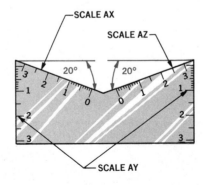

FIG. 272

Section 52 to lay out trimetric scales,
each of the three foreshortened scales
will be different.

Some recommended shapes for dimetric and trimetric scale templates
are shown in [273]. By using the interior portion of the template for lesser
angles, as many as three different sets
of angles for different viewing angles
may be included on one template.
Many drafting supply companies sell
commercially made dimetric and trimetric scale templates for commonly
used axis angles. Some of these scales
are designed to be attached to a drafting machine in place of the regular
scale [274]. Carefully done, a homemade template is equally as useful
and as accurate. Commercial scale
templates are generally preferred in
large illustration departments to en-
courage the use of uniform sets of axes
angles. In this way, drawings may be
worked on by different illustrators
without wasting layout and calcula-
tion time to derive a scale or trying
to match someone else's choice of
angles.

If a foreshortened scale for trimetric drawing has been laid out on
transparent material, it can be turned
over left for right to change the viewing angle. It can also be upended and
reversed for another selection of angles. Even when a scale containing
only one pair of angles is used, the
number of possible viewpoints available to the illustrator is greater in either
dimetric or trimetric than in isometric
(see Section 53—Selecting Axonometric Viewing Directions). This feature makes the dimetric and trimetric
systems more popular among illustrators who regularly work on large,
complex assemblies. It enables the
illustrator to draw a view more nearly
like that seen, for example, by a me-
chanic opening an overhead door or
looking for an adjustment point deep
down inside an equipment bay on an
aircraft.

50. CIRCLES IN DIMETRIC

When a circle occurs on a principal plane of an object, the angle of
the ellipse that represents it in a dimetric view will vary widely depending on the axes angles selected. The

Scales may be marked on blades for a drafting machine . . . or several sets of scales may be marked on a single template.

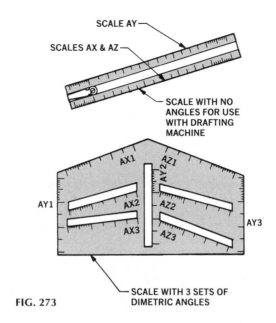

FIG. 273

Trimetric scales attached to a drafting machine in a position parallel to the trimetric axes.

FIG. 274

To find approximate ellipses angles for a given dimetric axis system . . . construct a dimetric cube using proper fore-shortened scales . . . draw a minor axis line through the center of each face in a direction perpendicular to the face . . . draw perpendicular major axes . . . try various angle ellipses equal in size to the cube's full size . . . select ellipses that are closest to being tangent at the midpoints of the sides.

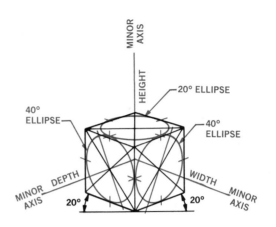

FIG. 275

ellipse angle always equals the angle that the circle's plane makes with the line of sight. As in isometric, the minor axis of an ellipse that represents a circle must follow the direction of a line that is perpendicular to the plane on which the circle occurs.

You can approximate the proper ellipse angle for a particular situation by constructing a dimetric cube for the axis system being used [275]. Be sure to use the proper foreshortened scales in laying out the width, height, and depth of the cube. Locate the center of each face at the intersection of diagonal lines drawn across corners. Draw a minor axis line through each center parallel to the width, height, or depth axis that represents the direction of a line perpendicular to the plane on which the ellipse lies. Draw a major axis line perpendicular to each minor axis. Then try various angles of ellipse template openings equal in size to the full (not foreshortened) size of the cube on the minor and major axes lines until you find ellipses that are closest to being *tangent* to the edges of the cube at their *midpoints.*

A more exact way of determining the proper ellipse angle for circles drawn on the true axonometric faces of an object is shown in [276]. The procedure is an extension of the method shown in [271] for constructing dimetric scales. To find the ellipse angle for the face on the left, extend line YX a convenient distance to point B. Project points Z′ and A parallel to YX to establish points C and D on a line drawn perpendicular to YX through B. Draw an arc of radius BC to intersect line AD at D′. Draw line BD′ and measure its angle with line XB. Thus, 41° is the required ellipse angle for the face on the left in this example. A similar construction can be made for the top face by extending line XZ to E and drawing an arc with radius EF to obtain point G. This gives you an ellipse angle of 21° for the top face. In dimetric the ellipse for the face on the right has the same angle as the face on the left since the axes angles and the scale ratios are the same. In trimetric an additional construction is required to find the third ellipse angle [293]. Since 41° and 21° ellipse templates are not normally available, the closest standard ellipse templates (40° and 20°) are used with no noticeable error in most cases.

Construction procedure for finding exact ellipse angles in dimetric.

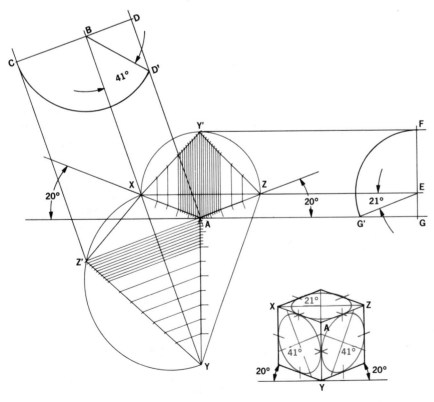

FIG. 276

Popular dimetric axes . . . scale ratios and ellipse angles for principal planes.

	Axis Angles		Scale Ratios			Ellipse Angles		
	Left	Right	Left	Right	Vertical	Left	Right	Top
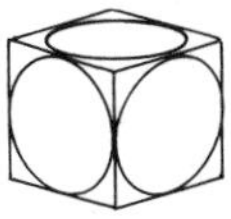	15°	15°	.73	.73	.96	45°	45°	15°
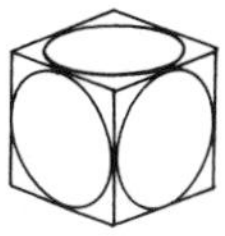	20°	20°	.75	.75	.93	40°	40°	20°
	25°	25°	.78	.78	.88	40°	40°	30°
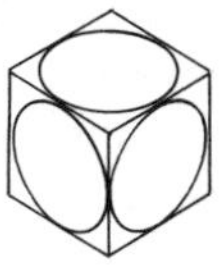 (isometric)	30°	30°	.82	.82	.82	35°	35°	35°
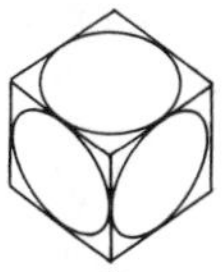	35°	35°	.86	.86	.71	30°	30°	45°
	40°	40°	.92	.92	.54	25°	25°	55°

	Axis Angles		Scale Ratios			Ellipse Angles		
	Left	Right	Left	Right	Vertical	Left	Right	Top
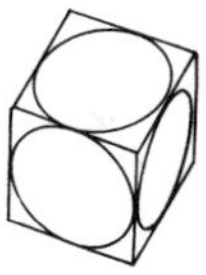	15°	60°	.96	.73	.73	45°	15°	45°
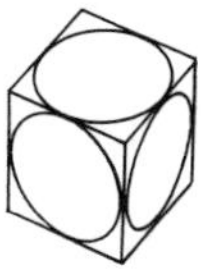	20°	50°	.93	.75	.75	40°	20°	40°
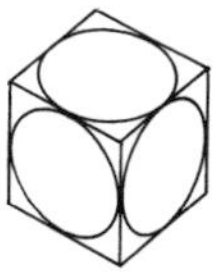	25°	40°	.88	.78	.78	40°	30°	40°
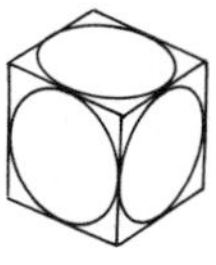	20°	35°	.86	.71	.86	45°	30°	30°
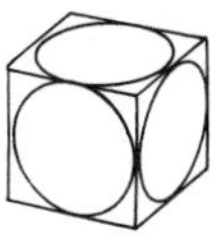	10°	40°	.92	.54	.92	55°	25°	25°

FIG. 277

Commonly used dimetric axis angles, scale ratios, and ellipse angles for principal planes are shown in [277]. Using these basic axes systems, almost any object can be illustrated effectively because of the large number of viewing directions possible with each one. This is discussed in Section 53—Selecting Axonometric Viewing Directions [303].

By adhering to a limited number of commonly used axis angles, the illustrator can standardize the equipment needed. Also, it will be easier to coordinate with a group of illustrators working together on common projects. Using standard axis angles, the required scale ratios and ellipse angles can be found directly in the table [277]. The lengthy scale construction procedures [267-271] and ellipse angle determination [276] will not be needed.

A scale for any known ratio is easily constructed using a technique similar to that used in [143] to create a foreshortened isometric scale. Fig-

Scales for known ratios can be constructed by projecting parallel lines from a full size scale . . . construction shown is for a 0.71 ratio.

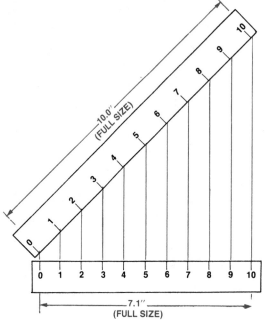

FIG. 278

Ellipse protractors are available for dimetric and trimetric . . . the angle must match the ellipse angle of the plane on which the protractor is used.

FIG. 279

ure [278] shows the construction of a 0.71 ratio scale. Use a full size scale to lay out a 7.1 in. distance on the scale being constructed. Then position the full size scale at an angle such that a full 10.0 in. distance and its subdivisions can be projected by parallel lines onto the new scale.

For circles occurring on principal planes of an object drawn in dimetric, follow the same basic procedures as described in Section 42—Circles in Isometric. For circles occurring on inclined and oblique planes, follow most of the procedures described in Section 44—Circles on Angled Surfaces. The basic principles, described in Section 45—Cylindrical Surfaces in Isometric, also hold true for dimetric and trimetric. In dimetric, standard ellipse templates are used because of the variety of angles and the necessity of always using foreshortened scales. The marked size on a template opening will match the full specified size of the circle because the major axis always appears true length when an axonometric drawing is laid out with foreshortened scales. In place of an isometric ellipse protractor, you must use a dimetric or trimetric ellipse protractor [279]. Select the proper angle protractor to match the ellipse angle of the plane on which the protractor will be used.

In many cases you can quickly approximate the dimetric or trimetric view of a circle by laying out an enclosing square on the angled surface [280]. Here, a *circle* has been created by drilling a round hole *perpendicular* to an inclined plane in object *A* and perpendicular to an oblique plane in object *B*. After transferring the enclosing square to the dimetric view, try various angle ellipse template openings of the specified size to find one that is closest to being *tangent* at the *midpoints* of the sides. This trial and error procedure can be refined if the direction of the minor axis of the ellipse can be easily found. Always remember the basic rule in axonometric that *the minor axis of an ellipse that represents a circle must follow the direction of a line that is perpendicular to the plane on which the circle occurs.*

Use an enclosing square to approximate an ellipse that represents a circle on inclined and oblique surfaces . . . select an ellipse that is closest to being tangent at the midpoints of the sides . . . to refine the selection, find the direction of a line perpendicular to the plane to orient the minor axis.

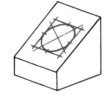

OBJECT A

OBJECT B

FIG. 280

You can approximate the dimetric or trimetric view of an ellipse on an angled surface by laying out an enclosing rectangle [281]. In this illustration a ***vertical*** hole has been drilled through the two objects. This produces ***ellipses*** on the inclined and oblique surfaces. Draw an enclosing rectangle around the ellipse and transfer it to the dimetric view. Try ellipse template openings of various sizes and angles to find one that is closest to being ***tangent*** at the ***midpoints*** of the sides. In this case, knowing the direction of a line perpendicular to the angled surface is of no value because the minor axis of an ellipse that represents an ellipse ***does not*** follow this direction.

51. DRAWING A DIMETRIC VIEW

To make a dimetric drawing of the shaft support bracket pictured in [282], use width and depth axis angles of 20°. In [275] you found that 20° ellipses would be appropriate for circles on the horizontal surfaces and 40° ellipses for circles on the vertical surfaces of a cube drawn with 20° axes angles. These ellipse angles are also found in the table [277] along with the foreshortened scale ratios. The width and depth axes require a scale ratio of 0.75, and the height scale is reduced to a 0.93 ratio. The shape of the bracket does not lend itself well to the enclosing box method of layout. Instead, the symmetrical nature of the part permits you to lay out the

Use an enclosing rectangle to approximate an ellipse that represents an ellipse on inclined and oblique surfaces . . . select an ellipse that is closest to being tangent at the midpoints of the sides.

OBJECT A

OBJECT B

FIG. 281

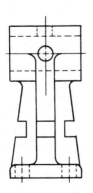

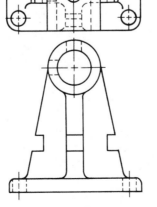

FIG. 282

Top, front, and left side views of a shaft support bracket.

major features separately around the axis of symmetry.

First, lay out the dimetric axes [283]. You can use the same technique for centering the drawing as you used for isometric [154, 155, 156]. Let the intersection of the three axes represent the left, front, bottom corner of the bearing bracket's base. Using the proper foreshortened dimetric scales, lay out the width, depth, and height of the base, and lightly draw in its basic rectangular outline. On the top surface of the base, establish the width and depth centerlines and lay out the crosslike intersection of the vertical support ribs on the surface.

At the center of the base, establish a vertical centerline [284]. Then draw the centerline for the horizontal hollow cylinder parallel to the 20° depth axis at the proper height. Locate the ends of the cylinder on the centerline, and through these points construct minor and major axes for the end ellipses. The minor axes are in line with the cylinder's centerline. The major axes are perpendicular. Using a 40° ellipse template, draw ellipses of the proper size for the inner and outer diameters of the cylinder. Join their outer edges with tangent 20° lines as shown.

Next, locate the intersections of the vertical support ribs with the outside of the cylinder. The tangency lines of the outer surfaces of the left and right ribs are located on the same level as the centerline of the cylinder [285]. Extend the height of the centerline around both sides of the cylinder to the center where the thickness of the ribs is laid out. Then drop parallel edge lines to the rib layout on the base. Lay out the rib notches parallel to the lines where ribs join the base.

Determine the location where the top of the front rib joins the underside of the cylinder by laying out its distance back from the front face of the cylinder. From here, drop parallel edge lines to the rib layout on the base. You can also locate a similar intersection line for the rear rib at this time to verify that this rib is not visible in the dimetric view. Complete the ribs by drawing their vertical intersection line with each other, the notches in each rib, and the elliptical

Draw a dimetric view of the shaft support bracket . . . draw dimetric axes at selected angle . . . lay out base of the bracket . . . locate rib intersections on top surface.

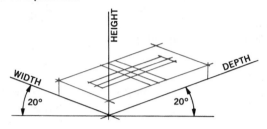

FIG. 283

Establish vertical centerline at center . . . draw horizontal centerline for cylinder and locate end surfaces . . . draw end ellipses and join their outer edges with tangent lines.

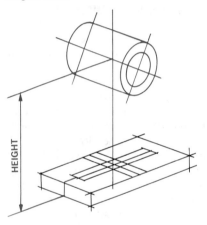

FIG. 284

Locate tangency lines where the ribs meet the cylinder . . . extend rib edges to meet layout on the base . . . draw intersection lines.

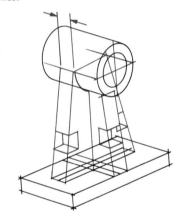

FIG. 285

Locate centers of holes in cylinder and base . . . establish axes for holes and draw ellipses . . . add fillets and rounds . . . darken visible lines.

FIG. 286

A round on a sharp edge is drawn with an ellipse template opening of the proper size and angle for that surface.

FIG. 287

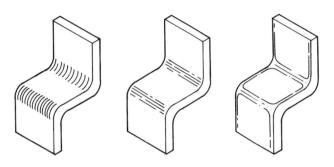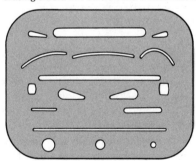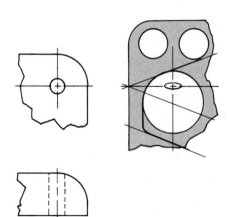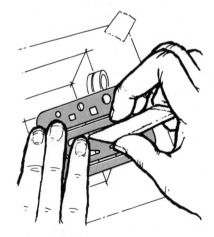

intersection line with the underside of the cylinder.

Finally, locate and draw the small holes in the cylinder and the mounting holes in the base [286]. In each case you must locate the beginning and ending points of each hole, draw minor and major axes, and select ellipse templates of the proper angle and size. You must also add fillets and rounds where required using appropriate ellipse templates corresponding to the sizes specified on the multiview drawing. When a production drawing calls for many small fillets and rounds, it is usually too time consuming to locate and construct all of their centerlines and axes and actually draw in the appropriate ellipses. Experienced illustrators simply fake in the appropriate arc segments with an ellipse or circle template.

In the case of a round on the sharp corner of a flat surface, use an ellipse template opening of the proper size and angle for that surface to draw in a small curve [287]. When the rounding occurs in two directions (a spherical radius), use a circle template since a sphere retains its true circular shape regardless of the viewing direction [288]. Figure [289] shows some of the common conventions used by illustrators to indicate rounded corners and edges. Frequently a production drawing will

Corners with a spherical radius are drawn with a circle template.

FIG. 288

Common conventions used by illustrators to indicate rounded corners and edges.

FIG. 289

carry a note that reads BREAK SHARP CORNERS. In this case the rounding is very slight and may not be needed on the technical illustration. If it is desired, illustrators usually use judgment as to whether to estimate the rounding freehand or to draw it with a small ellipse or circle template.

When you have completed a drawing, erase the various construction lines that you used to locate minor and major axes of ellipses, to project irregular shapes, and to define other constructions. Protect the drawn lines that are to stay by using an erasing shield [290]. After erasing the construction lines, go back and darken the visible lines of the object for greater clarity.

Exercise 24

Any of the objects illustrated in Section 90—Problems for Assignment are suitable examples to use in practicing the principles learned in the preceding sections on dimetric drawing. Enlarge the objects as necessary to suit the available or assigned drawing sheet size. Maintain the proportions shown as closely as possible. Use either the dimetric axis system and viewing direction that provides the best description of the object or the axis system and viewing direction assigned by your instructor. Make a quick sketch of each object first to obtain a clear understanding of the object and to be sure that the given views are correct. The sketch will help you visualize the finished illustration and aid you in positioning it on your drawing sheet. Use a grid underlay sheet

from Appendix C as an aid in sketching. To help select suitable problems, refer to the categories of objects listed in isometric Exercises 18 through 23. Use some of the same objects that you drew in these exercises, and compare the results.

When drawing is complete, erase excess construction lines with the aid of an erasing shield . . . darken the visible lines.

ERASING SHIELD

FIG. 290

Trimetric . . . the rotation and tilt angles are selected to position all three axes at different angles with each other and with the viewing plane . . . different scales must be used on each axis.

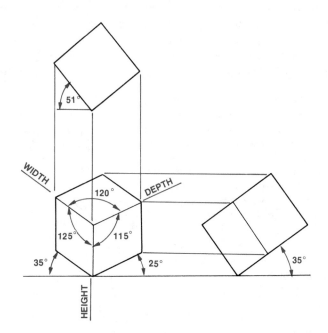

FIG. 291

Construction procedure for trimetric scales.

52. TRIMETRIC DRAWING

In *trimetric drawing* the width, height, and depth axes are drawn such that none of the angles between the axes are equal [291]. This is the result of rotating the object about a vertical axis a selected number of degrees so that two of the principal faces will be at unequal angles with the viewing plane. The object is then tilted forward about a horizontal axis a selected number of degrees so that the third face will be at a different angle with the viewing plane than the other two faces. The three axes will each be distorted a different amount depending on the angle of each with the viewing plane. In [291] the 125°, 120°, and 115° angles between axes are the result of a 51° rotation and a 35° tilt. The ability to position an object at any angle with the viewing plane gives trimetric an infinite amount of flexibility in viewing direction. Any face can be given any desired amount of visibility.

When the width, height, and depth axes angles for a trimetric drawing

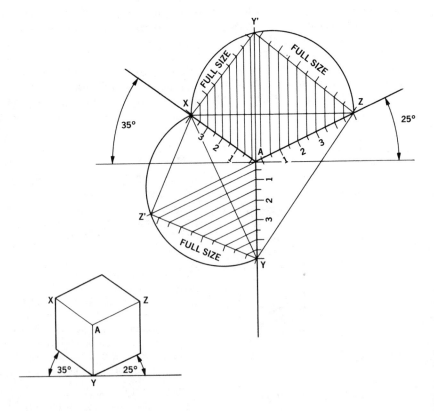

FIG. 292

Construction procedure for finding exact
ellipse angles in trimetric.

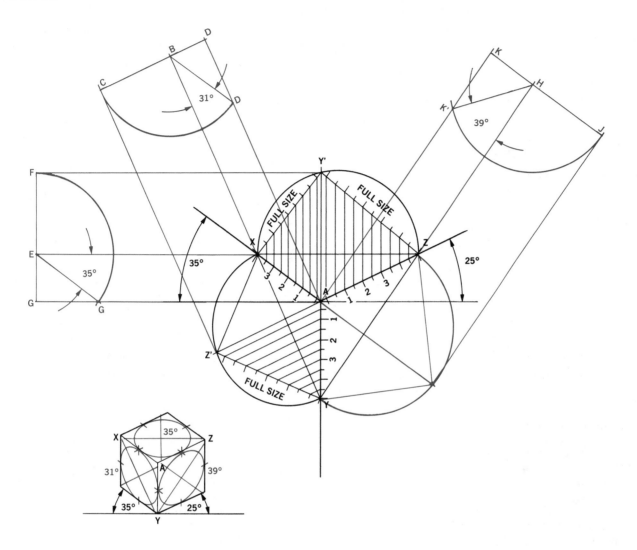

FIG. 293

have been chosen, their respective foreshortened scales are developed using the same construction as was used for dimetric [271]. The only difference is that the axes for the faces on the left and right are no longer equal. Figure [292] shows the scale development for 35° and 25° left and right axes and for the vertical height axis. The same basic procedure can be used for other axis angles. The construction for determining the proper ellipse angles to use on the principal faces is shown in [293]. This is the same procedure as was used for dimetric [276]. Standard 30°,

35°, and 40° ellipse templates will be used for this axis system.

Just as the interior portion of a dimetric scale template can be used to lay out several sets of angles, a trimetric scale can be similarly constructed for multiple angle use [273]. If you choose to make a multiple angle scale, color code or prominently mark each corresponding set of scales to reduce the possibility of accidentally using a scale that is not part of the selected group of three while making a drawing.

Some of the more commonly used sets of trimetric axis angles, scale ratios, and ellipse angles for principal

Popular trimetric axes . . . scale ratios and
ellipse angles for principal planes.

AXIS ANGLES		SCALE RATIOS			ELLIPSE ANGLES		
LEFT	RIGHT	LEFT	RIGHT	VERTICAL	LEFT	RIGHT	TOP
10°	20°	.825	.62	.95	50°	35°	15°
10°	30°	.90	.57	.95	55°	25°	20°
15°	20°	.79	.70	.95	45°	40°	20°
15°	30°	.85	.60	.95	50°	30°	25°
15°	45°	.81	.70	.85	50°	25°	35°
20°	30°	.825	.71	.90	45°	35°	25°
25°	35°	.86	.75	.82	40°	30°	35°
25°	45°	.90	.80	.73	35°	25°	45°

FIG. 294

Top, front, and left side views of an
adjusting block for a sewing machine.

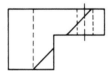

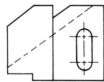

FIG. 295

Draw a trimetric view of the adjusting
block . . . draw trimetric axes at selected
angles . . . lay out an enclosing box.

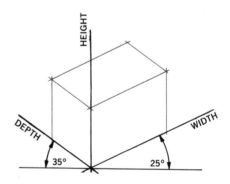

FIG. 296

The trimetric system might be used to draw the adjusting block for an industrial sewing machine shown in [295]. Axis angles of 25° and 35° are selected to best display the features of the block. You can use the same technique for centering the drawing as was used for isometric drawing [154, 155, 156]. The basic layout procedures are the same as those used for isometric and dimetric drawing. Start by drawing the 25° depth axis, the 35° width axis, and a vertical height axis passing through their intersection [296]. Lay out an enclosing box on the axis lines. Now lay out the visible surfaces that touch the top, front, and left sides of the box by transferring the X-, Y-, and Z-coordinates of their boundary lines from the multiview drawing [297].

Some of the boundary lines of the outside planes are also part of the boundaries of the visible interior surfaces that will be drawn next [298]. Draw the slot by locating its vertical centerline and the horizontal centerlines for the half circles at each end [299]. The direction of the minor axis

planes are shown in [294]. You can find the proper ellipses for other axis angles by using the procedures shown in [293]. You can also approximate them by constructing a trimetric cube as was done in [275] for dimetric. Angles chosen that are not shown in the table may result in the need for

an ellipse for which a template is not readily available. This could create unnecessary problems with your drawing. You can approximate the ellipse angles for inclined and oblique planes in trimetric in the same way as described in Section 50—Circles in Dimetric [280, 281].

lines of the ellipses that represent the half circles is established parallel to the depth axis. Draw the major axis lines perpendicular. Use a 40° template to draw the ellipse segments. Draw vertical lines tangent to the ellipses to define the edges of the slot. Erase excess construction lines and

Lay out the boundary lines of all planes that touch the visible faces of the enclosing box.

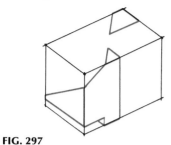

FIG. 297

Lay out the boundary lines of the visible interior planes.

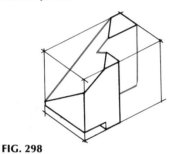

FIG. 298

Locate centerlines for the slot . . . establish axes directions and draw ellipse segments . . . draw tangent slot edge lines . . . erase construction lines and darken visible lines.

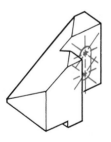

FIG. 299

darken the visible lines to complete the view.

The principle advantage of the trimetric system is the greatly increased variety of viewing directions that can be applied to an object. Many illustrators prefer to use dimetric drawing as the optimum technical illustration system because it goes a long way toward eliminating the boxy appearance of isometric drawings while requiring only two scales and two ellipse angles for principal planes. Although

trimetric often produces a more realistic looking drawing than dimetric, it is more difficult to work with because it requires three scales and three sets of ellipses. However, once you construct a permanent trimetric scale template, the main objection to trimetric drawing is eliminated. Keeping track of which of three ellipse angles to use on a principal plane is only slightly more complicated than keeping track of two. Many illustrators inscribe a sample ellipse and its angle into their scales just below the appropriate foreshortened scale to help them keep track of which ellipse to use with that axis.

Exercise 25

Any of the objects illustrated in Section 90—Problems for Assignment are suitable examples to use in practicing the principles learned in the preceding section on trimetric drawing. Enlarge the objects as necessary to suit the available or assigned drawing sheet size. Maintain the proportions shown as closely as possible. Use either the trimetric axis system and viewing direction that provides the best description of the object or the axis system and viewing direction assigned by your instructor. Make a quick sketch of each object first to obtain a clear understanding of the object and to be sure that the given views are correct. The sketch will help you visualize the finished illustration and aid you in positioning it on your drawing sheet. Use a grid underlay sheet from Appendix C as an aid in sketching. To help select suitable problems, refer to the categories of objects listed in isometric Exercises 18 through 23. Use some of the same objects that you drew in these exercises and in Exercise 24 (dimetric) and compare the results.

53. SELECTING AXONOMETRIC VIEWING DIRECTIONS

When starting a technical illustration, you must decide which face of a part or an assembly will be featured or turned most fully toward the viewer. The rule of thumb for making this decision is to feature the face that contains the most information for the viewer's use. As the examples in [300] show, through poor planning it is possible to orient an illustration so

that most of the essential information to be communicated is hidden. Poorly chosen views may illustrate features of the object that really do not need illustrating at all.

A good practice to follow is to orient the object so that the illustration shows that view of the object that the user of the illustration is most likely to see [301]. If the illustration is to be used to instruct the user in adjusting a control or in repairing a mechanism that is permanently mounted behind an access door or plate, then the

Poor view planning hides essential information.

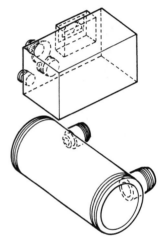

FIG. 300

Orient an object to show the view that the user is most likely to see.

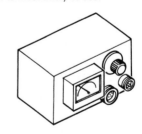

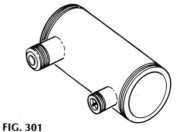

FIG. 301

drawing should show a view looking through the open door [302].

The viewing direction in axonometric can be changed by rotating the object about any of its three axes until the desired view is obtained. Figure [303], supplied by the Graphic-Standard Instruments Company, shows the many different views of a single object that may be drawn using the isometric axis system, a single dimetric axis system, and a single trimetric axis system. Axes can be reversed left for right or turned upside down to produce left or right empha-

The drawing should show the view of the object the user will see when using the illustration.

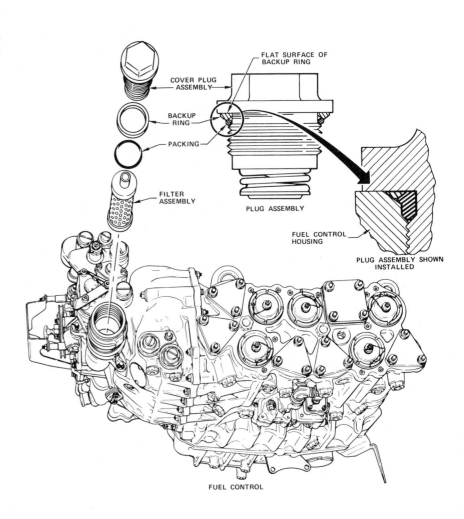

COVER PLUG ASSEMBLY

FLAT SURFACE OF BACKUP RING

BACKUP RING

PACKING

FILTER ASSEMBLY

PLUG ASSEMBLY

FUEL CONTROL HOUSING

PLUG ASSEMBLY SHOWN INSTALLED

FUEL CONTROL

FIG. 302

Change the viewing direction in axonometric by rotating the object about any of its three axes.

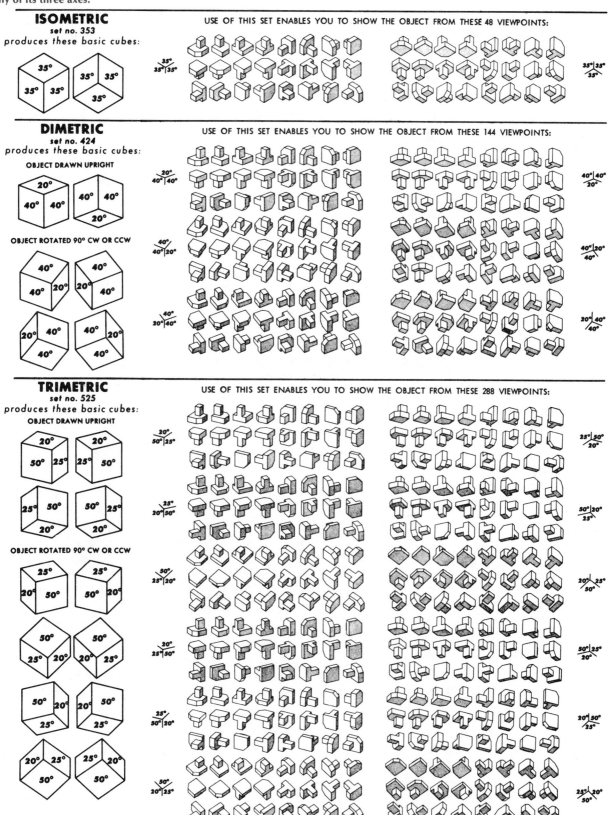

ISOMETRIC
set no. 353
produces these basic cubes:

USE OF THIS SET ENABLES YOU TO SHOW THE OBJECT FROM THESE 48 VIEWPOINTS:

DIMETRIC
set no. 424
produces these basic cubes:

OBJECT DRAWN UPRIGHT

OBJECT ROTATED 90° CW OR CCW

USE OF THIS SET ENABLES YOU TO SHOW THE OBJECT FROM THESE 144 VIEWPOINTS:

TRIMETRIC
set no. 525
produces these basic cubes:

OBJECT DRAWN UPRIGHT

OBJECT ROTATED 90° CW OR CCW

USE OF THIS SET ENABLES YOU TO SHOW THE OBJECT FROM THESE 288 VIEWPOINTS:

FIG. 303

Interior arrangement drawing of an automobile.

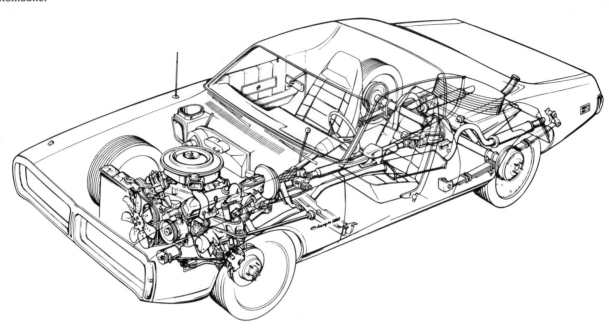

FIG. 304

sis or to provide worm's eye views or bird's eye views of the object.

Even more information can be included in a drawing by deciding whether it is appropriate to show the object as an interior arrangement, a cutaway, or an exploded assembly. These special types of views are described in the following sections.

Exercise 26

Draw one or more of the objects listed below (or any others of your choice from Section 90—Problems for Assignment) using several different viewing directions in isometric, dimetric, and trimetric, and compare the results. Refer to [303] for guidance in selecting views.

Probs. 4, 5, 6, 10, 11, 12, 19.

54. INTERIOR ARRANGEMENT DRAWINGS

Some special illustration techniques are often required with major assemblies that are made up of many component parts. These are used to illustrate better their method of operation, location of principal parts, or sequence of assembly [304].

Interior arrangement drawings show details inside a housing that is drawn to appear transparent . . . hidden lines are omitted.

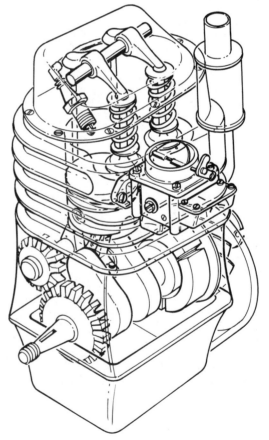

FIG. 305

An *interior arrangement drawing* depicts the object as though the outer shell were glass while all of the parts within are made of their normal material [305]. This kind of drawing is used primarily to familiarize the user with the location and size of the various parts that go to make up the whole assembly.

Drawing an interior arrangement is easier than it looks since in reality it is merely a group of drawings of smaller objects arranged to show their position in relation to one another. Although such drawings are time consuming, they are not difficult. Views from several directions may be needed, however, so that individual parts will not be obscured by other parts.

The easiest procedure for drawing interior arrangements is to use whatever natural sections occur in the object and locate the separate parts by their relationship within that section. Aircraft are divided into fuselage stations, wing stations, tail stations, and water lines (imaginary lines measuring the distance from the ground upward to locate aircraft features in the height direction) [250]. Similarly, ships are divided by keel stations, bulkheads, and decks. In the absence of any such systematic grid, uniformly spaced horizontal or vertical cutting planes can be used to provide a useful section breakdown.

When drawing each section, locate the individual parts using installation or assembly drawings. Always start drawing from the surface of the assembly nearest your eye so that as you move back into the drawing field and one part appears in front of another, there will be less for you to draw. You won't waste valuable time drawing items that will not be seen in the final illustration.

55. CUTAWAY DRAWINGS

Cutaway drawings are used to demonstrate the operating features and arrangement of parts inside complex assemblies [306]. Using this technique, the operation of most complex machines can be made understandable to laymen. An excellent example is the cutaway of a

Cutaway drawings show interior construction and operating features.

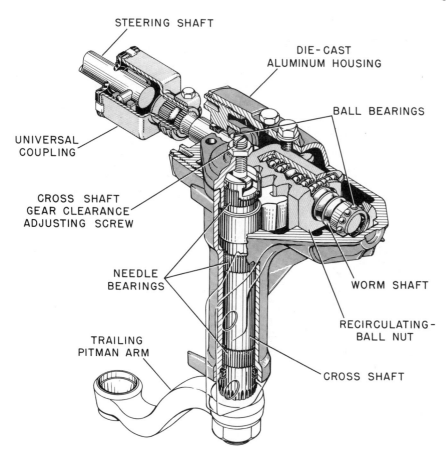

STEERING SHAFT

DIE-CAST
ALUMINUM HOUSING

BALL BEARINGS

UNIVERSAL
COUPLING

CROSS SHAFT
GEAR CLEARANCE
ADJUSTING SCREW

NEEDLE
BEARINGS

WORM SHAFT

RECIRCULATING-
BALL NUT

TRAILING
PITMAN ARM

CROSS SHAFT

FIG. 306

Cutaway drawing of a turbine engine.

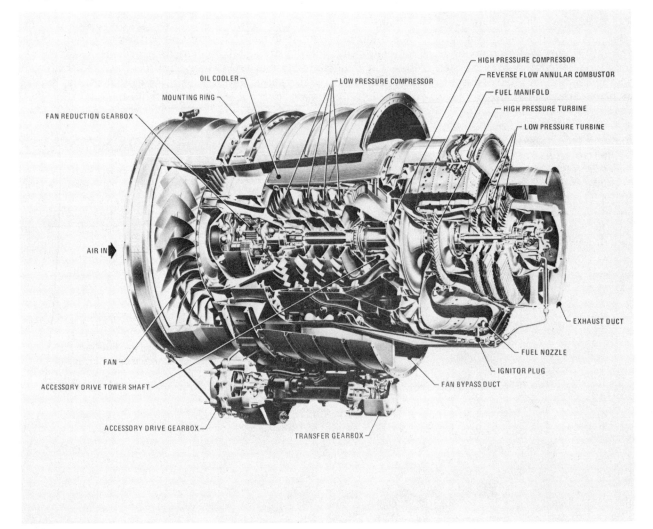

FAN REDUCTION GEARBOX

MOUNTING RING

OIL COOLER

LOW PRESSURE COMPRESSOR

HIGH PRESSURE COMPRESSOR

REVERSE FLOW ANNULAR COMBUSTOR

FUEL MANIFOLD

HIGH PRESSURE TURBINE

LOW PRESSURE TURBINE

AIR IN

EXHAUST DUCT

FUEL NOZZLE

IGNITOR PLUG

FAN BYPASS DUCT

FAN

ACCESSORY DRIVE TOWER SHAFT

ACCESSORY DRIVE GEARBOX

TRANSFER GEARBOX

FIG. 307

turbine engine [307]. Drawing a cutaway is no more complicated than drawing the component parts of the entire assembly. The only difference is that section view cuts are made through various parts at locations chosen by the illustrator.

Figure [308] shows an assembled bushing puller and its component parts. It is used to extract bushings from flywheels. In the following steps, you will construct a trimetric cutaway of this puller in a position half way through the operation of extracting a bushing.

(1) Lay out a set of trimetric axes with one axis extended to the right to serve as the centerline of the puller [309]. Draw a partial view of the flywheel starting with its outer surface positioned on the vertical axis. One quarter of the flywheel is removed (as in a half-section view in a multiview drawing) along the horizontal and vertical axes to expose the bushing recess.

(2) To show the bushing partially removed, locate its outer surface a short distance away from the inner surface of the recess in the flywheel [310]. Locate its opposite end also, and establish minor and major axes for the end ellipses. Using an ellipse template, draw the bushing lightly with the

Bushing puller assembly and its
component parts.

SLEEVE

COLLET

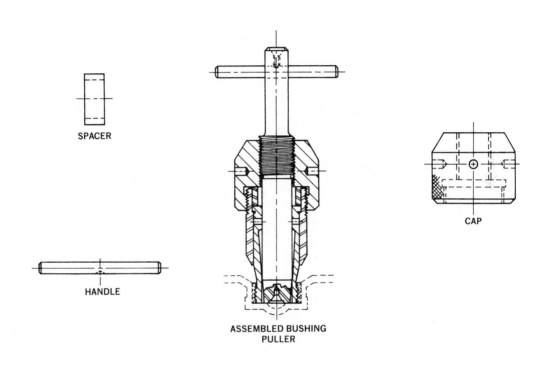

SPACER

HANDLE

CAP

ASSEMBLED BUSHING
PULLER

ROD

FIG. 308

Draw a trimetric cutaway of the puller . . .
draw trimetric axes at selected angles . . .
draw flywheel with a portion removed to
show the bushing recess.

FIG. 309

Draw the bushing in a partially removed
position . . . cut out a portion to match the
flywheel.

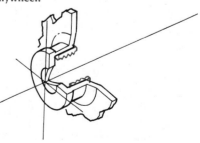

FIG. 310

Draw the puller rod with its end even with the inner face of the bushing recess.

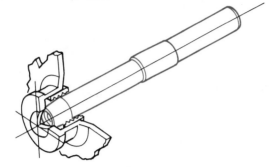

FIG. 311

Draw collet and sleeve around the rod . . . remove a quarter section.

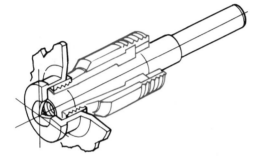

FIG. 312

Add spacer, cap, and handle . . . draw threads on the rod . . . add knurling and holes to the cap.

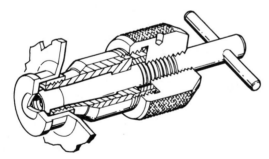

FIG. 313

An exploded drawing shows a product that has been pulled apart along its assembly centerline.

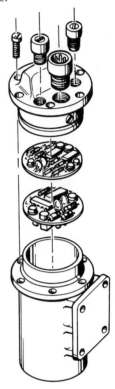

FIG. 314

bly drawing with one quarter removed. Draw the threads on the puller rod and show the handle. Add the small holes and the knurling on the cap. Add section lining on the cutaway sections. Erase construction lines and darken visible lines [313]. For clarity, centerlines are usually omitted in pictorial drawings unless they are needed for some special purpose.

You have drawn the bushing puller as a 90° cutaway. A 180° cutaway drawing has a 180° portion removed. Cutaway drawings may also be made with an irregular size portion removed to expose critical features of the assembly.

56. EXPLODED DRAWINGS

Exploded assemblies are used to illustrate the relative location of parts and subassemblies in complicated equipment. They are also frequently

same quarter section removed as the flywheel.

(3) Draw the puller rod along the centerline [311]. The end of the rod is drawn even with the inner face of the bushing recess. Since there is no internal detail to be shown for the rod, it is not sectioned.

(4) Draw the collet around the rod with its end even with the outer face of the bushing and the sleeve in the position shown on the assembly drawing. Remove a quarter section of the collet and the sleeve [312].

(5) Draw the spacer and the cap in the position shown on the assem-

used in parts catalogs to identify replacement parts and to do double duty as assembly aids for repair technicians.

An exploded view can be drawn to any scale using any of the axonometric drawing systems. The primary objective is to provide as much information in one illustration as possible. This makes the selection of the viewing direction of primary importance. It is also essential that illustrators have a thorough understanding of the assembly sequences of the objects being drawn.

Although a complicated exploded view may look frightening to a beginning illustrator, such drawings are really just a collection of single part illustrations arranged in their disassembly sequence. The example in [314] shows that no special instruction or practice is required to construct an exploded view. Lines parallel to the axes of the chosen drawing system are used as centerlines through parts and bolt holes to indicate where each part attaches to its mates.

When making an exploded view, occasionally the centerline path of one exploded view component will be blocked by another. In this case the part is jogged aside into a clear area [315]. The jog or offset is always done on the appropriate axis to maintain the viewer's orientation to the part's true location. Intersections of centerline paths should also be avoided by using offsets. More than one ex-

ploded drawing may be required to describe completely an assembly having many parts [316, 317].

Exercise 27

The objects listed below are suitable examples to use in practicing the principles learned in the preceding sections on interior arrangement, cutaway, and exploded drawings. Use the axonometric drawing system and viewing direction that provides the best description of the object or the system and direction assigned by your instructor. Make a quick

sketch first to obtain a clear understanding of the object and to be sure that the given views are correct. The sketch will help you visualize the finished illustration and aid you in positioning it on your drawing sheet. Use a grid underlay sheet from Appendix C as an aid in sketching. In planning your layout, it is well to think of a specific use for the finished illustration such as assembly or repair instruction, cataloging, or promotion.

(a) The following objects listed in Section 90—Problems for Assignment are suitable for exploded drawings.
Prob. 99 (bicycle crank locking pin)
Prob. 100 (gear puller)

More than one exploded drawing may be required to describe completely an assembly having many parts [317].

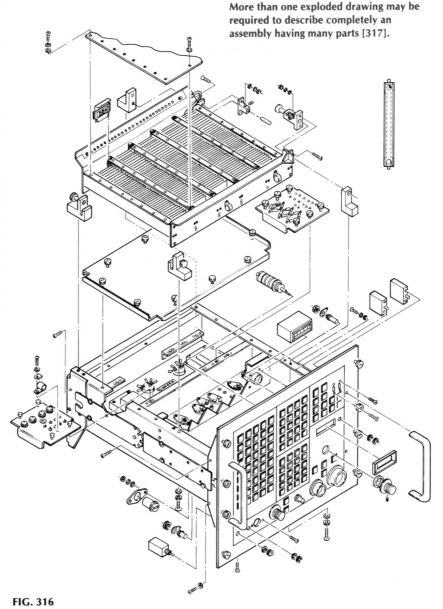

Centerline paths can be jogged to clear adjacent parts.

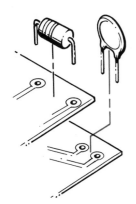

FIG. 315

FIG. 316

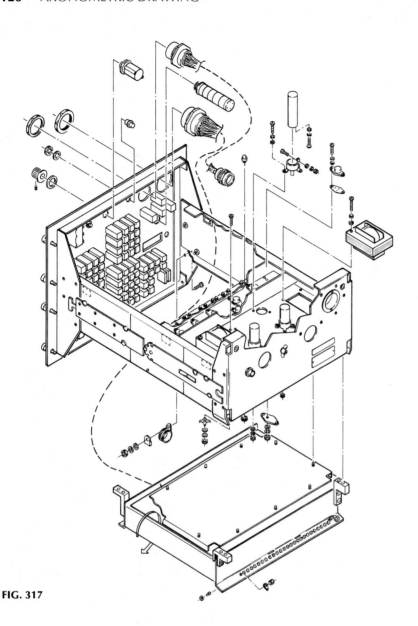

FIG. 317

(b) Good experience in making interior arrangement, cutaway, and exploded drawings can be obtained by disassembling common manufactured products such as the ones listed below:

Pencil Sharpener
Lead Pointer
Eraser Holder
Drafting Pencil
X-acto Knife
Mat Knife
Drawing Compass
Flashlight
Tire Pump
Bicycle Wheel Front Hub
Bicycle Wheel Rear Hub (with brake or gears)
Bicycle 10 Speed Derailleur
Tire Valve
Garden Hose Nozzle
Faucet
Light Fixture
Light Switch
Electric Outlet
Various Types of Adjustable Wrenches
Wheel Puller
Nut Cracker
Clip Board
Door Locksets
Lock Cylinder

Perspective Drawing

57. BASIC PERSPECTIVE PRINCIPLES

When you look at your surroundings, you see that objects located far away from you appear to be smaller. By virtue of the same optical phenomenon, any set of parallel lines (such as the edges of a highway or a set of railroad tracks) seems to converge at some distant point even though you know that they remain parallel for their entire length [318].

Objects located far away appear smaller . . . parallel lines seem to converge in the distance.

FIG. 318

At the point where the earth and the sky appear to meet, there is a dividing line that is called the **horizon.** This is the point where you cannot see any more of the earth—it is the limit of your vision. This line is most apparent at the seashore where your vision is not obscured by trees, mountains, or other attachments to the earth [319].

The horizon line is most apparent at the seashore.

FIG. 319

A full discussion of how we see is beyond the scope of this text. Briefly, humans see because modulated light rays are emitted as reflections from objects viewed. These rays form a cone as they focus into the eye [320].

"Seeing" is accomplished when objects reflect light rays.

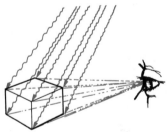

FIG. 320

They are focused onto a small spot on the back wall of the eye. Here, they are changed into electrical impulses that cause a series of electrical and chemical reactions in the nervous system. This causes visual perception. Even though several people may stand at the same location and view the same scene, the visual impression that each person experiences is unique. It is not exactly like that of any other person who has viewed the scene. However, the sum of the series of individual visual experiences is the same for each member of the group.

Perspective drawing enables the illustrator to make accurate scaled drawings in two dimensions that successfully imitate the three-dimensional visual perceptions of the mind. Before discussing the mechanics of perspective drawing, it is important to recognize that the position of the viewer with respect to the object is the factor that determines the size and shape of the object being viewed. In perspective drawing, the location where the viewer stands is called the **station point** [321].

The viewer's position determines the size and shape of the object . . . the station point is the location where the viewer stands.

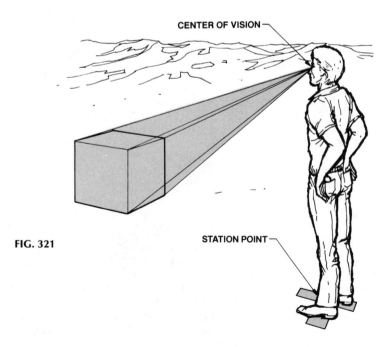

CENTER OF VISION

STATION POINT

FIG. 321

Imagine that an object is projecting visual rays to your eye in the form of a visual cone. Now imagine that the cone is intercepted by a sheet of glass large enough to rest on the ground. This sheet of glass is known as the *picture plane.* This plane serves the same function in perspective as the viewing plane does in the other drawing systems. Its bottom edge, resting on the ground, is called the *ground line* [322].

Light rays projected from an object form an image on the picture plane . . . the ground line is where the picture plane meets the ground.

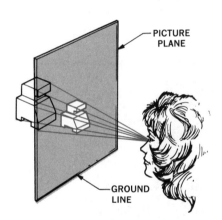

PICTURE PLANE

GROUND LINE

FIG. 322

If you (at the station point) are looking exactly through the center of the picture plane so that there is just as much of the horizon to the left as to the right, you are viewing the scene in what is called *parallel* or *one-point perspective.* Your vision is centered at a point that exactly bisects the horizon. This point is called the *center of vision.* In one-point perspective, the center of vision coincides with the point where the highway edges, railroad tracks, trees, and houses seem to converge [323]. This point is called the *vanishing point.*

If you move the station point either to the left or to the right of the center of the picture plane so that the center

of vision rests at a point on the horizon other than the exact center, you are viewing the scene in *angular* or *two-point perspective* [324]. Now the edges of the objects in the scene appear to converge on two different vanishing points, hence the name "two-point" perspective.

Parallel or one-point perspective . . . the station point is centered on the picture plane . . . your vision is centered on the horizon at a single vanishing point.

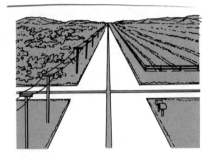

FIG. 323

Angular or two-point perspective . . . the station point is moved to the left or right . . . your vision is off-center on the horizon creating two vanishing points.

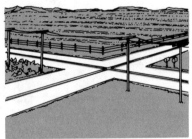

FIG. 324

When the station point is raised considerably, the edges of the objects will be seen to converge on three points, two on the horizon and one

below the station point where objects recede into the depths [325]. This *aerial* or *three-point perspective* is most commonly experienced when looking down from a very tall building.

The horizon line is always at eye level, whether you are lying down, standing up, or flying above the earth in an airplane. This means that when you look straight ahead, the center of vision always rests at some point on the horizon line [326].

Aerial or three-point perspective . . . the station point is raised considerably . . . a third vanishing point is created below the station point.

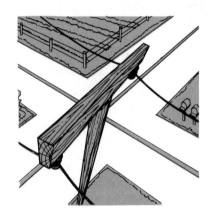

FIG. 325

The horizon is always at eye level . . . your center of vision always rests on the horizon when looking straight ahead.

HORIZON

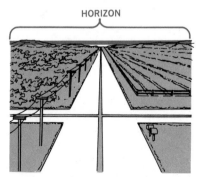

FIG. 326

58. PERSPECTIVE DRAWING AIDS

There are several commercially available devices that the illustrator may use for assistance in making perspective drawings. Some systems are based on special tools, resembling T-squares and captive triangles; others are complete drawing board assemblies [327]. The most commonly used aids, however, are a series of printed perspective underlay grids that are available from several commercial sources [328].

Many types of perspective drawing aids are commercially available.

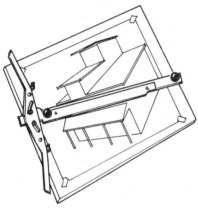

FIG. 327

Perspective grids are the most popular drawing aids.

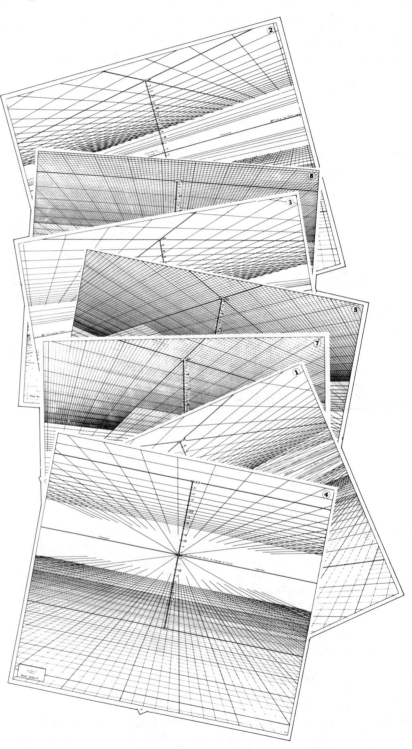

FIG. 328

In this section, you will construct several grids, one each for use in making one-point perspective views, two-point perspective views, and three-point perspective views. Commercially available sets of grids normally include a one-point grid and several two-point grids having different viewing directions.

Before beginning to construct the grids, you should be aware of some characteristics of perspective drawing. It is possible to make perspective drawings by projecting directly from the views of a multiview drawing of an object. It is also possible to make perspective drawings by using a construction process that is roughly equal to the construction of the perspective grid. Either of these operations is costly and unnecessarily complicated. Therefore, most professional illustrators either construct or buy a set of perspective grids that best suits their everyday needs. Once you understand the steps of construction, you can construct a perspective grid for any specialized purpose or view. The best perspective drawings are usually those that present the object as it would normally be seen by the viewer, avoiding extreme and unusual viewing angles.

Typically the construction of a perspective grid large enough to be useful requires that the overall layout be quite a bit larger than the final grid size to accommodate the locations of the vanishing points and the station points. If the vanishing points and station points are located too close together, the grid will produce drawings that are severely foreshortened. This causes a distorted appearance. To avoid this the grid construction should be made on a large sheet of paper or drafting film on a full size drafting board whenever possible. If you construct your grids on plastic drafting film, they will be more stable and durable. In addition, a two-point grid on film may be turned over left for right to be used as a basis for an opposite viewing direction.

59. ONE-POINT PERSPECTIVE GRIDS

The first grid that you will construct will be a grid for parallel or one-point perspective. The viewing direction produced by this type of perspective is used primarily for interior views of rooms or objects such as airliners or submarines. One-point perspective is not the most useful type of perspective, but it is the simplest system and therefore the easiest to learn to construct. The following steps are required:

(1) First, establish a station point (*SP*) near the bottom of your sheet [329]. This point represents the location on the ground or on some supportive surface where the observer is standing [321]. In one-point perspective, mark the station point at the bottom of a line that bisects vertically the viewing area of the layout. Next establish the center of vision point *CV*. This is the point on the horizon where the viewer's eye is centered. Assuming an average viewer's eye level to be about 165 cm (5 ft-5 in) above the ground, the center of vision should be at that scale height above the station point on the vertical line. For most purposes, it is marked about one third of the way down from the top of the layout area [330].

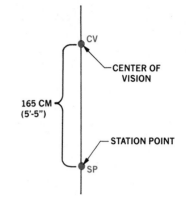

Establish station point near bottom of sheet . . . center of vision is directly above at viewer's eye level.

FIG. 329

Draw a one-point perspective grid . . . mark the center of vision about one third down from the top of the layout area . . . draw the horizon line passing through the center of vision.

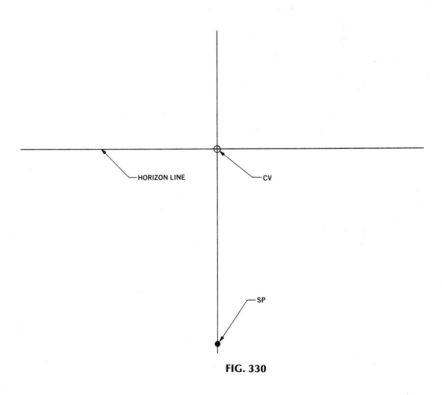

FIG. 330

(2) Now you can draw the horizon line as a horizontal line passing through *CV* [330]. The center of vision always rests on the horizon when the viewer looks straight ahead.

(3) The next step is to lay out the picture plane [331]. This represents the area that was described as a vertical sheet of glass with its bottom edge resting on the ground. It intercepts the reflected light rays from the object being viewed. A good size for general use is 45 × 60 cm (18 × 24 in). You can use any proportion that your layout sheet will accomodate. Lay out the rectangle so that approximately one third of its height is above the horizon line.

(4) On the bottom and right side edges of the picture plane, lay out scale divisions spaced 1.0 cm (0.4 in) apart [331]. The bottom of the picture plane extending to the right and left is also graduated. This will be the permanent scale reference for your grid. It should be precisely drawn. In use, the increments may be assigned any value, from millimeters to miles, depending on what is appropriate for the illustration. Scales are frequently placed on the *SP/CV* line itself. This results in a vertical scale in the center of the picture plane. The location of the vertical scale is arbitrary, but remember that when using the grid all dimensions taken from the scale, regardless of its location, must be projected along the established perspective lines to the site of the drawing on the grid to achieve correct foreshortening.

(5) Draw a series of lines connecting *CV* with the scale markings on the bottom of the picture plane [332]. In one-point perspective, the center of vision is the single vanishing point for all parallel depth lines.

Draw the picture plane with about one third of its height above the horizon . . . accurately space scale divisions on the bottom and right edges.

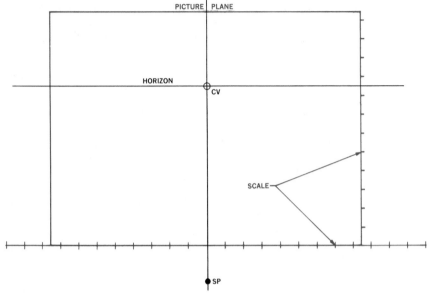

FIG. 331

Draw lines from the bottom scale marks to the center of vision . . . the center of vision is the single vanishing point in one-point perspective.

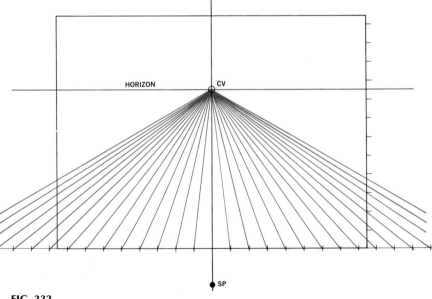

FIG. 332

(6) Place the needle point of a large compass on *CV* and the compass lead on *SP* [333]. Swing an arc upward to the right until the arc intersects the horizon line at a point called the **measuring point** (*MP*). Draw a straight line from the bottom left corner of the picture plane to the measuring point. This line is the **measuring line.** Trim the angled lines from the center of vision at the left and right edges of the picture plane.

(7) Draw a horizontal line at each point where the measuring line intersects one of the angled lines that meet at *CV* [334]. For clarity and ease of use, stop the horizontal lines a short distance below the horizon line when they become too closely spaced to be clearly useful.

Swing an arc from the station point to the horizon line to establish the measuring point.

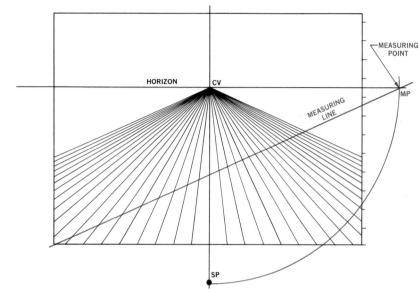

FIG. 333

Draw horizontal lines through the points where the measuring line intersects the converging lines.

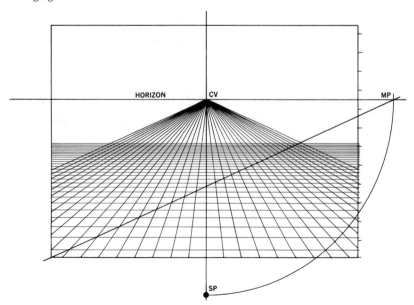

FIG. 334

(8) Turn the layout sheet around so that the bottom is now at the top and repeat steps 4 through 7, using the point of intersection of the station point line and the picture plane top edge as the new station point (*SP*) [335].

(9) Return the layout sheet to its original position and trim the sheet to the edges of the picture plane, or leave a small margin all around [336]. Erase construction lines and arcs. This grid is suitable for making one-point perspective views from a normal viewpoint for average size adults. It can also

Turn the layout around so that the top is at the bottom . . . repeat the grid construction procedures using a new station point at the picture plane edge.

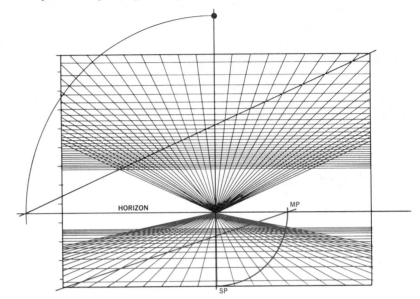

FIG. 335

Return the layout to the original position . . . trim the borders and erase construction lines and arcs.

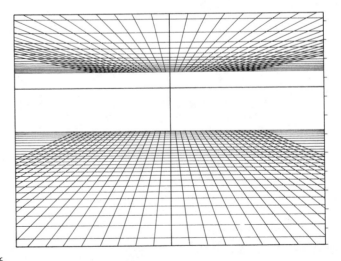

FIG. 336

be used in the inverted position for views looking upward at overhead objects [337].

Invert the grid for drawing overhead objects.

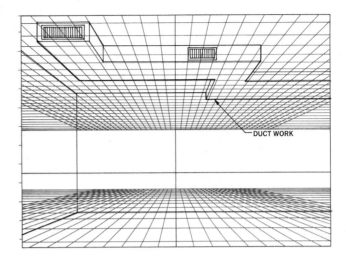

FIG. 337

60. DRAWING A ONE-POINT PERSPECTIVE

Look at a portion of the one-point grid. Notice its resemblance to a tiled floor in a large room [338]. Each tile square has the width and depth dimensions assigned to each scale mark on the bottom and side edges. For instance, if you decide that each of the scale marks represents one centimeter, then each of the tiles on the floor and ceiling are one centimeter square.

This grid system provides a width and depth scale for the measurement of any object. To obtain a height measurement, it is necessary to refer to the vertical scale on the right edge of the picture plane. It is important to note, however, that these height measurements are only true at that location in space represented by the picture plane. As objects recede in space toward the vanishing point, they must appear to grow smaller in size. To accomplish this, you must project height measurements made on the picture plane scale back from the bottom edge of the picture plane along appropriate grid lines. As the grid lines converge, they will automatically reduce the height.

As an example, find the height of the vertical line *AB* that starts at a certain point *A* on a grid by moving the point forward along a grid line until it meets the bottom edge of the picture plane at *A'* [339]. Determine the height *A'B'* of a vertical line drawn at *A'* by a horizontal projection from the right edge height scale. This true height can then be projected back along a grid line to a point *B* directly above point *A*.

A portion of the grid resembles a tiled floor . . . each square tile has the dimensions of the edge scales.

FIG. 338

Establish the height of a vertical line *AB* . . . move forward from point *A* on a grid line to point *A'* on the picture plane edge . . . project the true height of *AB* from the right edge scale to a point *B'* above *A'* . . . move point *B'* back along a grid line to *B* above point *A*.

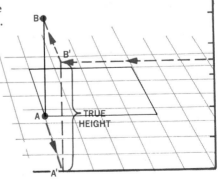

FIG. 339

Figure [340] shows how a cube 4 units on a side would be laid out on a grid. Select a 4-unit wide by 4-unit deep base on the grid. Extend the depth border lines to the width scale at the bottom edge of the picture plane. Draw vertical lines at these points to meet a horizontal projection line from the 4-unit height mark on the right edge scale. From the tops of these vertical lines, draw converging depth lines to the vanishing point. The intersections of these converging lines with vertical lines erected at the four corners of the base locate the corners of the top surface and establish the cube's height. Finally, darken the visible lines of the cube.

Circles in perspective are treated in much the same way as in axonometric drawing. You can obtain the most natural appearing ellipse in perspective by drawing a perspective square that just encloses the circle [341]. Try various angles and sizes of ellipse template openings until you find one that is closest to being *tangent* at the *midpoints* of the sides. As in axonometric drawing, position the minor axis of an ellipse that represents a circle to follow the direction of a line that is perpendicular to the plane on which the circle occurs. In this example the minor axis follows the vertical height axis. Since the perspective square is narrower at the rear than at the front, no perfect tangential ellipse is available, and a compromise selection is made in the interest of saving time.

Off-axis lines and irregular shapes are laid out by plotting points in exactly the same way as in the various axonometric drawing systems. In fact, the presence of the perspective grid lends itself even more conveniently to the use of this method.

As an example of one-point perspective drawing, draw a view of the locating bracket shown in [342]. Using a one-point perspective grid as an underlay beneath your drawing vellum or film, proceed with the following steps:

Draw a perspective cube . . . select a 4-unit square base on the grid . . . project the width forward to the bottom edge . . . draw vertical lines at the 4-unit height projected from the right edge scale . . . project the height back to vertical lines drawn at each corner of the base . . . darken the visible lines of the cube.

FIG. 340

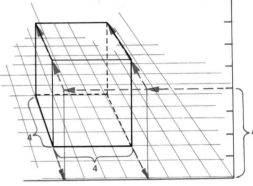

Use an enclosing square to draw perspective circles . . . select an ellipse that is closest to being tangent to the midpoints of the sides of the perspective square . . . the minor axis of an ellipse that represents a circle follows the direction of a line perpendicular to the surface.

FIG. 341

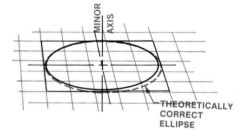

Two views of locating bracket.

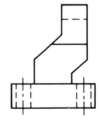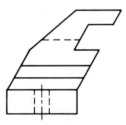

FIG. 342

(1) After selecting a suitable scale, lay out the rectangular bottom surface of the guide bracket [343]. Select a location on the grid that will best display the features of the bracket.

(2) Project the front right corner of the base forward along a grid line to the bottom edge of the picture plane and draw a vertical line. Project the height of the base to this line from the right edge height scale. Now project this height back along a grid line to a point directly above the front right corner of the base [344]. Lay out the upper surface of the base at this level, and join it to the bottom surface with vertical corner lines. Draw the intersection lines of the upper portion of the bracket on the top surface of the base.

(3) Draw the horizontal top surface of the bracket by laying out its boundary lines on the same plane as the bottom surface of the bracket and then projecting directly upward to a height established in the same way as was done in step (2) [345].

Draw a one-point perspective of the bracket . . . lay out the bottom surface on the grid.

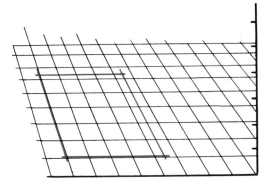

FIG. 343

Project the width forward to the bottom edge . . . project the height of the base from the right edge scale . . . project the height back to the vertical lines at the corners of the base . . . draw upper surface of the base . . . lay out intersection lines for upper portion of the bracket.

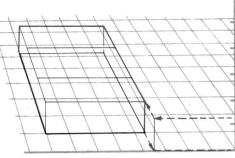

FIG. 344

Lay out boundary lines of the horizontal top surface on the same plane as the bottom surface of the bracket . . . project the boundary lines upward to a height established by projection from the right edge scale.

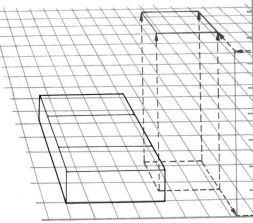

FIG. 345

(4) Complete the upper portion of the bracket by locating the beginning and ending points of the boundary lines of its visible off-axis surfaces and locating the slot [346].

(5) To show the visible mounting hole in the base, construct an enclosing square on the top surface of the base [347]. Draw an ellipse that is closest to being tangent at the midpoints of the sides. Darken the visible lines of the bracket, and erase construction lines.

Now that the view is complete, you can see how the positioning of the base of the bracket in step (1) affected the visibility of the bracket's features. The farther to the right or left from the vertical center of the viewing area that an object is drawn, the more of one face or the other that will be exposed in the one-point perspective view.

Exercise 28

Many of the objects in Section 90—Problems for Assignment are suitable examples to use in practicing the principles learned in the preceding sections on one-point perspective drawing. Enlarge the objects as necessary to suit the available or assigned drawing sheet size. Maintain the proportions shown as closely as possible. Use an available one-point grid or construct your own following the procedures in Section 59. Use either the viewing direction that provides the best description of the object or the viewing direction assigned by your instructor. Make a quick sketch of each object first to obtain a clear understanding of the object and to be sure that the given views are correct. The sketch will help you visualize the finished illustration and aid you in positioning it on your drawing sheet. Use a grid underlay sheet from Appendix C as an aid in sketching. To help select suitable problems, refer to the categories of objects listed in isometric Exercises 18 through 23. Use some of the same objects that you drew in these exercises, as well as in dimetric and trimetric, and compare the results and effort required.

61. TWO-POINT PERSPECTIVE GRIDS

In the one-point perspective view of the locating bracket, you were

Complete the upper portion of the bracket by locating end points of the boundary lines of each visible plane.

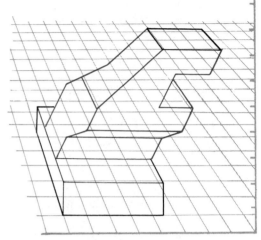

FIG. 346

Construct an enclosing square for the visible mounting hole . . . select an ellipse that is closest to being tangent at the midpoints of the sides . . . darken the visible lines and erase construction lines.

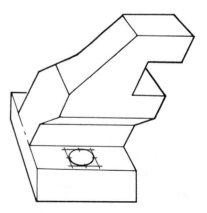

FIG. 347

looking in-line with the center of the viewing area. With the exception of room interiors and a very few other situations, this is an unusual viewing angle. It is more likely that you would view an object of this type from a location somewhat off-center. This more natural viewing condition can be achieved in illustration work by using two-point perspective.

To create a grid for two-point perspective, the following steps are required:

(1) On a large sheet of paper or drafting film, establish a station point (*SP*) near the bottom about one third of the way from the left edge instead of the center as was done for one-point perspective [348]. Draw a vertical line through the station point, and locate the point that represents the center of vision (*CV*) about one third of the way down from the top of the layout area. Draw a horizontal line representing the horizon through *CV*.

(2) Starting at *SP*, draw a line upward to the left at an angle of 60° with the horizontal [349]. Label its point of intersection with the horizon as the left vanishing point (*LVP*). At a 30° angle with the horizontal, draw a line upward to the right from *SP*. Label its intersection with the horizon as the right vanishing point (*RVP*). Now, try placing a drawing triangle on your layout with the vertex of the right angle at *SP*. By pivoting the triangle to the right and left, you can visualize various combinations of angles to the vanishing points that might be used for making other two-point perspective grids. The angle between the vanishing point lines does not have to be 90°. Making it larger or smaller produces other view-

Draw a two-point perspective grid . . . locate the station point and the center of vision on a vertical line . . . draw horizon line through the center of vision.

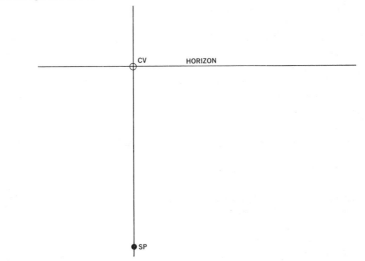

FIG. 348

Draw a 60° line from the station point to establish the left vanishing point on the horizon . . . draw a 30° line to establish the right vanishing point on the horizon.

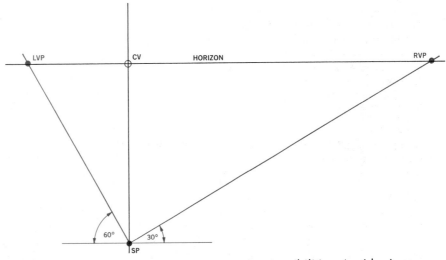

FIG. 349

ing possibilities. Avoid using extremely small angles from the horizontal to either of the vanishing points. Not only are such views usually disturbing to the eye, but they also fail to deliver much useful information to the viewer. They also create unnecessary difficulty for the illustrator in drawing circular or irregular shapes within the narrow included angles.

(3) Draw the picture plane outline, and mark scales along the bottom, top, and right edges exactly as was done for the one-point perspective grid [350].If the same set of scales and the same picture plane size is used throughout all of the perspective grids constructed, you will finish with a matched set of grids that you can use easily and interchangeably through a series of drawings. The basic relationship of scale and size eliminates the annoyance of changing scale or finding that one grid is the wrong size for a particular object.

(4) The next step is to draw a line from each scale mark on the bottom edge line to the left vanishing point (*LVP*) [351]. A similar set of lines is then drawn to the right vanishing point (*RVP*).

(5) Now draw lines from the scale marks on the top edge of the picture plane to *LVP* and *RVP* [352]. For clarity, leave a narrow clear zone above and below the horizon line. Lines in the area near the horizon produce extreme foreshortening that is not useful and is best eliminated [353]. Some illustrators prefer to draw in every fourth or fifth line to the vanishing points with a heavy double weight line to aid in rapid scaling of objects in the field of the drawing. Now trim back the layout sheet to the outline of the picture plane and remove the construction lines [354].

Draw the picture plane . . . mark scales along the bottom, top, and right edges.

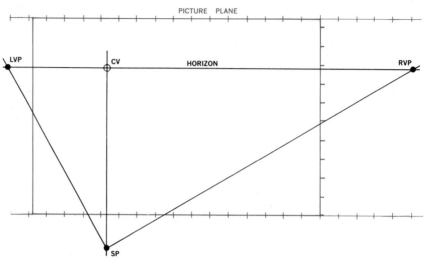

FIG. 350

Draw converging lines from the bottom edge scale marks to the vanishing points.

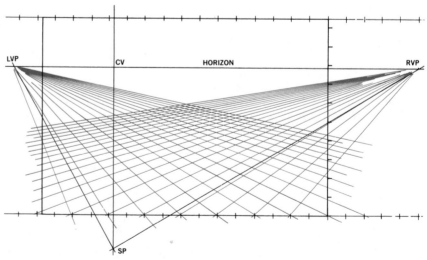

FIG. 351

Draw converging lines from the top edge scale marks to the vanishing points.

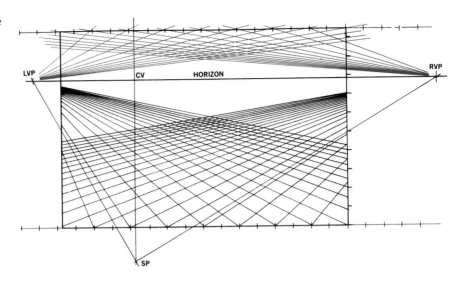

FIG. 352

Omit useless grid lines from the narrow area above and below the horizon line.

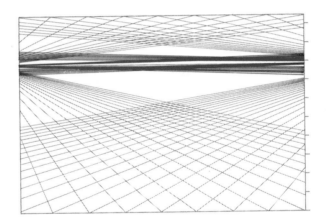

FIG. 353

Trim the layout back to the picture plane . . . erase construction lines.

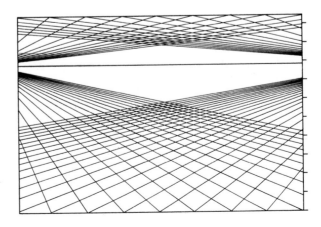

FIG. 354

If you carefully consider the viewing direction with respect to your two-point perspective grid, you will see that this one grid is capable of providing eight different viewing directions. For a four-sided object, this would make possible thirty-two different views of the same object if the grid is turned upside down, reversed left for right, and the orientation of the object is changed left for right [355]. Because of this feature, only a limited number of perspective grids are necessary to provide the illustrator with a large number of viewing directions for use in making perspective drawings.

62. DRAWING A TWO-POINT PERSPECTIVE

Figure [356] is a multiview drawing of a pivot block for an earth moving machine. Using the two-point perspective grid as an underlay, select a suitable viewing direction.

Start the layout of the pivot block by drawing the outline of the bottom surface [357]. Next, lay out the ver-

A single grid can be used for many different views of an object.

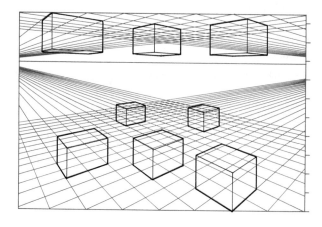

FIG. 355

Top, front, and right side views of a pivot block for an earthmover.

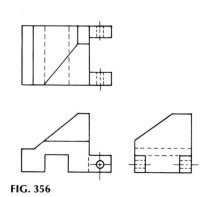

FIG. 356

Draw a two-point perspective of the pivot block . . . select a suitable viewing direction and lay out the bottom surface.

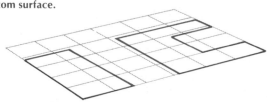

FIG. 357

tical left side and front planes [358]. Make height measurements in the same way as you did on the one-point perspective grid [339]. Follow this by laying out the three visible horizontal surfaces. By joining some of the lines just drawn, the boundaries of the two visible off-axis planes can now be easily completed [359]. Lay out enclosing squares for the hole circles. Select an ellipse template opening that is closest to being tangent at the midpoints of the sides, and draw the ellipses [360]. Darken the visible lines and erase the construction lines.

Exercise 29

Most of the objects in Section 90—Problems for Assignment are suitable examples to use in practicing the principles learned in the preceding sections on two-point perspective drawing. Enlarge the objects as necessary to suit the available or assigned drawing sheet size. Maintain the proportions shown as closely as possible. Use an available two-point perspective grid or construct your own following the procedures in Section 61. In constructing your own grids, the following angles are recommended: 30° to the right and 60° to the left; 20° to the right and 40° to the left; 15° to the right and 25° to the left. Use either the viewing direction that provides the best description of the object or the viewing direction assigned by your instructor. Make a quick sketch of each object first to obtain a clear understanding of the object and to be sure that the given views are correct. The sketch will help you visualize the finished illustration and aid you in positioning it on your drawing sheet. Use a grid underlay sheet from Appendix C as an aid in sketching. To help select suitable problems, refer to the categories of objects listed in isometric Exercises 18 through 23. Use some of the same objects that you drew in these exercises, as well as in dimetric and trimetric, and compare the results and effort required.

63. THREE-POINT PERSPECTIVE GRIDS

Three-point (aerial) perspective is by far the most difficult of the drawing systems to project accurately. Most professional illustrators do not use it at all. Instead, where the illustration requires this type of view, they will add freehand modifications to a pro-

Lay out the visible vertical and horizontal surfaces.

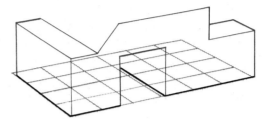

FIG. 358

Complete the boundary lines of the off-axis planes.

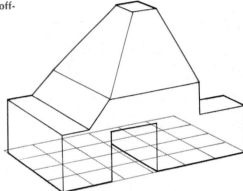

FIG. 359

Lay out enclosing squares for the hole circles . . . select ellipses that are tangent at the midpoints of the sides . . . darken visible lines and erase construction lines.

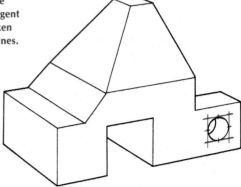

FIG. 360

jection made on a two-point perspective grid. For most situations, the third vanishing point is not required, and it really adds little to the realism of the illustration. Three-point perspective is usually used only to draw aerial views of such objects as tall buildings, chemical processing towers, space launch gantrys, or other very large and unusual objects. Figures [361] and [362] are examples of smaller objects drawn in three-point perspective.

The construction of a three-point perspective grid is confusing because of the many lines involved. After completion, it may be even more confusing to use unless some cleanup is done. After constructing the three-point grid, trace it onto a clean sheet, eliminating all construction lines in the process. The grid will also be easier to use if the sets of lines converging toward each of the three vanishing points are drawn or inked using different colors. Since a very large layout is required to produce a much smaller usable grid area, draw the construction on as large a sheet as space will allow. Lastly, a three-point perspective drawing is more subject to distortion than any other type due to the short distances that usually result between the center of vision and the vanishing points. For this reason, the vanishing points should be placed as far out as possible.

A three-point perspective grid is constructed as follows:

A three-point perspective of a piston and connecting rod assembly.

A three-point perspective drawing of a control mechanism.

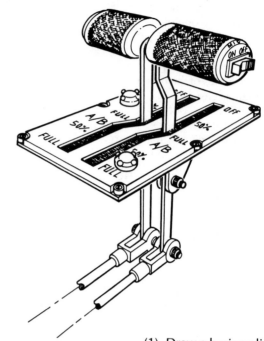

FIG. 361

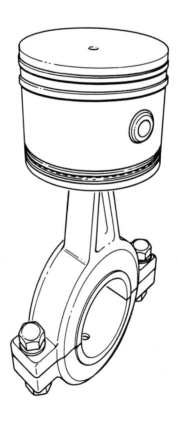

FIG. 362

(1) Draw a horizon line near the top of your sheet [363]. Mark a left vanishing point (*LVP*) and a right vanishing point (*RVP*) at the extremes. Bisect the horizon line between the vanishing points, and label this point *CV* for center of vision. Below the horizon line, draw an arc that is centered on *CV* and passes through *LVP* and *RVP*.

(2) Slightly to the right or left of the center of vision (approximately a fifth of the distance from *CV* to *LVP* or *RVP*), drop a vertical line to the bottom of your layout [364]. Label the bottom of this vertical line *VVP* for vertical vanishing point. Label the point where the arc is intersected by the vertical line *SPV* for station point vertical. Starting at *LVP,* draw a line to *VVP.* Draw another line from *RVP* to *VVP.* Bisect these two lines and label each center *CV*.

Draw a three-point perspective grid . . . draw horizon line at the top of the sheet . . . mark left and right vanishing points at the extremes . . . mark center of vision at the middle . . . draw an arc from *LVP* to *RVP*.

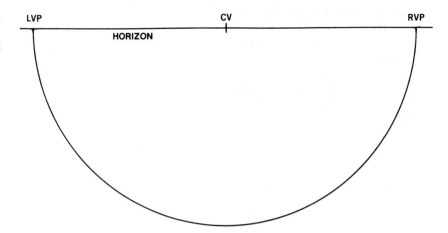

FIG. 363

Draw a vertical line to the right of the center of vision . . . mark the vertical vanishing point at the bottom of the line . . . mark *SPV* at the intersection of the arc with the vertical line . . . draw lines from *LVP* and *RVP* to *VVP* and label their centers *CV*.

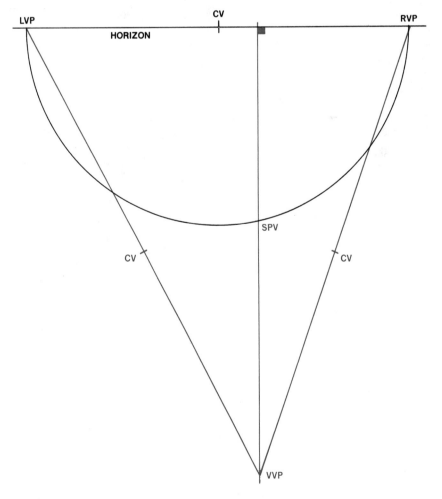

FIG. 364

(3) From *LVP* draw a line perpendicular to the line from *RVP* to *VVP*
[365]. Label the intersection point
of this line with *RVP–VVP* as *R*.
From *RVP* draw a line perpendicular to the line from *LVP* to *VVP*.
Label its intersection with *LVP–
VVP* as *L*.

Draw a line from *LVP* perpendicular to
RVP-VVP . . . label the intersection *R* . . .
draw a line from *RVP* perpendicular to
LVP-VVP . . . label the intersection *L*.

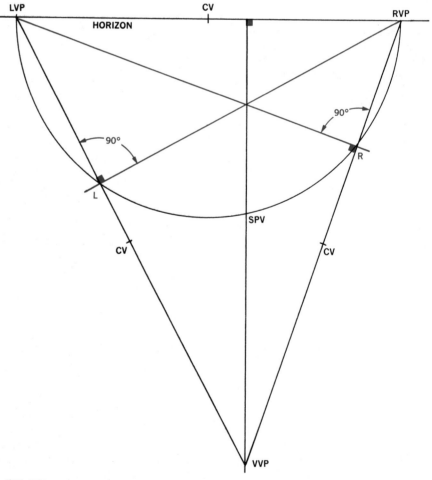

FIG. 365

(4) Using the *CV* point on the *LVP–VVP* line as a center, swing an arc from *LVP* to *VVP* [366]. Label the point where this arc intersects line *RVP–L* as *SPR* for station point right. Using the *CV* on line *RVP–VVP* as a center, swing another arc from *RVP* to *VVP*. Label its intersection with *LVP–R* as *SPL* for station point left.

Draw an arc from *LVP* to *VVP* . . . its intersection with *RVP-L* is labeled *SPR* . . . draw an arc from *RVP* to *VVP* . . . its intersection with *LVP-R* is labeled *SPL*.

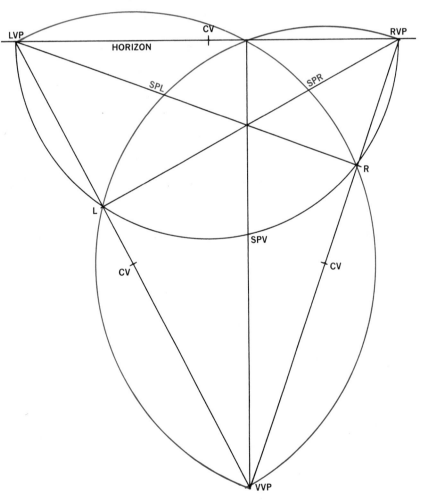

FIG. 366

(5) Draw a line parallel to the horizon through *SPV* [367]. Divide this line into appropriate scale increments, and draw lines from the scale marks to *LVP* and *RVP*. This provides a scaled perspective grid for drawing the horizontal faces of an object.

Draw a horizontal line through *SPV* . . .
mark scale increments on this line . . .
draw converging lines from the scale
marks to *LVP* and *RVP* to form a grid for
horizontal surfaces.

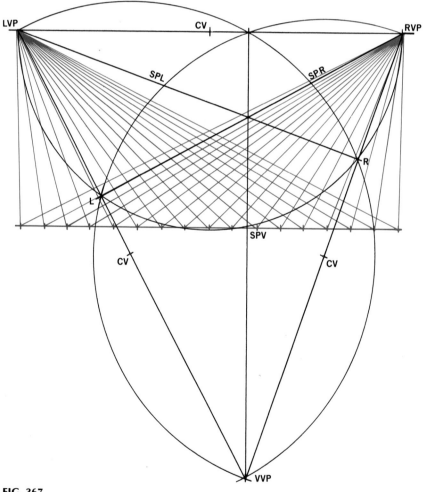

FIG. 367

(6) Draw a line through *SPR* that is parallel to the line *LVP–VVP* [368]. Mark the same scale increments on this line, and draw lines from the scale marks to *LVP* and *VVP*. The result is a grid for use with vertical faces vanishing to the left.

Draw a line through *SPR* and parallel to *LVP-VVP* . . . mark the same scale increments on this line . . . draw converging lines from the scale marks to *LVP* and *VVP* to form a grid for vertical surfaces vanishing to the left.

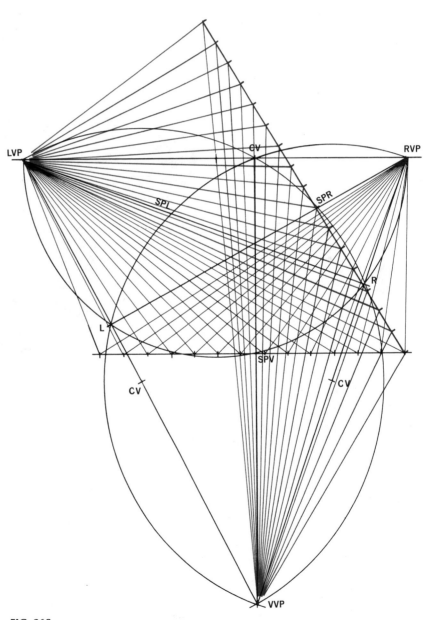

FIG. 368

(7) Draw a line through *SPL* that is parallel to *RVP–VVP,* and mark the same scale increments on it [369]. Draw lines from the scale marks to *RVP* and *VVP*. This grid is for use with vertical faces vanishing to the right.

(8) At this point, the grid layout is complete. It is advisable to erase

Draw a line through *SPL* and parallel to *RVP-VVP* . . . mark the same scale increments on this line . . . draw converging lines from the scale marks to *RVP* and *VVP* to form a grid for vertical surfaces vanishing to the right.

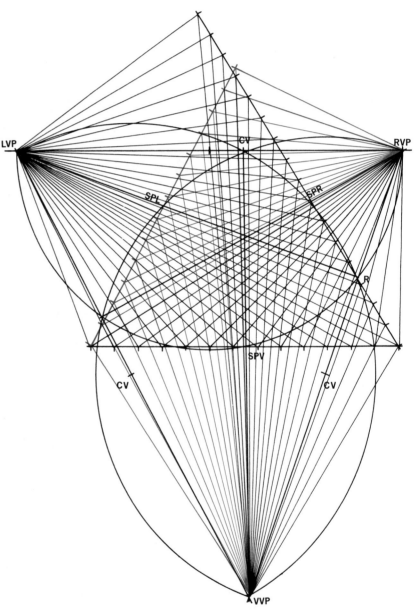

FIG. 369

all construction lines or trace the grid onto a clean sheet. Retain only the triangular central portion of the grid [370]. Eliminate all of the arcs and unnecessary radial lines from the vanishing points. It is wise to retain and darken the perpendiculars drawn through each of the station points. If you concentrate on the intersection of these three perpendiculars, you will see the basic width, depth, and height axis system that was used in axonometric drawing. This will also help you visualize how the grid pattern relates to each of the principal faces of an object.

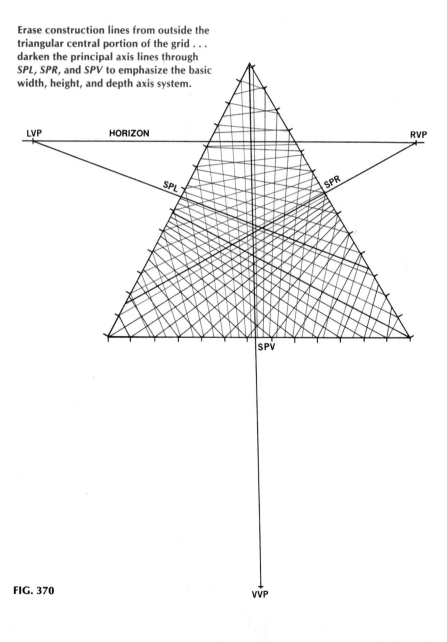

Erase construction lines from outside the triangular central portion of the grid . . . darken the principal axis lines through *SPL, SPR*, and *SPV* to emphasize the basic width, height, and depth axis system.

FIG. 370

64. DRAWING A THREE-POINT PERSPECTIVE

To see how a three-point perspective grid is used to draw objects, first draw a cube that measures 4 units on a side. Make a quick sketch to determine a suitable viewing direction. The base *ABCD* of the cube is then located on the grid in a position that will produce the desired view [371]. Lay out the 4 units of width and depth along their respective grid lines.

On a three-point perspective grid, height measurements are made differently than on one-point and two-point grids. Since the three-point grid has converging height lines, it is not necessary to move a line forward to the edge of the picture plane to lay out its true height. To establish the height of the cube, locate point *E* 4 units above point *A* on the height grid line passing through *A*. Then draw lines *EF* and *EH* along width and depth grid lines passing through *E* until they meet the height grid lines rising from *B* and *D*. Draw lines *FG* and *HG* along grid lines from *F* and *H* until they intersect at *G* on a height line rising from *C*. Note that when drawing objects where the measurements do not fall exactly at a grid crossing, you can easily estimate the direction of intermediate grid lines converging to the same vanishing points.

A multiview drawing of a spacer block is shown in [372]. Using these views, draw the filler block in three-point perspective. First select a suitable viewing direction by sketching a box that would enclose the block. Locate the base of the enclosing box on the grid in a position that will give the desired view [373]. Now lay out the other faces of the enclosing box. Then draw the horizontal and vertical surfaces of the filler block that touch these faces. Locate the boundary lines of the other surfaces by projecting inward along the grid lines [374]. Draw holes by laying out enclosing squares and selecting tangent ellipse template openings. Darken the visible lines of the filler block and erase the construction lines.

Draw a three-point perspective cube . . . locate a 4-unit square base *ABCD* on the grid . . . establish the 4-unit height of the cube on the height grid lines passing through the corners of the base . . . darken the visible lines of the cube.

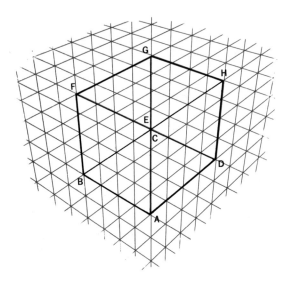

FIG. 371

Exercise 30

Many of the objects in Section 90—Problems for Assignment are suitable examples to use in practicing the principles learned in the preceding sections on three-point perspective drawing. Enlarge the objects as necessary to suit the available or assigned drawing sheet size. Maintain the proportions shown as closely as possible. Use an available three-point grid or construct your own following the procedures in Section 63. Use either the viewing direction that provides the best description of the object or the viewing direction assigned by your instructor. Make a quick sketch of each object first to obtain a clear understanding of the object and to be sure that the given views are correct. The sketch will help you visualize the finished illustration and aid you in positioning it on your drawing sheet. Use a grid underlay sheet from Appendix C as an aid in sketching. To help select suitable problems, refer to the categories of objects listed in isometric Exercises 18 through 23. Use some of the same objects that you drew in these exercises, as well as those in dimetric and trimetric, and compare the results and effort required.

Top, front, and right side views of a spacer block.

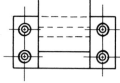

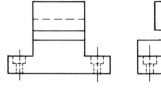

FIG. 372

Draw a three-point perspective of the filler block . . . select a suitable viewing direction by sketching an enclosing box . . . lay out the enclosing box on the grid . . . lay out the boundary lines of all surfaces that touch the visible faces of the box.

Project inward along the grid lines to locate the boundary lines of the interior surfaces . . . add holes by laying out the enclosing squares and drawing ellipses tangent at the midpoints . . . darken visible lines and erase construction lines.

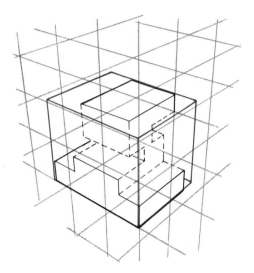

FIG. 373

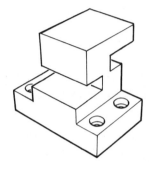

FIG. 374

Oblique Drawing

65. OBLIQUE DRAWING PRINCIPLES

The oblique drawing system is entirely different from the axonometric and perspective drawing systems, although some of the construction procedures are similar. The oblique system is fundamentally different because the observer's line of sight is at an angle with the viewing plane. The object is oriented with one principal face parallel to the viewing plane to reduce distortion and to simplify the drawing procedures. The description of the oblique system has been left until last because of its infrequent use in professional technical illustration.

The oblique system uses the multiview projection of the most important face of an object as a beginning point. This face appears undistorted just as in the multiview drawing because it is placed parallel to the viewing plane [375]. The other faces are drawn using parallel edge lines following a depth axis drawn at an angle with the horizontal width axis. The angle of the depth axis changes with changes in the direction and angle of the observer's line of sight with the viewing plane. This provides varying amounts of visibility for the faces of the object that are not parallel to the viewing plane.

Oblique drawing . . . one face appears undistorted just as in the multiview drawing.

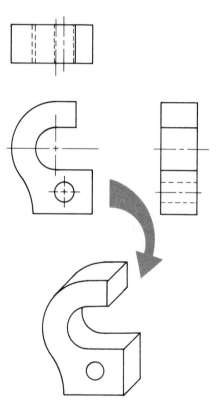

FIG. 375

In theory, the depth axis can be drawn at any angle with the horizontal except 90°. The scale used for the depth axis can also be varied to provide the most natural looking representation of the object. The basic form of oblique drawing uses a 45° angle for the depth axis and the same scale on all three axes [376]. A less distorted appearance of the object can be obtained by reducing the depth scale to ¾. If it is desired to provide better visibility to the top surface, the depth axis may be drawn at 60° with the horizontal. A ¾ scale for depth provides a pleasing appearance at this angle also. To increase the visibility of the side surface, a 30° depth axis angle may be used. A ¾ scale for depth is also desirable for this angle.

Drawings resulting from use of the oblique drawing system are so distorted from normal human vision that the system is rarely used by professional illustrators. The only real advantage is that it is easy to lay out irregular contours on the undistorted front face. This advantage quickly disappears, however, as the illustrator gains experience in using the axonometric drawing systems. Engineers frequently find the oblique system easy to use for quick freehand sketches.

Years ago, when oblique drawings were more popular, the term *cavalier oblique* was used to describe the basic type of oblique drawing made at a 45° angle and using the same scale on all three axes [377]. If the scale on the receding axis was reduced to ½ while still holding a 45° angle, the result was called a *cabinet oblique.* This reduces the overall size of the illustration and relieves some of the depth distortion while maintaining the ease of using a readily available 45° angle and ½ size scale.

The angle and scale of the depth axis may be varied to minimize distortion and to vary the visibility of the faces that are not parallel to the viewing plane.

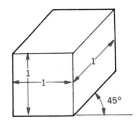

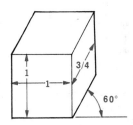

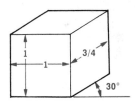

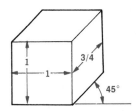

FIG. 376

In cavalier oblique, depth is drawn full scale . . . in cabinet oblique, depth is half scale . . . axis angle is 45° in both cases.

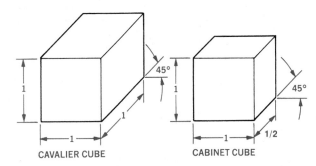

CAVALIER CUBE   CABINET CUBE

FIG. 377

66. DRAWING RECTANGULAR OBJECTS

Objects that are basically rectangular should be oriented in oblique drawing so that the face of the object having the most complex contours appears as the front face [378]. This is so that any surfaces of the object that are parallel to the front face will appear identical to their description in the multiview drawing. The layout procedure will be much easier. Care should also be taken to orient the object so that important features are not hidden behind other features or on the unseen side of the oblique view [379].

The procedures used for drawing an oblique view are very similar to those used for axonometric drawing. The process is simplified, however, by being able to transfer the frontal surfaces directly from the multiview to the oblique drawing. All surfaces parallel to the front face will appear undistorted. Measurements on or parallel to the width and height axes will be the same as on the multiview drawing. Depth measurements must be made in accordance with the depth angle and scale chosen for the oblique drawing.

In laying out the bearing support shown in [380], start with an enclosing box [381]. Draw the planes and lines or points that lie on the faces of the box first. Then draw boundary lines of the visible interior surfaces by plotting the width, height, and depth coordinates of their end points [382]. Since the circles are located on planes parallel to the front face, draw them with a circle template. As with other forms of pictorial drawing, hidden lines are normally omitted. Centerlines are seldom shown unless they are needed to clarify a special situation or to show a dimension.

Orient objects so the most complex contours are parallel to the undistorted front face.

FIG. 378

Select a viewing direction so important features are not hidden.

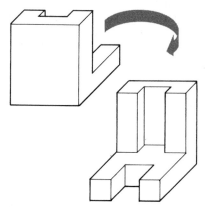

FIG. 379

Top, front, and right side views of a bearing support.

FIG. 380

Draw an oblique view of the bearing support . . . draw an enclosing box . . . lay out the boundary lines of the planes that touch the visible faces of the box.

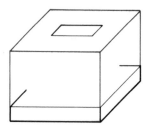

FIG. 381

Lay out the boundary lines of the visible interior surfaces . . . draw circles with a circle template . . . omit hidden lines.

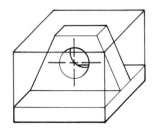

FIG. 382

67. DRAWING CYLINDRICAL OBJECTS

The oblique system is especially useful for drawing cylindrical objects because the object can usually be oriented so that the circular surfaces are either on or parallel to the undistorted front face [383]. In this position you can easily sketch or draw them with a compass or circle template. If the majority of the features of an object are cylindrical (as in a threaded shaft, a gear cluster, or a camshaft), you can make the drawing with more precision and accuracy, as well as ease, if you can use standard tools to draw these features.

In laying out a cylindrical object such as the one shown in [384], it is best to start by drawing its longitudinal axis at the chosen oblique angle. Then locate the centers of the front and back surfaces [385]. Lightly draw the circular outlines of these surfaces to aid in positioning the centers so that the oblique view will fit well in your drawing area. Mark the centers of the circular front and back surfaces of each cylindrical portion of the object on the axis line [386]. Draw light construction lines perpendicular to the axis at each center to help locate the ends of arcs and the starting points for tangents. Now draw the visible portions of the circles and arcs with a compass or a circle template. Draw tangent edge lines for each cylindrical portion parallel to the axis to complete the drawing [387].

Cylindrical objects . . . orient so the circular surfaces can be drawn undistorted.

FIG. 383

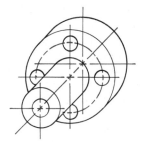

Two views of a typical cylindrical object.

FIG. 384

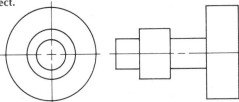

Draw an oblique view of a cylindrical object . . . draw oblique axis . . . locate the centers of the front and back surfaces . . . lightly draw front and back circles to help position the view.

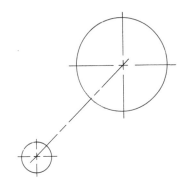

FIG. 385

Mark centers of the front and back surfaces of each cylindrical portion . . . draw light lines perpendicular to the axis at each center to locate ends of arcs and tangent points . . . draw visible portions of circles with a compass or a circle template.

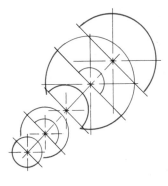

FIG. 386

Complete each cylindrical portion by drawing tangent edge lines parallel to the axis.

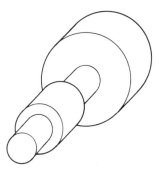

FIG. 387

When circles or arcs occur in an oblique drawing on surfaces that are not parallel to the front face, they must be represented by ellipses. Approximate these by drawing an oblique representation of a square that is tangent on all sides of the circle [388]. Try various angles and sizes of ellipse template openings until you find one that is closest to being *tangent* at the *midpoints* of the sides. The rule used on axonometric drawings for orienting the minor axis of an ellipse in the direction of a line perpendicular to its plane *does not* hold true in oblique drawing.

Because of the severe distortion of especially the side faces in oblique, the ellipses will also appear very distorted. Sometimes you can obtain better results in drawing an approximate ellipse by using one of the ellipse construction techniques shown in Appendix A. However, this is usually too time consuming for professional applications unless the ellipses are especially large or of unusual size.

Exercise 31

The objects listed below and illustrated in Section 90—Problems for Assignment are suitable examples to use in practicing the principles learned in the preceding sections on oblique drawing. Enlarge the objects as necessary to suit the available or assigned drawing sheet size. Maintain the proportions shown as closely as possible. Use either the oblique axis system and viewing direction that provides the best description of the object or the axis system and viewing direction assigned by your instructor. Make a quick sketch of each object first to obtain a clear understanding of the object and to be sure that the given views are correct. The sketch will help you visualize the finished illustration and aid you in positioning it on your drawing sheet. Use a grid underlay sheet from Appendix C as an aid in sketching. If you have drawn any of the objects listed below in axonometric or perspective, compare your finished oblique drawing with the drawings made in the other systems for degree of realism obtained and amount of effort required.

(a) The following objects are basically rectangular with straight lines.
Probs. 3, 5, 12, 20, 27, 33.
(b) The following objects are basically rectangular with circles and arcs.
Probs. 38, 40, 43, 46, 62, 65.
(c) The following objects are basically cylindrical.
Probs. 52, 53, 55, 56, 57, 58.

Use an enclosing square to draw circles on surfaces not parallel to the undistorted front face . . . select an ellipse that is closest to being tangent at the midpoints of the sides.

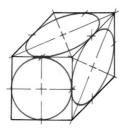

FIG. 388

Technical Illustration Drawing Techniques

Technical illustrators also draw charts and diagrams.

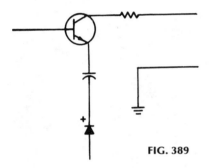

FIG. 389

68. SPECIAL DRAWING TOOLS

So far the most common drawing systems have been discussed, and you have learned how to construct special scales, templates, and grids to make illustration easier than by direct projection from multiview drawings. These aids and a great many more besides are also commercially available. The construction techniques have been described so that you can better understand how to use these aids. Also, under adverse con-

ditions, you can build what you need to be effective when commercial aids are not available or are not quite suited to the individual job.

The explanations, so far, have been oriented to drawing individual parts or assembled objects. Technical illustrators, however, also draw a great many abstract or nonobjective things such as flow charts, schematics, charts, graphs, nomographs, and block and logic diagrams [389]. These, too, are more easily drawn using commercially available aids and shortcuts. (For detailed information

on making various types of electronic drawings including block and logic diagrams, see Beakley, Autore, and Alf, *Electronic Drafting*, Bobbs-Merrill, Indianapolis, 1982.)

Since illustrators often work at home as well as in a drafting room, it is usually preferable to acquire those tools that are the most portable. Avoid purchasing the more elaborate specialized drawing boards and associated equipment unless there is sufficient demand for the types of drawings that can be made more economically with them.

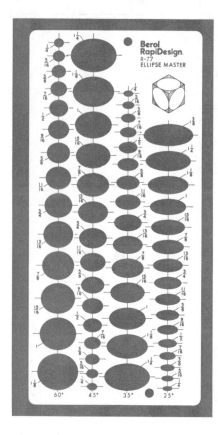

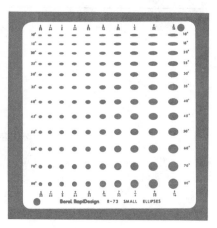

Ellipse templates are available in 5° increments from 10° through 80° and in sizes from 3 to 175 mm and $\frac{3}{32}$ to 7 in. across the major axis [390]. Large ellipse templates are quite expensive and are used infrequently, so they are provided in most studios for the illustrators. If this is not the case, the ellipses needed can be drawn smaller and enlarged with a copy camera.

In addition to ellipse templates, there is a wide variety of special templates designed to assist in drawing

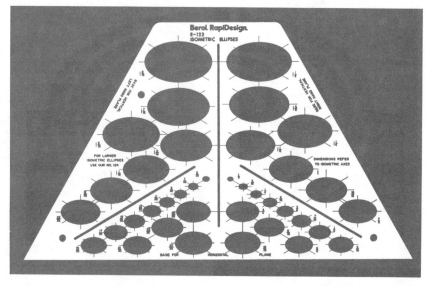

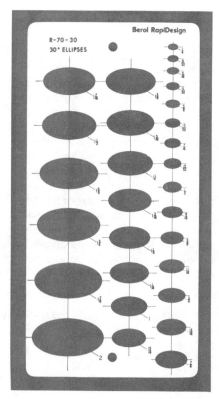

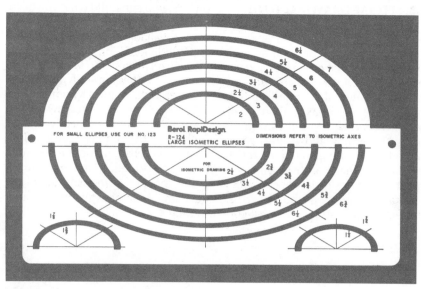

FIG. 390
Ellipse templates are available in a wide variety of sizes and angles.

repetitive objects. There are templates for the heads of various types of screws and bolts, and also for nuts, threads, springs, and rivets that are commonly used by illustrators whose work is chiefly mechanical [391]. In the electronics field, there are logic, schematic, and computer flow diagram templates [392]. Literally hundreds of templates are available for all kinds of specialized purposes. In addition you can use a piece of plastic and cut your own templates for arrowheads, wavy break lines, and so forth.

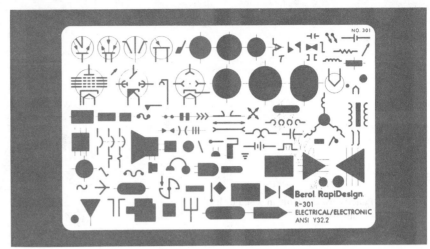

FIG. 392

Special templates are available for electronic and computer diagrams.

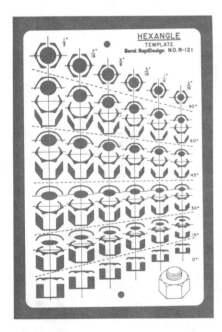

Special templates speed up the drawing of common parts.

69. DRAWING WITH PENCILS

When you have practiced basic drawing procedures enough to become proficient at laying out individual parts and assembled products in one or more drawing systems, you should begin to concentrate on the methods to be used to make your drawings reproducible in a clear and professional manner. Although pencil illustrations are used in some studios as the regular production method, they are not generally considered professionally acceptable. When using pencil, it is difficult to maintain good control of line weights and densities. This in turn makes reproduction into plates for printing much

more difficult than necessary. If the illustrator's work is not easily and clearly reproducible, it has little commercial value.

Pencils are graded as to density [393]. Starting at H, in ascending order, the grades are H, 2H, 3H, and so on to 9H. Each of these grades has successively harder lead than the last and consequently makes lighter lines.

Pencil leads are graded from very hard (9H) to very soft (6B).

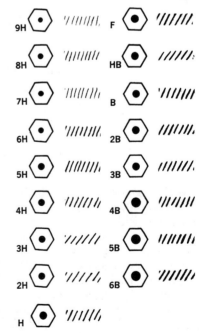

FIG. 393

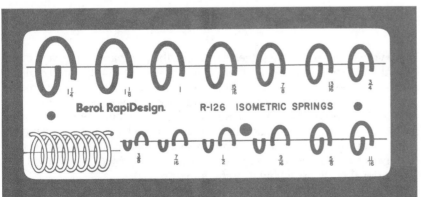

FIG. 391

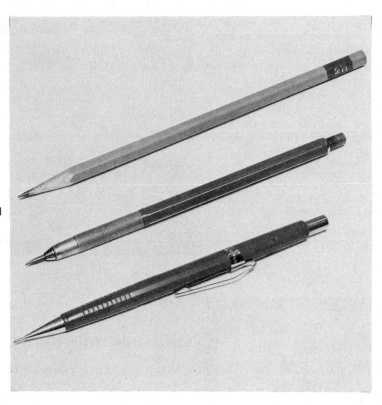

Pencils are available in wood or lead holder styles.

FIG. 394

Ultra-thin lead holders require no sharpening or pointing.

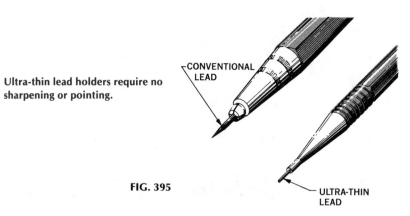

CONVENTIONAL LEAD

ULTRA-THIN LEAD

FIG. 395

Below H the grades run F, HB, B, 2B, 3B, through 6B, each being successively softer and consequently producing darker lines. All of these grades are available in regular wood drafting pencils or as leads to be inserted in mechanical lead holders [394]. The newest in mechanical holders use 0.3 mm (0.012 in), 0.5 mm (0.020 in), 0.7 mm (0.028 in), or 0.9 mm (0.036 in) diameter ultra-thin leads [395].

These very fine leads are designed to help the illustrator maintain more consistent line widths as the lead wears away on the abrasive drawing surface. They also save time since no sharpening or pointing is required.

The three chief objections to pencil drawing are: (1) the lead is reflective under the intense lighting used in reproduction and tends to reflect light back into the camera thus weak-

ening the photographed image of the lines; (2) it is nearly impossible to produce a reasonably complex drawing with good black reproducible lines and still keep the drawing reasonably clean; and (3) it is very difficult to maintain even line weights that are consistent throughout the drawing.

When pencil drawings are desired, there are ways to combat the

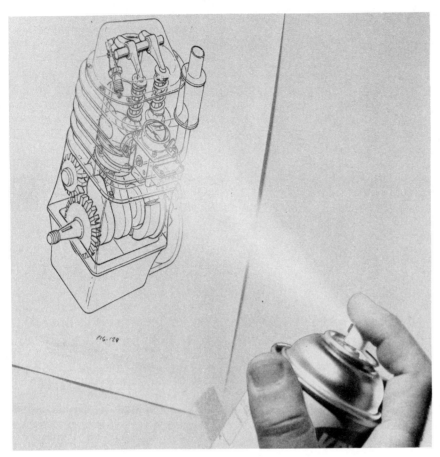

Spraying with a fixative reduces smudging.

FIG. 396

problems associated with them. First, to reduce the smudging of the lead, spray the finished drawing with a good grade of matte workable fixative [396]. Most of the available fixatives are based on acrylic lacquers or enamels, and the coating of these finishes tends to darken the pencil lines by 10 to 20 percent. Since most drawings are revised several times, it is important to remember to use the "workable" variety. This means that the fixative can be removed with an eraser and the line work changed with relative ease.

To help keep your drawing clean, there are a number of drafting compounds available that you can lightly sprinkle onto the drawing surface while you work. These compounds are finely ground eraser crumbs that prevent graphite smears caused by sliding triangles and templates across the drawing surface. Unfortunately, their tendency is also to erase some

of the density of the drawn lines while removing the unwanted smudges.

Finally, to keep line weights under control as much as possible, keep your pencil (or any other drawing instrument) as nearly perpendicular to the drawing surface as possible. As you move the pencil along a straight edge or within a template opening, develop the habit of slowly rotating the pencil to distribute the wear evenly around the sides of the point [397]. A pencil used in lettering should also be rotated slightly between strokes or letters to maintain uniform line weight.

When drawing with a conventional pencil or a lead holder, use a pencil pointer frequently. Be careful to wipe the lead clean and to break off the needle point by shaping the lead on a piece of scrap paper. Avoid leaning the pencil lead against the edge of a template or straight edge where the lead might be cut or notched by the edge.

Slowly rotate the pencil to wear the point evenly.

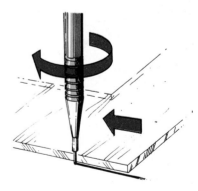

FIG. 397

70. DRAWING WITH INK

The preferred method of finishing technical illustrations is to ink them. A wide selection of inks and pens is

Various types of technical pens are available.

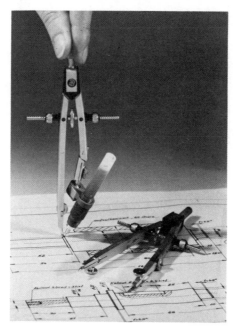

FIG. 398

Ink lines on plastic drafting film are easily erased with a slightly moistened eraser.

FIG. 399

available [398]. Several choices of drawing surfaces are available to take ink readily. Normally, the material on which ink drawings are made is laid over an original pencil layout. For this reason, transparency is a de-sirable quality. The materials usually used for ink drawings are specially finished types of vellum paper or plastic drafting film.

Since the various kinds of India inks used are usually water based, any oily deposits on the drawing surface from fingerprints or processing will form a resistance to the ink causing it to fail to stick uniformly to the surface. This condition can be corrected on any surface by sprinkling some inking powder ("pounce") on the surface and rubbing the entire area to be inked. After the surface has been cleaned, be sure to wipe the powder away with a tissue or brush before beginning to ink or the powder residue will clog your pen points. Special liquid cleaners are also sold for use on plastic drawing film.

The least expensive and most commonly used drawing surface is a good grade of vellum. The surface takes ink readily, dries rapidly enough to be satisfactory, and can be pounced as necessary. Small incorrect portions of inked lines can be chipped from it with success. Large errors are more difficult to erase. For these errors, an abrasive ink eraser is required. If not used carefully, the surface of the vellum can be easily damaged. When inking on vellum, be careful of the drag of some styles of pen points across the surface of the vellum. Too much pressure, holding the pen at an angle, or too frequent retracing of a line can result in the pen point digging into the surface and causing the ink to blot.

The original cost of plastic drafting film is more than for other materials. This is largely offset by its greater durability, dimensional stability, and ease of erasing. The surface of the plastic film that makes it suitable for inking is a thin coating that is applied to one or both sides of the film at the factory. This can be destroyed by too much erasing or chipping and is then difficult if not impossible to restore well enough to reink. Some illustrators rub the surface with a small piece of soapstone to restore its inkable qualities. This technique, however, is of limited value. Erasing on plastic film is best done with a slightly moistened plastic or soft rubber eraser [399].

Small corrections in inked lines, such as overrun corners, are usually made with an X-acto knife or other sharp blade. Using a light touch and scraping the blade across the ink will chip away the ink and leave a clean edge after a little practice [400].

71. LINE WEIGHTS

There are good and necessary reasons to pay particular attention to the weight of the lines that you use to draw an illustration. Line "weight" refers to the width or thickness that distinguishes different types of lines. The first and simplest reason has to do with reproducibility of the lines by photolithography or any of the direct

Small ink corrections can be made by scraping with a knife.

FIG. 400

image plating systems for printing. Cameras photograph the white of the paper and the black lines represent an area where no image is recorded.

With this basic understanding, you can see that the blacker and thicker the line, the easier and more successfully it will reproduce. The lithographic films used for such reproductions are typically blind to a light blue color. A pencil having this shade of color (referred to as "nonphoto blue") is used to mark corrections or notes on reproducible original drawings. Many pencil leads and some types of inks used in black "throw-away" pens contain just enough blue pigment to make reproduction of them difficult. Red, on the other hand, reproduces just as well as black and is used frequently as a substitute for black in keylining and other production techniques that will be described later.

Technical pens are available in a wide range of point sizes to produce different line widths [401]. Unfortunately, many of the sizes are too fine for good, consistent reproduction on film or printing plates. The amount of size reduction of the reproduction

governs what will be reproducible. Most camera/film combinations will reproduce well almost any weight line at the same size with no reduction. Most drawings for reproduction, however, are drawn oversize so that they will require some reduction.

Oversizing is done to provide a convenient working size for the illustator and also because small errors, such as line weight inconsistencies or overrun corners in an inking, will be unnoticeably small when the drawing is reduced [402]. Com-

Drawing oversize helps hide small errors when the illustration is reduced for final use.

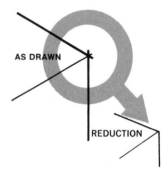

FIG. 402

Point sizes and line widths for technical pens.

FIG. 401

Clean pens with ultrasonic cleaners.

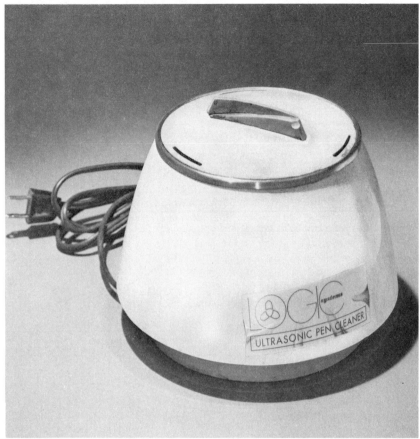

FIG. 403

Closely spaced parallel lines will "melt together" when they are reduced unless they are spaced carefully.

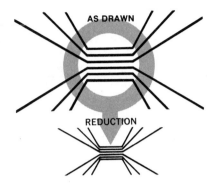

FIG. 404

sonic cleaners that are available in most large drafting rooms [403].

Parallel lines that are spaced too closely will "melt together" when reduced unless proper care is taken in their spacing [404]. For reductions of 50 percent or more, use a reducing lens to check the original drawing to be sure that the spacing will be adequate after the reduction is made. Adequate spacing is also important on schematics or other types of diagrams that must be clearly read. On these drawings, maintain a minimum space between parallel lines of 3 mm (⅛ in) at the final reproduced size. This spacing is the minimum amount to make it easy for the reader to trace out individual lines and circuit paths. If the parallel lines occur in an illustration of an object where it will not be necessary to trace individual paths, the rule of practice is that the space between the lines should be as great as the width of the lines themselves.

Another reason for being careful about using different line weights is that, if properly used, they can become a part of the visual language of drawing and can communicate important information about the object being illustrated. If a fine line is drawn crossing a heavy line, or a wavy or rough textured line is drawn crossing a straight or smooth line, the straight, smooth, or light line in all cases appears to lie behind the other in space

monly, illustrations are reproduced at 50 and 67 percent of original size. That is, the original was twice or one and one-half times the size of the final copy. For reproductions within this range, a good working rule is to use no line weight smaller than that produced by a 0 size pen. This means approximately a 0.35 mm (0.0138 in) width line. If the reproduction is to be at a size even smaller than 50 percent, the original line width must be increased accordingly.

Selecting the best line width to use does not always dictate a specific size pen point. The line width produced by a certain point size will vary slightly with the brand of pen, the cleanliness of the pen, the technique of the user, the brand and condition of the ink being used, the type of vellum or film

on which the drawing is made, and sometimes even the weather. These variables will be quite noticeable to the beginning illustrator but are of less concern to the professional illustrator who is drawing on a regular basis. Equipment, technique, maintenance, and drawing material become standardized with frequent use, and the working environment becomes more stabilized. Generally, a pen point will produce a slightly wider line on plastic drawing film than on vellum. Large users of technical drawing inks seldom have a problem with pens that clog from old ink. Keeping the ink flowing freely in a pen is much less of a problem when that pen is used every day. However, it must still be cleaned periodically. This is simplified by using the ultra-

[405]. This optical illusion can be useful in creating drawings that appear to have a third dimension or depth.

If, when inking a drawn object, you select two line weights of 0 and 3 or 4 [0.35 mm (0.0138 in) and 0.80 mm (0.0315 in) or 1.2 mm (0.0472 in)] you can create the illusion of depth. Picture the object as if it were floating in space [406]. Note all of the edges that have open space behind them. These are the edges of the object that you could reach around with a hand and feel only empty space. Ink all of these edges with the heavier weight line. All of the remaining edges that represent "interior" edges (edges surrounded by material) should be inked with the lighter weight line.

It is also true that a line that contains a break appears to recede behind a crossing line that is continuous [407]. Using this principle, break any sets of lines at the point where they would enter or disappear behind another surface. Make the break with a knife blade held perfectly parallel to the predominant surface. The break should be about the same size as the weight of the line being broken.

Compare two inkings of the same object—one with only one line weight and no breaks and one with different line weights and breaks [408]. You will see that the second appears to have more depth dimension and "reality" than the first.

A fine straight line appears to lie behind heavy, wavy, or textured lines.

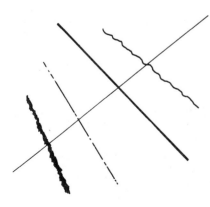

FIG. 405

To create the illusion of depth . . . imagine the object to be floating in space . . . ink the outside edges that you could reach around with heavier lines.

FIG. 406

Break a line just before it crosses behind another line to give the illusion of depth.

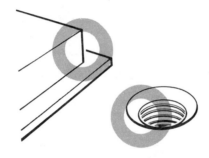

FIG. 407

72. PRINCIPLES OF SHADING

The ability to see objects is based on the reflection of light off of their surfaces. A normal function of light is its counterpart—shade. Shadows are the absence of light or a lower level of light reflectivity. This is caused by blocking light or by the bouncing of light off of an irregularly reflective surface. Shadows are a normal part of our visual experience, and they too help to define the shape or position of objects as well as some of their other characteristics.

If an object is floating some distance off the ground, it casts a shadow that visually helps you determine that it is floating [409]. If the same object is lighted the same way and is sitting very close to the ground, it casts a

Varying line weights and line breaks provide depth and realism.

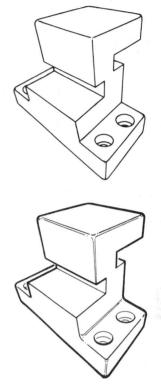

FIG. 408

The position of a cast shadow helps you visualize the location of an object.

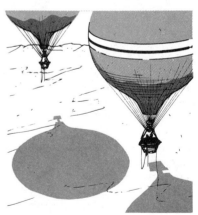

FIG. 409

shadow that helps you understand that it is just barely floating.

In most of our experience, light comes from somewhere overhead. This may be from the sun or from

Light usually comes from overhead . . . the shadow is seen toward the bottom.

BALL
CAUSES
LIGHT BLOCK
OR SHADOW

FIG. 410

ceiling lights in a building [410]. Lighting from below is unusual and its effects are not as firmly planted in our memories. As a result, the positions of shadows help us orient objects with respect to up and down. The shadow side of an object is generally assumed to be the down side or toward the bottom.

There are two kinds of shadows—those that appear on the surfaces of an object opposite the light source and those that are cast onto the ground or onto adjacent objects or surfaces [411]. Cast shadows used in illustrations frequently obscure neighboring objects or surfaces, particularly when drawing assemblies. For this reason, they are usually omitted for clarity. Since cast shadows are seldom used by technical illustrators, their construction will not be discussed here.

Shadows appear on the unlit side of an object . . . they are also cast onto the ground or adjacent objects.

FIG. 411

Since the presence of light and shade is a visual supplement that helps us see and understand objects, you should be prepared to use them to enhance the quality of drawings. Much can be learned by observing the effect of light and shade on four common geometric solids: a cone, a sphere, a cube, and a cylinder [412].

Light and shade effects on common geometric solids.

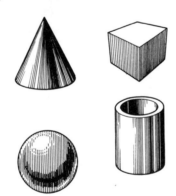

FIG. 412

A large number of objects are composed of these shapes in combination or in part.

If a single source of light exists in the upper left hand corner of the drawing area, areas of light and shade will be produced on solids in the way shown in [412]. An upper left position of the light source is a standard location in technical illustration work [413]. Again, a uniform approach to this type of detail helps the reader make uniform interpretations.

If light and shadow conditions are taken strictly from a single light source, the objects will possess great dark areas and cast heavy dark shadows [414]. The presence of heavy shadows in a technical drawing is undesirable since the shadows will very likely obscure valuable information about one side of the object. In addition, in real life it is unusual to have an object lighted by only a single light source. Even when this is true, the surfaces that surround the object tend to be reflective and will consequently throw some additional light back onto the dark side of the object

Upper left is the standard light source position for technical illustration.

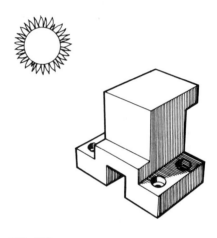

FIG. 413

With a single light source, objects have great dark areas and cast heavy dark shadows.

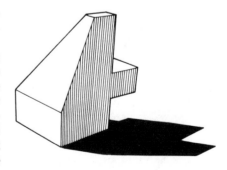

FIG. 414

[415]. This requires that the shaded surfaces on an object be depicted with gradual darkening of tone. Drawings of this type are known as **continuous** or **full tone drawings** in contrast to **line drawings** where the only two values are black and white and the full range of gray tones is not used.

Surrounding surfaces reflect light back onto the dark side of an object.

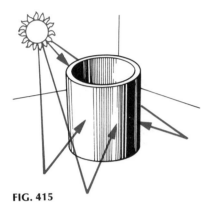

FIG. 415

73. BLOCK SHADING

Most technical drawings are line drawings, and it is desirable to keep them like this to reduce the cost of preparation and reproduction. In keeping with this, the system used to add a useful amount of shadow to line drawings is called **block shading.** In block shading a slight shadow effect is drawn on the right side and bottom of an object [416]. This is based on the standard assumption that the light source is located in the upper left hand corner of the drawing.

You can often add block shading by merely thickening the lines in the appropriate areas [417]. Where polished metal is the material of the object, it is more common to use sequentially a solid dark area to represent the shaded area, a white space to represent the reflected light from whatever the object rests upon or is surrounded by, and a thinner dark area to represent background reflections [418].

Some thought must be given to maintaining continuity in your shading. For instance, consider a piece of

tubing that drops down a very nearly vertical path, crosses left to right, and continues on an oblique angle [419]. Note how the "right side and bottom" location of the shadowed area changes as the configuration of the tube changes. The edges of most objects are given a slight radius to prevent sharpness and to remove burrs or tooling marks. When drawing an

Block shading . . . a slight shadow effect is drawn on the right side and the bottom.

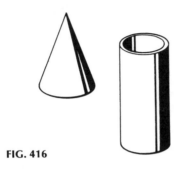

FIG. 416

Block shading can often be done by thickening lines in appropriate areas.

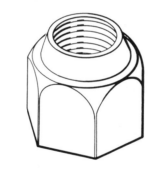

FIG. 417

On polished metal, the solid dark area is the shaded area . . . the white space is reflected light from whatever the object rests on . . . the thinner dark area is background reflections.

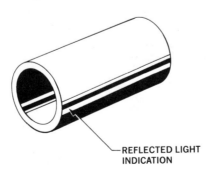

REFLECTED LIGHT
INDICATION

FIG. 418

Maintain continuity . . . the shading on the right side and bottom changes with the bends in the tubing.

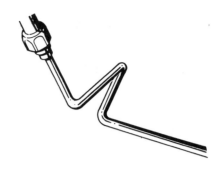

FIG. 419

"interior" line, a few random, short breaks in the line will suggest light reflecting from such an edge and relieve the sharp-edged appearance of a line [289].

74. SPECIAL SHADING TECHNIQUES

Block shading is the simplest and cleanest method of shading technical drawings without obscuring some of the object's features. There are other shading methods, however, that can be used to accomplish the same purpose. These methods still allow the printing advantage of being able to reproduce the illustrations as line drawings.

Using a series of straight or curved parallel lines to develop tones of gray or shade is known as **straight line shading** [420]. When lines are added that run in opposite directions to the

Straight line shading . . . parallel lines are used to develop tones of shade.

FIG. 420

Cross hatching . . . shading produced by crossing sets of parallel lines.

FIG. 421

Stipple . . . shading tones produced by varying the density of a close pattern of dots.

FIG. 422

straight line shading, this is known as *cross hatching* [421]. A close pattern of dots that changes tonal ranges by more or fewer dots in a given area is known as *stipple* [422]. Figure [423] shows stipple used in combination with block shading.

All of these methods can be reproduced in line negatives that are used in the printing process. When done by hand, however, these shading methods are expensive in terms of the illustrator's time. All of the basic patterns mentioned and a great deal more are available in the form of *adhesive* or *transfer sheets.* With adhesive sheets, an illustrator can select the pattern desired and apply it to the drawing, cutting away with a knife the area that should remain clear of shade [424]. The desired portion is then burnished (pressed down) with a plastic tool designed for this purpose or pressed firmly with the edge of a triangle or template to positively

stick the adhesive-backed, trimmed portion of the sheet to the drawing.

Transfer sheets are used by selecting the desired pattern and simply placing it over the area to be shaded. A pencil or similar tool is then rubbed over the top of the sheet where the

Shading patterns are available on adhesive sheets to save time.

FIG. 424

Block and stipple shading applied to a cutaway drawing of an automobile engine.

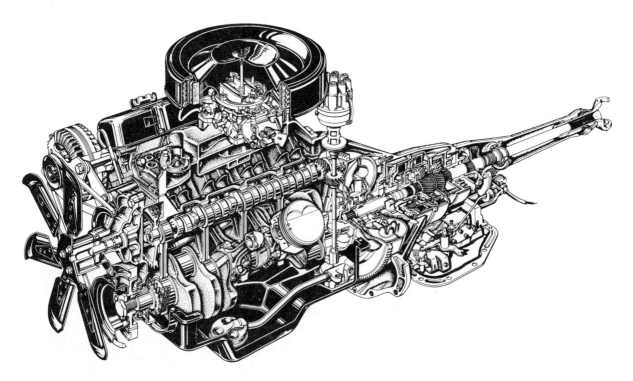

FIG. 423

tone is desired [425]. The ink image transfers from the backing sheet to the surface of the drawing and can be made relatively scratch resistant by applying a light coating of fixative.

A variation of the adhesive and transfer shading sheets is a type of illustration board coated with shading patterns in both straight line and cross hatch as well as dot patterns. When you complete an inked drawing on this board, the shading patterns may be exposed where desired by painting the board with a developer solution [426].

Exercise 32

Select several of the illustrations that you drew in previous exercises. Redraw them in ink using line weight and shading techniques learned in Sections 70 through 74. Consider the purpose for which the illustrations might be used and also possible methods that might be used to reproduce the finished illustrations.

75. CONTINUOUS TONE DRAWINGS

All of the various means of adding shading to line drawings that have been discussed so far use small increments of black either in the form of lines or dots to produce tone variations. That is to say, there are no real shades of gray in the drawing although the patterns, when reproduced small enough, will appear to the eye to represent shades of gray.

Shading patterns on transfer sheets are rubbed onto the desired area.

FIG. 425

Shading patterns on special types of illustration board are exposed by painting with a developer.

FIG. 426

You can complete a technical drawing in such a way that it has the appearance of a black and white photograph having a full range of shades of gray from white to black. The procedure to do this is referred to as **rendering.** The most common use for such drawings is in advertising or promotional literature. Straight technical illustration done for manufacturing and assembly instruction is seldom completely rendered.

Although there are an infinite number of tints of gray that are possible, the graphic arts industry generally recogizes 10 to 15 steps of gray. On the graphic arts **step wedge** used to measure the tonal quality of film and plates, the grays have values assigned according to their density [427]. The lightest step is said to be a 10 percent gray, the next 20 percent, and so on to 100 percent of full black. This designation is used to re-

fer to the resulting gray values that are obtained when the step wedge is photographed as a part of a printing negative. The step wedge illustrated is marked in photographic densities. Properly exposed, these densities will produce the appropriate percent dot in the proper location on a litho negative.

The term **continuous tone** is used to describe an illustration or a photograph that has a full spectrum of gray values (from black to white) used in its composition. Continuous tone art may only be completely reproduced by continuous tone photography. To reproduce the gray tones accurately, the rendering must be placed in front of a camera, and a black and white negative must be shot and printed. This is the same way that you take a black and white photograph of a person or a scene.

If this were the only way to reproduce continuous tone illustrations, they would be useless for mass reproduction since photographic prints are expensive. A nearly perfect representation of the gray tones can be achieved by converting the continuous tone art to what is called **line copy.** Line copy contains only black and white. When you prepare a rendering or a continuous tone photograph for printing by converting it to line copy, the process is called **halftoning** and results in what is called a **halftone negative.** This negative is then used to prepare the printing plate.

In order to reproduce shades of gray on a printing press with only one run of black ink, the shades of gray must be printed in a manner similar to the technique used in stipple shading.

A graphic arts step wedge assigns values to shades of gray according to density.

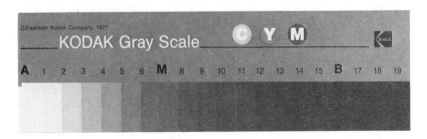

FIG. 427

A continuous tone illustration photographed through a halftone screen produces a dot pattern on a printing negative.

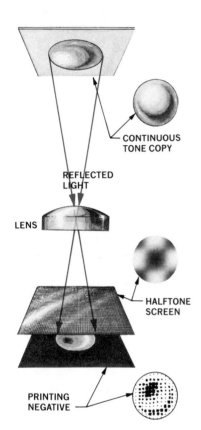

FIG. 428

Enlarged view of the halftone screen.

That is, the tones must be reproduced as a series of dots. The blacker the tone desired, the denser the dot pattern. The lighter the tone desired, the less dense the dot pattern.

To produce the dot pattern, the continuous tone illustration or photograph is photographed onto a line negative through a *halftone screen* [428]. The halftone screen is composed of a grid of photographic squares that are nearly transparent at the center and darkly shaded at the edges. This effect present in each square of the halftone screen is known as *vignette*. When magnified it looks like [429]. As light reflects from the surface of the art, it is transmitted to the negative only through the halftone screen. Where the reflected light is intense (as reflected from a light or white area), the light intensity tends to burn through the vignetted area failing to expose only the small dot area where the corners of the vignettes are joined and densest. On the negative, this results in a highlight dot or an area that will reproduce a very light tone of gray.

Where the reflected light intensity is low from the dark part of the original drawing or photograph, only the clear area in the center of the vignettes will be exposed resulting in a small shadow dot image on the negative. In the middle tone area, where the gray is theoretically composed of 50 percent black and 50 percent white, the image produced is a checker pattern in which the reproduced vignette squares of black and white are of equal size.

76. OPAQUE WATER COLOR RENDERING

Tubes of opaque watercolors, called *retoucher's grays,* are available that are graded to correspond to the gray scale reproduction standard [427]. That is, the grays are labeled 10 through 50 percent gray by 10 percent increments. In most cases, values above 50 or 60 percent gray are intended to be mixed by the addition of black to the darkest gray.

Retoucher's grays are said to be *opaque* because if a mistake is made in the rendering, it can be corrected by painting another tone over the error and the second coat will cover the

FIG. 429

Squeeze various shades of retoucher's grays into the compartments of a plastic box.

FIG. 430

first. For this reason, retoucher's grays are an excellent media for beginners to use in learning to render.

A successful working setup can be assembled by squeezing out the contents of the tubes into a compartmented plastic box of the type normally used to hold screws, nails, or fishing lures [430]. Allow the paint to dry thoroughly. When dry, the paint can be easily reconstituted by dip-ping a watercolor brush in water and dampening the cake of color until the desired consistency for rendering (about the thickness of cream) is achieved.

Use retoucher's grays on either watercolor paper or a good grade of illustration board. The board is preferable for this kind of work since it resists the wrinkling and warping that is common with watercolor papers.

77. BRUSHES AND THEIR USE

Brushes made to be used with water colors range in size from the smallest 00 through quite large #8 and #9. Brushes also have various names to describe their shapes. *Flats* have rectangular ends, *rounds* have round ends, and *brights* have pointed ends

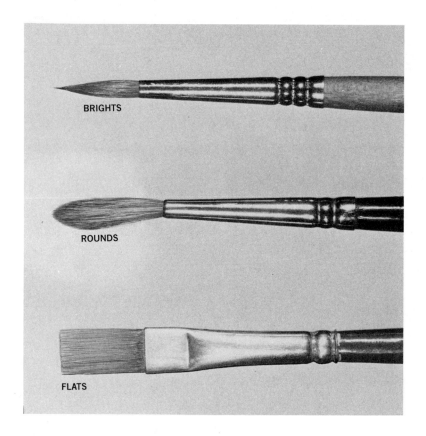

BRIGHTS

ROUNDS

FLATS

Brushes are available in different sizes and shapes.

FIG. 431

[431]. For most purposes, it is enough to have one high quality, pointed watercolor brush made of sable of about #2 or #3 size and one flat brush that is either ½ or ¾ in. wide.

There is no universally accepted **best** way to hold a brush. Whatever grip is most comfortable and effective for you is probably the correct one to use. The paint should be applied evenly and generally should be stroked on in only one direction. Avoid pushing down or scrubbing with the brush. Such use is too hard on expensive brushes and produces no special effect that is not possible in some less destructive way.

78. RENDERING TECHNIQUE

Since technical subjects are so filled with straight lines, the drawing of straight lines is one very useful technique to practice and learn well. It is not easy to rule a straight line freehand with a brush. An all metal ruler or a wooden ruler with an inserted metal edge will assist you in guiding the brush. Steady the hand that holds the ruler by resting your knuckles on the drawing board surface [432]. Practice gripping the brush firmly so that the ferrule cannot slip up or down in your grip while resting the fingers of the brush hand on the face of the ruler as a guide. When the whole arrangement is steady, move the brush carefully but smoothly along the ruler's metal edge. Be careful not to change the pressure on the brush or the thickness of your line will change accordingly. After a little practice, you should be able to draw a line that is quite straight and reasonably consistent in weight.

As your first rendering project, try to duplicate the step wedge with your own retoucher's grays. Start by making a border around each area to provide practice in ruling with a brush. Remember that it is necessary to mix all of the gray values above 50 or 60 percent that you will need.

Guide the brush along the edge of a ruler to draw straight lines.

FIG. 432

In order to keep your tray colors pure, do any mixing on a pallette made of a piece of glass or acetate or use a commercial water color pal-

A typical work station . . . colors are always mixed on a palette.

FIG. 433

lette [433]. Another aid to cleanliness is to use two pots of water. After brushing each density of paint, always wash your brush out first in one pot and then rinse it in another. The first pot will become dirty very quickly but the water in the second will re-main relatively clean for a long time. This cleaner pot should be used when you are mixing colors.

When you have practiced enough to feel somewhat confident, choose one of your technical drawings as the subject of your first rendering. Start by transferring the drawing to a piece of illustration board. This can be done best by using some homemade carbon paper. To make carbon paper, start with a piece of thin tracing paper and a cotton wad. Dump the graphite powder from your pencil pointer onto

To make carbon paper for transferring drawings . . . dump graphite powder from pencil pointer onto tracing paper.

FIG. 434

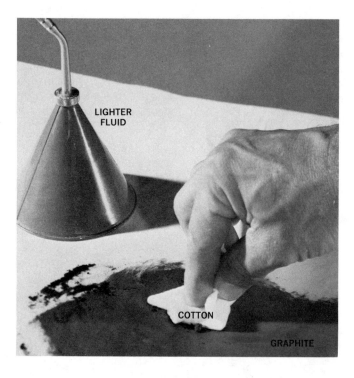

Soak cotton wad with lighter fluid . . . wipe graphite evenly over the paper.

FIG. 435

the tracing paper [434]. Soak the cotton with standard cigarette lighter fluid or rubber cement thinner and wipe the graphite evenly over the paper, wetting the cotton frequently [435].

Tape the drawing that you have chosen to render to the illustration board at the top edge only. Slip the prepared carbon paper, graphite side down, under your drawing and use it as you would regular carbon paper to transfer the lines of the drawing. Since only regular graphite is being transferred to the illustration board, you will have no erasing problems as you would with commercial carbon paper.

Shades of gray can be blended with a wet brush.

FIG. 436

When you have transferred the drawing, refer to the geometric solids that are shown with line shading in [412]. Assuming the same light source (upper left hand corner), use various shades of gray to shade the surfaces of your object. Use the line shading of the solids as a guide to placing light and shade tones.

Retoucher's grays do not lose their solubility after they have been applied to the illustration board. This gives rise to a simple technique for blending subtle graduations of tone. If you paint a series of stripes of graded grays varying from light to dark on a surface so that they physically touch, you can blend one into another with a brush dampened with clean water [436]. Be careful to continue to work from light to dark so that any pigment that gathers in the brush will be blended in the right direction. For parts made of bright metal, the tonal rendering should resemble that in [437].

A typical opaque gray rendering.

FIG. 437

An airbrush is a miniature spray gun.

FIG. 438

79. AIRBRUSH RENDERING

The retoucher's grays that are used in hand brush rendering were originally developed for use in retouching photographs. They were later modified for use in an airbrush for both rendering and retouching.

The **airbrush** is a miniature spray gun with both fluid and air controls located in a plunger on its top [438]. Paint is placed in a fluid cup attached to the side, and the airbrush is driven with an available source of compressed air or inert gas. Usually airbrushes are used with cylinders of carbon dioxide (CO_2) or compressed air that are equipped with pressure regulators. This provides some mobility and interchangeability within the studio. For normal operation, the regulator is set between 140 and 170 kilopascals (20 and 25 pounds per square inch) pressure. This varies with the type of gun used.

An airbrush is capable of delivering a variety of tone or color widths, from a broad swath down to a line as fine as a normal pencil line. The width

The width of line produced by an airbrush depends on the distance between the tip and the illustration . . . for a fine line, the tip is close.

FIG. 439

depends on the distance between the tip and the board or photograph [439, 440].

You can learn to control an airbrush skillfully by practicing drawing lines with the airbrush in the space between the lines of type in a standard newspaper column or in an ad-

For a wider line, the tip is farther away.

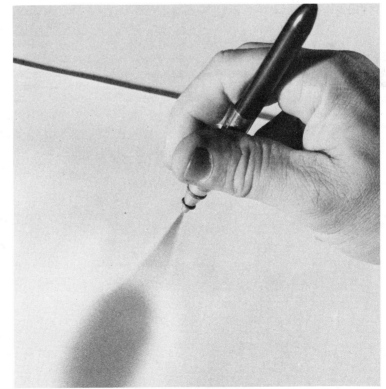

FIG. 440

Practice airbrush control by drawing lines between lines of type.

FIG. 441

To make frisket material . . . place plastic wrap in a box.

vertisement [441]. This teaches airbrush control in tight areas. It also develops the ability to stop and start the spray flow accurately at the right place.

When preparing a drawing to be airbrushed, you must be extremely careful to keep the surface of your drawing clean. The oil present in fingerprints will resist the paint and cause it to bubble on the drawing surface.

Any spray gun, even when used by an expert, deposits overspray in unwanted areas. To prevent this, a mask or **frisket** is used. Frisket material with adhesive backing is sold commercially in rolls. You can make it by coating thin plastic wrap with undiluted rubber cement. Use a large flat box with one corner cut out to coat the plastic. Place the plastic wrap in the bottom of the box [442] and pour unthinned rubber cement over it

FIG. 442

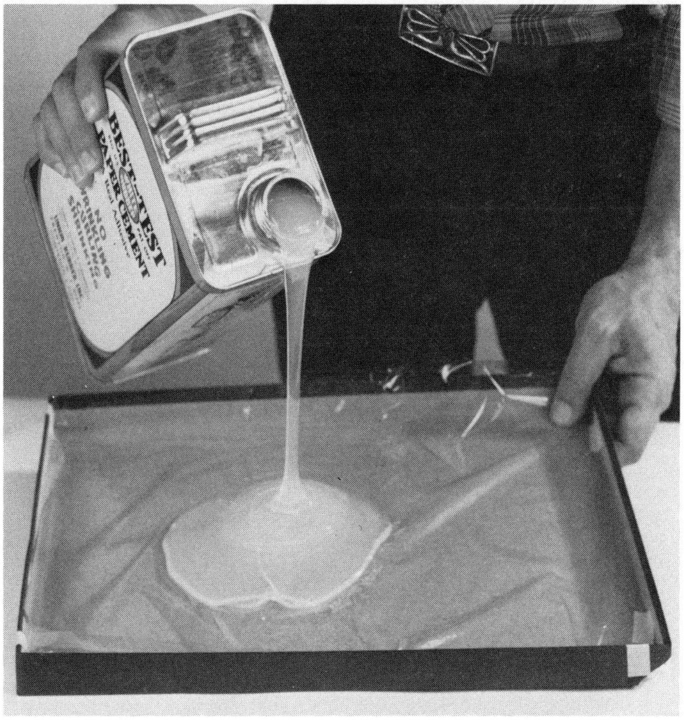

Pour rubber cement over the plastic.

FIG. 443

[443], allowing the excess to drain back into the can [444]. Let the cement dry. This homemade frisket is superior for retouching use because it remains nearly water clear throughout the operation.

Place the frisket material on the drawing or photograph to be air-

Drain excess cement back into can.

FIG. 444

Friskets and guides are used to mask areas from unwanted airbrush spray . . . lay frisket material on the illustration.

FIG. 445

brushed [445]. Using a very sharp X-acto or frisket knife and very light pressure, cut out the area in which you wish to work [446]. After a lot of practice, most retouchers cut out the area of the whole object or a large part of it and use homemade guides cut from stiff plastic sheets to mask

Using a sharp knife, cut out work area.

FIG. 446

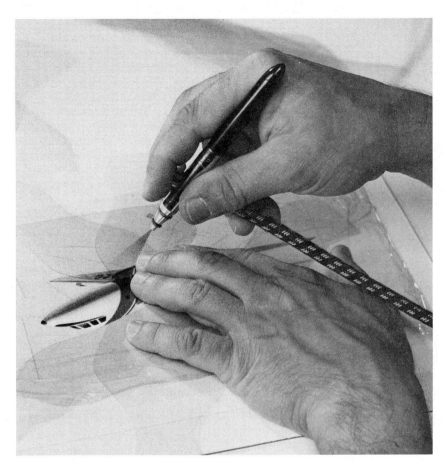

Use plastic guides to help control spray in small areas.

FIG. 447

Rendering with a handbrush.

FIG. 448

off or protect small areas of the object [447]. The guides are held in place and moved about with the left hand while the airbrush is used in the right.

The paint consistency used in an airbrush should be the same as that used with a hand brush. This is usually about the consistency of melted ice cream. Follow the manufacturer's specifications if you must thin the paint. Do not use a sable brush to load paint into the cup. Loose fibers of a sable brush are fine enough to travel through the airbrush fluid passages and become trapped in the fine tip. A good tool for loading paint is a cut down oil paint brush of reasonable size. The hog bristles commonly used in oil paint brushes are too thick to become trapped in the airbrush tip. The relatively stiff bristles of these brushes are also more effective in quickly working the paint to a usable consistency.

Figures [448, 449] show a comparison of rendering the same draw-

Rendering with an airbrush . . . produces smoother coverage and more subtle blending than handbrushing . . . the handbrush is still needed for edges and small features.

FIG. 449

An airbrush rendering of a cutaway of an internal combustion engine.

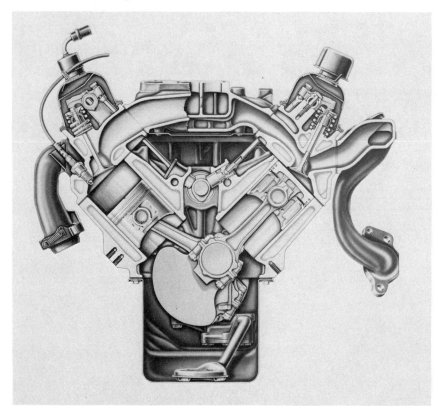

FIG. 450

ing using hand brush and air brush techniques. When reproduced, little difference is apparent except for the smoother coverage of tone and the more subtle blending of the airbrush rendering. Note that even though an airbrush is capable of producing quite small detail, the hand brush is still needed for edges and small features. Figure [450] is an airbrush rendering of a more complex object.

An airbrush can be used with retoucher's grays, dyes, or watercolor. In some cases it has also been used with acrylic and lacquer colors. There is no restriction as long as the pigment is thin enough to pass through the brush and does not produce unacceptable cleaning or drying time.

When you are finished using an airbrush, clean it by running at least six full cups of water or solvent through the system. If the airbrush should become clogged with dried pigment,

follow the manufacturer's recommendations for cleaning. The tip ferrule should be used only to adjust the spray for fine or coarse texture.

80. PHOTO RETOUCHING

Photo retouching has become a very popular and widely used method of technical illustration. If the object to be illustrated exists, it can frequently be photographed more economically than it can be drawn. However, the photograph usually is not quite right for the purpose intended. Perhaps the object was photographed in a shop background that detracts from the image, or the object is a slightly different appearing model than the one desired, or maybe it was incomplete at the time it was photo-

graphed. In such cases, retouching can make the necessary changes.

The same techniques and tools used to make airbrush renderings are used to retouch photographs. The main emphasis here is to retouch the photo in such a way that the retouching is not detectable in the final reproduction. This calls for excellent drawing skills and enough practice to ensure very close tone matches between the photo and the paint.

Photographs do not use isometric, dimetric, or even trimetric drawing systems. They are not even good perspective likenesses because of the distortions created by the curvature of the camera lens. Any alterations that are added to a photo will blend in most successfully when drawn in perspective, but take care to match any apparent lens distortion that the photograph contains.

It is almost impossible to draw on a photo successfully with anything but a handbrush. Any other instrument will cut emulsion or dent the photo paper so that the imperfection will reproduce. Conversely, nothing erases so easily as photographic paper. A damp cotton swab is all that is required.

When retouching the surface of a photograph, clean the entire surface before beginning to work. Although there are commercial cleaners made for this purpose, most professional retouchers use a cotton wad moistened with saliva. The mild acid solution present in human saliva is an excellent cleaner for human finger prints. It eliminates residual photo chemistry left over from the developing process as well.

Figures [451] through [454] show some "before and after" examples of photo retouching. In reality, photo retouching is nothing more than making a photographically perfect rendering of something on an existing photograph so that it is not apparent that the photograph has been treated at all. The key to successful photo retouching, like all illustration techniques, is careful and continuous practice.

Photo retouching . . . before . . .

FIG. 451

. . . and after.

FIG. 452

Photo retouching . . . before . . .

FIG. 453

. . . and after.

FIG. 454

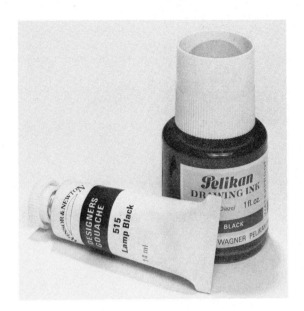

FIG. 455

81. WASH RENDERING

All of the examples of renderings previously discussed have used photo retoucher's grays that are opaque and can be readily corrected by over-painting. Wash renderings are made with only one color—basic black. They will reproduce exactly like the opaque grays.

A *wash* is a dilute solution of black paint or ink that is gray rather than black. Since a wash is transparent, any mistakes made in applying the wash requires a total restart. There is no effective way of correcting a wash rendering so that it will not be no-ticeable in the final reproduction. Some very minor corrections can be made with retouch grays, but nothing of any magnitude can be corrected by this method.

Washes can be made from India ink or any black pigment, but lamp-black water color is usually preferred for this purpose [455]. This is due to the smoothness of its texture and the success with which it can be extended with water.

Making the washes is best done in a deep dish water color pallette or a series of small bowls. Start with a very dark (nearly black) solution of paint

DERIVATIVES

"MOTHER"

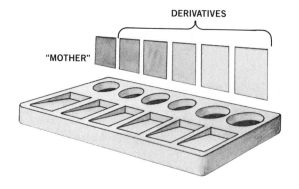

The mother wash is a very dark solution of paint and water . . . other shades are derived by adding more water.

FIG. 456

A typical wash rendering . . . the white is the illustration board.

FIG. 457

and water in good quantity. This is known as the **mother wash** [456]. Transfer a quantity of this solution to each of the pallette wells or bowls, adding ever increasing amounts of water to each one.

Test each solution on a scrap of illustration board and add water or color to each until you reach the range of gray tints that you want. Anything on an illustration that must be perfectly white, such as a highlight from a shiny piece of metal, must be the pure white of the illustration board [457]. This generally means that wash illustrations will be somewhat darker than normal to make the white of the board appear brighter.

Wash drawings can be made either with handbrushes or with an airbrush. Take special care in using the airbrush because the consistency of the paint is thinner than normal airbrush color. The thinner solution has a tendency to splatter.

Wash renderings are difficult to make unless you have practiced a great deal and perfected your brush technique. This rules them out for popular usage. However, they are so effective for some types of renderings (large expanses of glass or transparent materials, for instance), that they are often used by professional illustrators.

Exercise 33

Select several of the illustrations that you drew in previous exercises. Redraw them and use the rendering techniques learned in Sections 75 through 81. Select an appropriate material for each object. Consider the purpose for which the illustrations might be used and also how the finished illustrations might be reproduced.

Special Illustration Techniques

82. COPYING AND REPRODUCTION TECHNIQUES

Illustrations are often used several times before they are changed very much or discarded. The most economical way to repeat these illustrations is through some form of copying machine. If small changes are necessary, they can be easily made on a photostat or xerographic-type print. Line drawings reproduce well as photostats or PMTs (photo mechanical transfers). Either of these is considerably cheaper to use than any kind of photographic print that requires a film negative. If you have made a layout of an illustration that is several times larger than the final copy needs to be, an intermediate photocopy to reduce it closer to final size will save you from inking or finishing any more detail than is necessary. This will help reduce the cost of the illustration.

If the same element appears in twenty or more illustrations, consider drawing it once and having it printed on adhesive-backed material so that it can simply be cut out and applied wherever and whenever it is needed [458]. This happens frequently when making a series of detailed illustrations of systems contained within a master framework (automobiles, airplanes, and so forth) to show the location of the subsystem within the whole. Electronic diagrams make extensive use of preprinted standard components such as transistors, resistors, and terminal areas.

A feature that is repeated on several illustrations can be drawn once . . . copies can be printed on adhesive-backed material.

FIG. 458

83. PREPARING AUDIO-VISUAL MATERIALS

A good illustration of a product will usually be used for many different purposes. It will probably be printed, photographed into slides or overhead transparencies, or made into an instructional tool or a sales device. The end use dictates how much detail should be included and how boldly the drawing should be finished. For instance, the line weights in a line drawing should be doubled if you are aware that the drawing will be used to make a 35mm slide [459]. The heavier line weights are required for audio-visual aids because pro-

jected light tends to undercut and visually reduce the weight of lines.

For either printing or photographing, the rendering of drawings should be minimized to increase reproducibility and to make them easier to read. The tendency is for beginning illustrators to "overrender" their drawings in the belief that they are making them easier to understand. *Unfortunately, the effect is just the opposite.* The emphasis should always be placed on making the illustration say what it should say in the clearest, most uncluttered way.

Line weights should be doubled on drawings used to make 35mm slides.

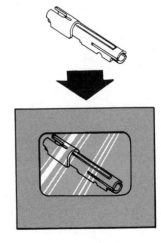

FIG. 459

When making up charts and graphs, for instance, you should consider the proportions of the scales. Do they make the information in the curve more or less obvious? If the information is not readily understandable, consider changing the proportion of one scale to another to emphasize the data being represented. Figure [460] shows a curve that fails to communicate the impact of the information that it contains. By reproportioning the scales in [461], the information receives proper emphasis.

Poor scale proportions . . . the curve fails to communicate.

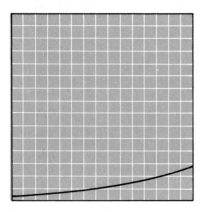

FIG. 460

Reproportioning the scales gives meaning to the relationships in the data.

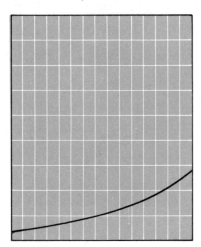

FIG. 461

84. PROPORTIONAL DIVIDERS

One of the handiest and most versatile tools an illustrator can use is a set of proportional dividers [462]. Proportional dividers have two sets of scales inscribed on their face. One is marked for lines and the other is marked for circles. For example, when the locking screw is released and the cursor set to 3 on the lines scale, a line measured with the large pointer end of the dividers automatically appears a third as long at the small pointer end. If the scale is set at 4, the points at the small end are set at a quarter of the spacing set on the large end. Using the scale adjustment of the proportional dividers provides a fast means of rescaling or reproportioning any straight line. This is especially valuable when working with different scale ratios in dimetric and trimetric.

The divider's scale marked for circles is used to divide circles into equal segments. If the lock is released and the cursor set at 7, a positioning of the large divider tips at a spacing equal to the radius of a circle provides a setting between the small points that, when stepped off on the circle's circumference, will divide it into seven equal arc segments. A typical divider has a scale that permits dividing a circle into six through thirty-six segments.

Frequently, an illustrator will have to make a scale drawing from a photograph. Spending some time with trial and error settings on a proportional divider will considerably reduce the labor necessary to do the job. The trick is to find some object in the photo that will provide a scale reference. For instance, a pen or pencil or match book cover can be used. Setting the scale on the basis of a common, relatively fixed size object, will provide the clue to working out the scale for the entire drawing.

85. CALLOUTS

Most technical illustrations are annotated. That is, they carry notes or numeric keys known as *callouts* that point out various parts or features of

Proportional dividers are useful for rescaling lines and for dividing circles into equal arcs.

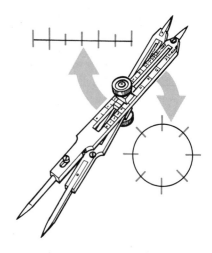

FIG. 462

the illustration. This is especially true when making a drawing of assembled parts or an exploded drawing. Callouts may be used to identify specific parts, to instruct the viewer how to maintain or install certain features, or to identify the assembly sequence of a given device. Placing the callouts on the drawing is the illustrator's responsibility. Over the years several different methods have been used.

Various types of ink lettering devices are available for use with technical pens (see Appendix A [A-35]). In one style (commonly referred to as Wrico) the pen is guided by holes in a template. In the other (commonly referred to as Leroy) the pen is held in a scriber that follows grooves in a template. Templates for both of these systems are available in a variety of letter and number styles and sizes. Usually the scribers are adjustable to vary the slant of the letters. The use of these instruments requires skill and considerable practice. Neither system is used very frequently today by professional illustrators because of the additional amount of labor costs that result.

More commonly, callout lettering is now produced on a variety of typing or typesetting devices that are faster, cheaper, and more reliable. Many callouts are done on electric typewriters, using the various styles of interchangeable type elements that

A Kroy lettering machine prints type on adhesive-backed tape.

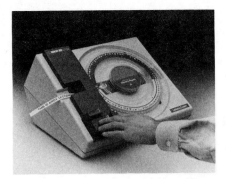

FIG. 463

are available for each machine. Other typing devices range from specialized, desk-top sized units, like the Kroy lettering machine [463], to large phototypesetters, like the Mergenthaler V.I.P. 2000 or the Autologic APS-μ5 [464], that are used to set the type for publications.

A computerized phototypesetter . . . and a sample of type sizes and styles produced on it.

ABCDEFGHIJKLMNOPQRSTUVWXYZ
abcdefghijklmnopqrstuvwxyz
1234567890

ABCDEFGHIJKLMNOPQRSTUVWXYZ
abcdefghijklmnopqrstuvwxyz
1234567890

ABCDEFGHIJKLMNOPQRSTUVWXYZ
abcdefghijklmnopqrstuvwxyz
1234567890

ABCDEFGHIJKLMNOPQRSTUVWXYZ
abcdefghijklmnopqrstuvwxyz
1234567890

ABCDEFGHIJKLMNOPQRSTUVWXYZ
abcdefghijklmnopqrstuvwxyz
1234567890

ABCDEFGHIJKLMNOPQRSTUVWXYZ
abcdefghijklmnopqrstuvwxyz
1234567890

ABCDEFGHIJKLMNOPQRSTUVWXYZ
abcdefghijklmnopqrstuvwxyz
1234567890

ABCDEFGHIJKLMNOPQRSTUVWXYZ
abcdefghijklmnopqrstuvwxyz
1234567890

ABCDEFGHIJKLMNOPQRSTUVWXYZ
abcdefghijklmnopqrstuvwxyz
1234567890

ABCDEFGHIJKLMNOPQRSTUVWXYZ
abcdefghijklmnopqrstuvwxyz
1234567890

FIG. 464

A recent development by Koh-I-Noor is an electronically controlled lettering and symbol generating instrument [465]. The plotter with its motorized pen and keyboard can be attached to a drafting machine. A large variety of preprogrammed standard or custom letter and symbol template modules can be inserted in a microprocessor-based controller and activated by the plotter keyboard to print directly on a drawing. Another style of electronic lettering machine is available from AlphaMerics [466].

Callouts produced on an electric typewriter may be typed on a variety of prepared materials that are already backed with an adhesive. Phototypeset callouts can be mounted on the drawing with double-sided adhesive sheets or with wax or rubber cement.

The motorized pen of the Koh-I-Noor lettering and symbol generating instrument prints directly on a drawing.

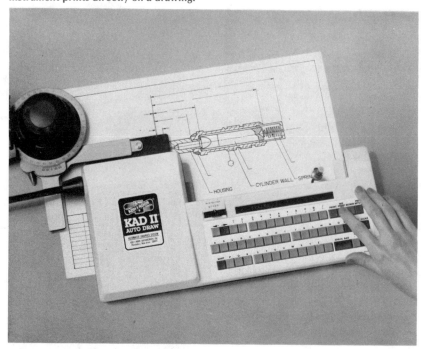

FIG. 465

The Alpha Merics electronic lettering machine.

FIG. 466

When arranging callouts on a drawing, it is common to use leaders with arrows to point to the part or feature being identified [467]. There are some rules that govern how this should be done:

(1) If the callouts are a series of numbers or letters, label them in clockwise order beginning at the bottom left [468]. The circles or "balloons" enclosing the numbers or letters should be a uniform size and arranged in an orderly pattern.

(2) Make leaders either all straight or all curved lines [469]. If curved, use only simple, one-direction curves. Leaders must not cross each other.

(3) Start each leader in line with the center of its balloon [470]. Arrow points should just touch the edge—not the interior—of the object. A leader connected to a dot can be used to designate an area or surface [471].

(4) If you use leaders and arrows with a white edge, orient the white edge to agree with the light source used in the illustration [472].

Callouts identify parts or features on assembly and exploded drawings.

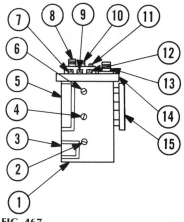

FIG. 467

Label numbers clockwise starting at the bottom left . . . the balloons are uniform in size and arranged in an orderly pattern.

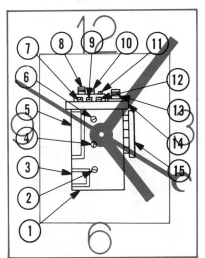

FIG. 468

Leaders should be either all straight lines or all simple curves . . . leaders must not cross each other.

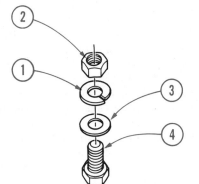

FIG. 469

A leader starts in line with the center of its balloon . . . the arrow point just touches the object.

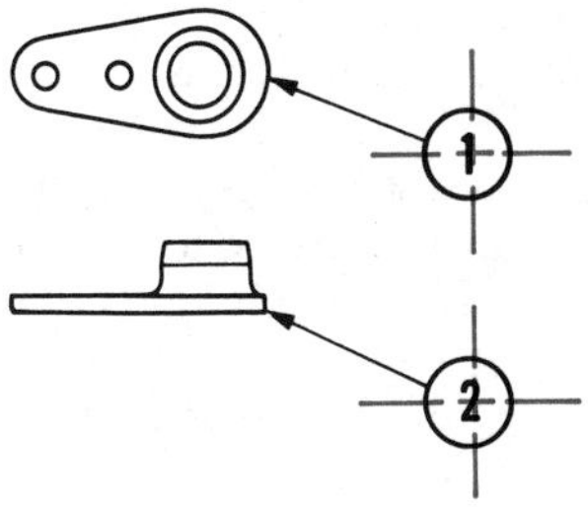

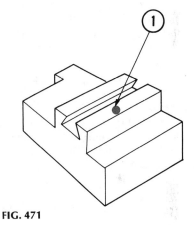

FIG. 470

A leader connected to a dot identifies an area.

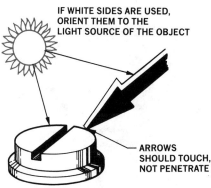

FIG. 471

Any shading used on arrows must agree with the light source used on the drawing.

IF WHITE SIDES ARE USED, ORIENT THEM TO THE LIGHT SOURCE OF THE OBJECT

ARROWS SHOULD TOUCH, NOT PENETRATE

FIG. 472

86. REPRODUCTION OF ILLUSTRATIONS IN COLOR

Color is used frequently to emphasize the information prepared by illustrators. Normally this is in the form of a second or third color added at the printing stage of reproduction. The color may be applied to lines or areas and may be solid (100 percent) color or various shades (percentages) of color. Even if a second color is not used, it may be desirable to print parts of an illustration in different shades of black to emphasize certain features. To accomplish this, the illustrator must understand the fundamentals of mechanically separating those portions of the artwork that require printing in different colors or shades.

Mechanical separation is required to break a drawing into separate images for each portion that is to be printed in a different color or shade of color. The camera can then be used to make separate negatives for each image to make the printing plates. Separation is also required when lines or areas of a black and white illustration are to be printed in different shades of gray (different percentages of black). In making the separation, all of the solid black image is placed on a basic piece of artwork and each image with a color or a shade of color or of black is placed on a separate overlay [473].

Each part of an illustration to be printed in a different color or shade requires a separate overlay.

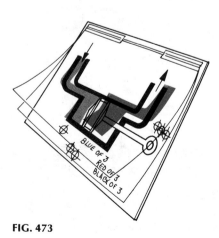

FIG. 473

A shade of color or of black in an area is obtained by the printer "stripping" (inserting) screened negative material in the designated area. This screened material, called a **tint block,** is related to the graphic arts step wedge discussed in connection with halftones [427]. The screening allows only a percentage of the area to be reproduced on the printing plate by transforming it into a certain density of dots [474]. Commercial tint block negatives are available in 5 percent increments to produce 5 to 95 percent of solid color.

Tint block screening allows only a percentage of an area to be reproduced on a printing plate by transforming it into a certain density of dots.

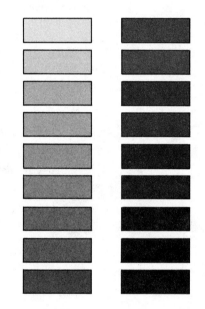

FIG. 474

All you must provide at the illustration stage is a "window" in which these mechanical tints can be placed. A window in a negative is merely a clear area where a tint block of a halftone negative of a photo or rendering can be taped to the line negative to be reproduced on the printing plate. A negative that contains both line and halftone elements is called a **combination negative.** You must also provide a method by which the printing plates can be accurately registered or reassembled and a set of instructions to tell the printer what color or per-

cent of color or black to put in each area.

In order to prepare a window, determine the size and location of the tint or halftone and lightly draw it in. Then fill this area with a red or dark amber adhesive-backed film that is trimmed to the outline. When photographed, this area will produce a clear portion or "window" in the negative. Commercially available material for this purpose is sold under a variety of trade names. It is commonly referred to as "red zip," "rubylith," or "amberlith."

As an alternate to the window method for colored or shaded areas, commercial illustrators have traditionally used a system called **keylining.** A keyline piece of art uses only a red or black outline on the base art to designate a window area. Draw all of the solid color or shaded portions of an art layout on the base artboard without overlays. Then attach a transparent tissue overlay to the base art. On this overlay you will note the various colors and shades that are desired in the outlined areas.

The actual mechanical separation of the various portions is then accomplished in the printer's shop by a negative stripper. The stripper makes an overlay, cuts windows, and locates tints where indicated. This overlay is used in contact with the printing plate during exposure rather than using negatives for the purpose. The term **keylining** originates from the "keyline" used to outline the tint and halftone areas on the original art. The keyline system is popular because it is less expensive to have overlays made by a negative stripper than by a more highly paid illustrator or designer.

87. PREPARING COLORED ARTWORK

First, securely mount the basic black artwork to an illustration board using rubber cement or some other method that does not allow the drawing to move. On the sides of the drawing outside the image area, locate two or three accurate register marks [475]. A **register mark** is a "bull's eye" or "target" in the shape of a cross contained in a circle. This is the system by which the printer maintains the color and shade plates in perfect register (alignment) with the black plate. Preprinted register marks are available as transfer sheets or on adhesive backing. Matching register marks are placed on each overlay in the artwork to produce marks on each printing plate.

Colored or shaded areas are produced by providing a window in a negative for the printer to strip in a tint block or to leave open for a solid color area. To do this, place on the overlay a mask or silhouette of the desired area that accurately fits the outline appearing on the basic artwork [477]. Use red or amber transparent material to make the mask.

ting is complete and all of the excess material has been removed from the overlay, place a tissue over the overlay. Then burnish the red zip or other material to make sure that it adheres well. Complete the overlay by specifying the required percentage of color or black on the margin.

You can hinge additional overlay sheets to the basic artwork to provide other colored lines or areas. Each overlay sheet must have register marks placed on it that perfectly match those on the basic artwork and overlays underneath [478]. That is, the register mark circles must coincide perfectly, and the lines of the cross must be exactly one on top of another. No part of the register mark on the board should be seen underneath the one on the overlay. For best accuracy when drawing register marks with ink, use the thinnest line weight available. Prepared stick-on register marks are more precise, faster, and easier to use.

Register marks are required to align overlays.

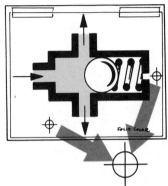

FIG. 475

Place "red zip" masks on the overlay to produce colored or shaded areas.

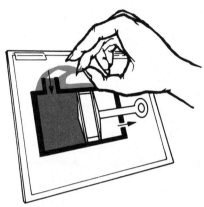

FIG. 477

On top of the black image artwork, secure a sheet of clear plastic at the top with tape. This overlay sheet will carry the image for the second color. If this image is line art, draw the lines in black ink directly on the clear plastic [476]. On the border outside the image area, note whatever percentage of color is desired. A certain percentage of black is specified if the lines are to be printed in a gray shade.

Place the red zip or amberlith adhesive film on the overlay and smooth it out to remove wrinkles and bubbles. Then cut it precisely to match the area where you want the second color. Take care in cutting the color film to prevent cutting through the plastic overlay sheet. When the cut-

All overlay sheets are hinged to the basic artwork . . . register marks control alignment.

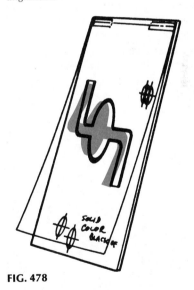

FIG. 478

Draw lines in black on clear plastic overlays . . . note the color and percentage of color on the edge.

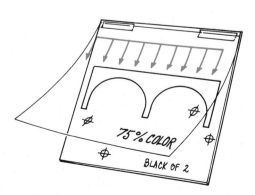

FIG. 476

Finally, tape a tissue sheet over the basic artwork and the plastic overlays [479]. The whole set is then protected from damage by adding a heavy paper overlay cover (flap).

A tissue sheet and a heavy paper flap protect the artwork from damage.

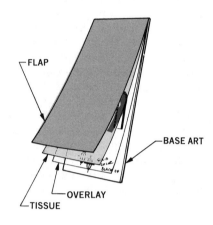

FLAP

BASE ART

OVERLAY

TISSUE

FIG. 479

Technical illustrations are sometimes rendered in full color. The reproduction of full color, continuous tone illustrations is a specialized process done through photolithography. The procedure is called a four-color process because all of the colors, tints, and shades of the original art must be reduced to negatives and plates representing just four colors—cyan, yellow, magenta, and black—for the printing press.

The original art is placed in a litho camera and four separate halftone negatives are made. The first is exposed through a red filter, which subtracts the magenta and yellow light reflected from the art, leaving only an image of the cyan content of the art on the negative. The second is exposed through a green filter, which subtracts the cyan and yellow, leaving only the magenta content to be recorded. The third is exposed using a deep blue or violet filter to subtract the cyan and magenta so that only the yellow image remains. Finally, a weak black halftone is shot through a salmon, neutral density filter.

Each of the dot patterns created by the halftone process is precisely angled away from the axis of the others so that when printed one on top of the other, the dots actually lie next to one another forming a four-colored rosette pattern. When this pattern is printed in cyan, yellow, magenta, and black, the dots of the halftone process are too small to be resolved individually by the human eye. The viewer sees their varied sizes and combinations of sizes as a good reproduction of all of the hues, tints, and shades present in the original art. Magenta dots in proper combinations with yellow dots reproduce reds, oranges, and all of their tints. When cyan is added to the combination, violets, red violets, and purples result. Removing most of the magenta content from a given area produces blues and greens of all shades. The highlight areas in the illustration are produced by the white of the paper, while the black printing supplies the detail in the shadow areas produced by saturate amounts of the other hues.

A computer aided drawing work station.

FIG. 480

88. COMPUTER AIDED ILLUSTRATION

The development of the digital computer and microprocessor technology has begun to make an impact on the illustration profession just as it has touched almost every other modern occupation. Any drawing system (except strictly free-hand drawing) can be modeled mathematically. This enables it to be expressed in a computer program. A program is the means by which the computer is taught to recognize and execute simple repetitive commands that are expressed in some language that the machine understands. Figure [480] shows a complete computer aided drawing work station.

Graphic information is entered into the computer at a CRT terminal.

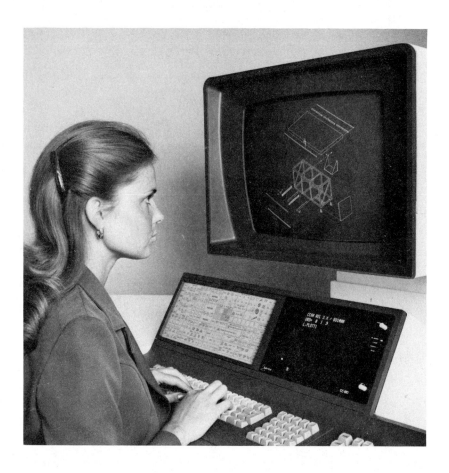

FIG. 481

Most computer installations that can be used for graphics work use a CRT (cathode ray tube) terminal to enter information into the computer [481]. These terminals resemble TV sets that have a set of typewriter keys attached to them. The operator places a description of the object into the computer by a process called *digitizing*. In digitizing, the width, height, and depth coordinates of the beginning and ending points of all lines describing the contours of a part are typed into the terminal. The points can also be entered by mounting a drawing on a digitizing table and locating the points with a special pen that is wired to the computer. The central processing unit of the computer applies the digital dimensions to the mathematical program for the drawing system desired. The resulting line drawing is displayed on the terminal screen.

When all of the dimensional data have been entered and the computer has displayed the drawing on the CRT screen, the operator can make changes or corrections. These are commonly made using a light pen or a joy stick to "draw" the change on the face of the screen. The changes can also be made using the pen on the digitizing table [482]. The keyboard on the terminal can be used to apply any callouts or identification that may be desired on the various parts in the finished illustration.

In more powerful computer graphics systems, if the operator needs to study the object from various viewing directions, the object can be rotated by the computer to other positions, usually with the use of a single function key on the terminal keyboard [483]. This is a great advantage in technical illustration because once data describing an object is in memory, the object can be viewed very quickly in any position.

The number of possible views surpasses even the large number of viewing possibilities shown in [303] because the computer can use an infinite number of axonometric axis systems instead of just the three systems used in this figure.

After the object is rotated into the most effective viewing direction on the screen, the picture can be printed and used either directly or as an underlay to make a finished technical illustration. This saves endless hours of plotting complex details especially when circles and curved surfaces are involved.

The more powerful computer graphics systems can also enlarge or reduce the size of views and add surface texture to line illustrations. Shades and shadows can also be added. Color is available on many systems. On very advanced systems, color can be added in various densities giving the illusion of air brushing.

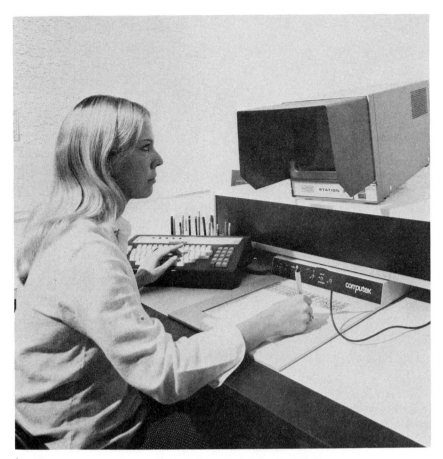

Changes to the computer image may be made with a digitizing pen.

FIG. 482

Some computer programs permit rotating an object on the screen to show different viewing directions.

FIG. 483

In large industries where all of the parts of a complex product, such as a turbine engine, have been recorded in the computer's memory, the pictures of the parts can be brought up on the computer screen and assembled. The assembly drawing can then be used as the basis for interior arrangement and cutaway illustrations, or the parts can be moved out along desired axes to create exploded views. Again the viewing direction can be readily changed at the touch of a button to develop the ideal view.

Large computer graphics systems are capable of storing a library of ready-made symbols for schematics and other specialized diagrams. A computer system capable of producing axonometric and perspective views can also easily plot a wide variety of bar charts, nomograms, curves, and other graphic presentations [484]. In many cases, these can be produced in color as well as in black and white.

FIG. 484

Charts and graphs can also be plotted using a computer graphics system.

A photo plotter produces lithographic film negatives or positives from digitized data.

FIG.485

When a drawing or a diagram has been created and corrected to the satisfaction of the operator at the terminal, a command is given to the computer to print the results. Depending on the selection of peripheral equipment available to the computer, it can write the instructions for creating the illustration on magnetic disc or tape storage for later use, or it can draw the picture directly on a plotter [485, 486, 487]. Some plotters produce drawings on paper or drafting film while others plot drawings directly on lithographic film, ready for quantity reproduction. Other peripherals can be added to the computer-aided drawing system to produce the desired illustration on microfilm or microfiche.

Computerized illustration is now a reality. It will become even more common as the cost of equipment and operations continues to decrease as a result of continuing technological advancement. It is just another of the tools that an illustrator can use to communicate technical information more effectively.

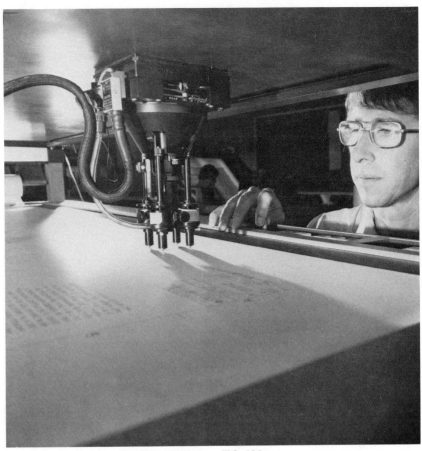

FIG. 486
A line plotter produces line drawings from digitized data.

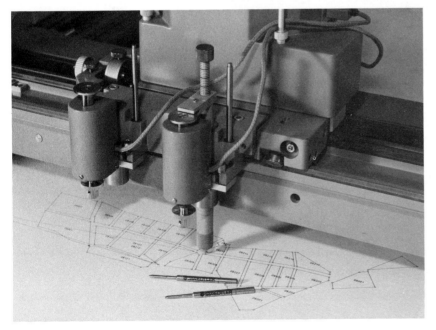

A close-up view of the drawing head on a line plotter.

FIG. 487

Professional Portfolio

89. THE MILES HARDIMAN STUDIO

To conclude this text, we believe that it is important that you see some examples of a professional technical illustrator's work. At our request, one of the nation's premier technical illustrators, Miles Hardiman of Littleton, Colorado, made available for this use a random selection of some of his recent work. This selection of drawings is presented for your review.

All of the drawings were done originally in full color. Unfortunately, it has not been possible to duplicate the work here in its original color, so some of the emotional impact built into each drawing is missing. Note the diversity of subjects and the exacting attention to detail of each drawing. In every case the subject was developed from idea sketches.

There are no photographs included in the portfolio. All are original drawings. Mr. Hardiman believes that the technical illustrator should have the touch of a fine artist. In this way the end result is not only a correct mechanical drawing but also a good finished artistic painting.

Mr. Hardiman is known for his realistic airbrush illustrations, often mechanical in nature. He has become famous for his ability to build up a realistic appearing product illustration from engineering drawings. He has won several Andy, C.A., Belding, and Print awards.

We are pleased to be able to present some examples of Miles Hardiman's work on the following pages.

Miles Hardiman

FIG. 488

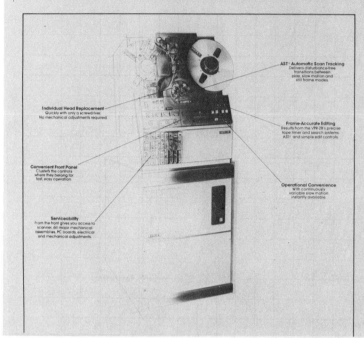

FIG. 489

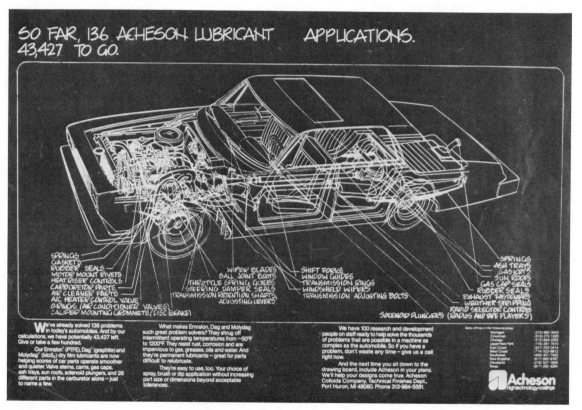

FIG. 490

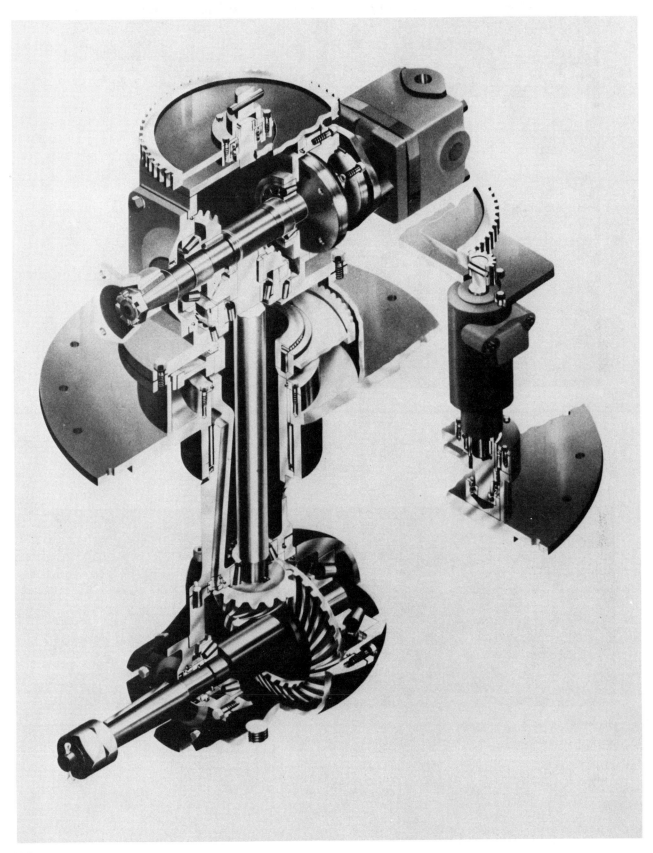

FIG. 491

FIG. 492

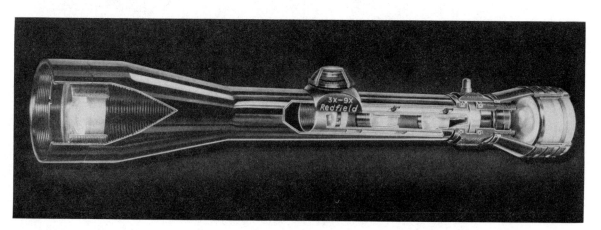

FIG. 493

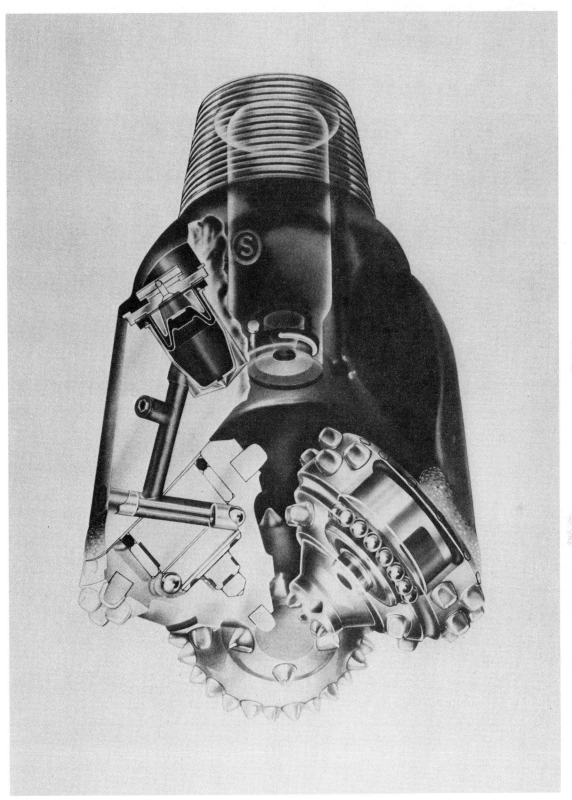

FIG. 494

FIG. 495

FIG. 496

Hello Milwaukee.

A great beer doesn't change. Olympia never will.

FIG. 497

FIG. 498

FIG. 499

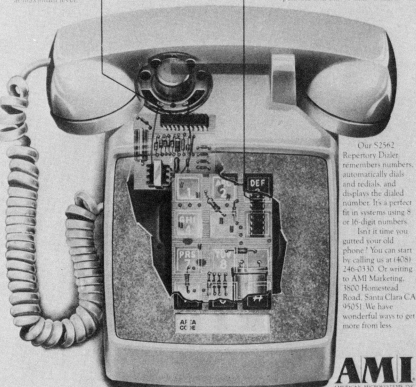
FIG. 500

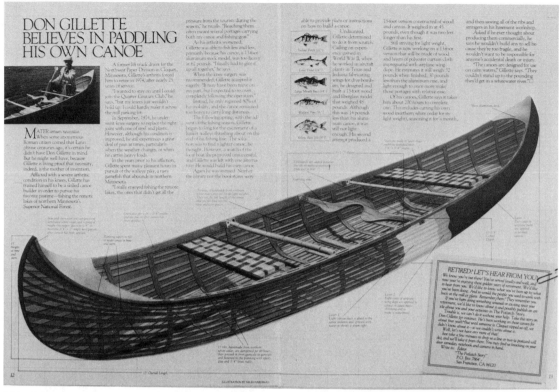

FIG. 501

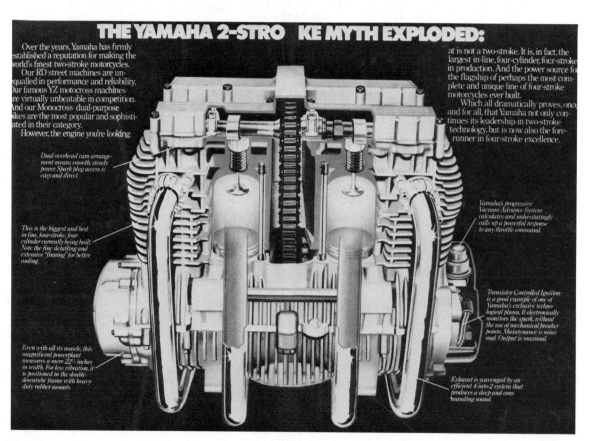

FIG. 502

Why you should use your head when choosing a helmet.

At Yamaha we feel that with a little careful thought, your helmet will do more than simply harmonize with the color of your bike's tank.

To get maximum penetration resistance without needless bulk, we urge you to look for an outer shell fabricated from layers of aircraft-quality fiberglass, not plastic.

The layers should be hand-applied. This costs more, of course. But it's the only way to eliminate weak spots and hidden air pockets that can cost you more than money.

As for the inner layer, insist on the finest quality expanded polystyrene. Because, unfortunately, if this layer doesn't absorb the impact of a fall, your head will.

Look for straps, a D-ring and a helmet shield that have been tested for strength and durability.

And for superior night visibility, you'll no doubt want your helmet to have a highly reflective decal which also forms an attractive design.

If you find a model with most of these qualities, you probably have yourself a pretty fine helmet.

If you find one with all of these qualities, then you've found yourself a Yamaha.

Military-grade tubular nylon

Multiple layers of hand-laid fiberglass

Thick expanded polystyrene

Soft foam comfort padding

Helmet shield tested for strength and durability

Reflective Yamaha decal

Lacquer finish with clear polyurethane protective coating

When you know how they're built, you'll buy a Yamaha.

FIG. 503

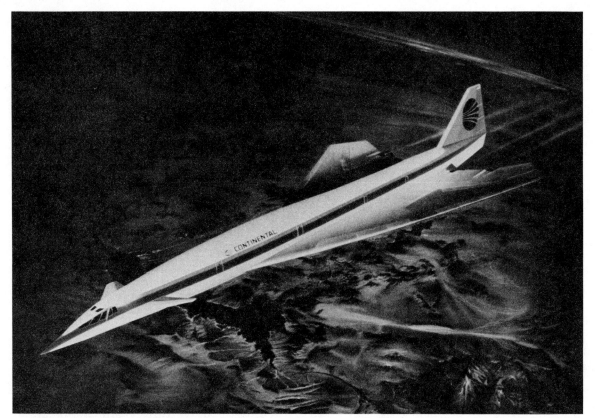

FIG. 504

FIG. 505

FIG. 506

FIG. 507

FIG. 508

The Yamaha DT 100:
Designed for the camping family.
And the family camper.

The mid-size Yamaha DT 100 Enduro is an outstanding machine for the camping family.

It's not tiny like many camper bikes. Yet the DT 100 isn't a large bike either, so adults and youngsters can handle it with ease. And it's easy to load onto your bumper carrier.

But the intermediate size of the Yamaha DT 100 is only part of the story.

Another is the engine. The DT 100's dependable two-stroke engine, displacing 99cc's of power and coupled to a five-speed transmission is well-suited to both on-street and off-road riding.

The patented Torque

Induction intake system provides ready power, particularly at low rpm's. And Yamaha's Autolube automatically mixes the oil and gas.

The frame is lightweight and strong. It's the same type we use on Yamaha off-road competition bikes.

You'll find the steering geometry is superb for negotiating narrow forest trails. And the long-travel

suspension helps provide greater control for rough, off-road riding.

But the Yamaha DT 100 Enduro is also legal on city streets. For those times when you have to come out of the woods and into the jungle.

When you know how they're built, you'll buy a Yamaha.

FIG. 509

FIG. 510

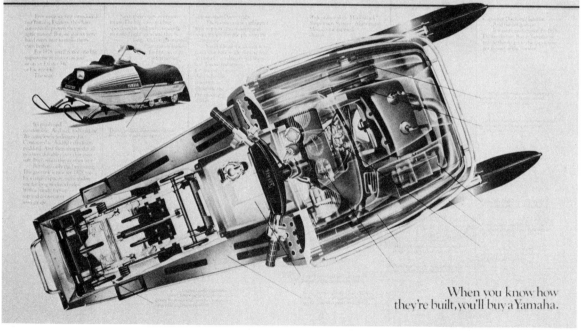

FIG. 511

Exercises

90. PROBLEMS FOR ASSIGNMENT

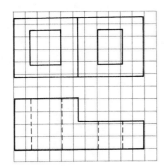

PROB. 1

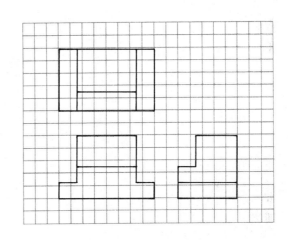

PROB. 2

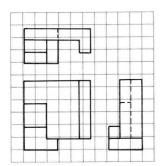

PROB. 3

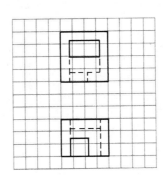

PROB. 4

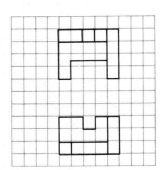

PROB. 5

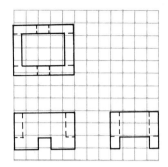

PROB. 6

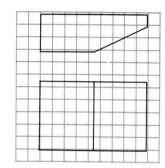

PROB. 7

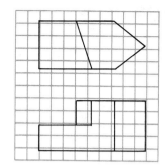

PROB. 8

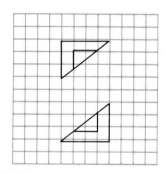

PROB. 9

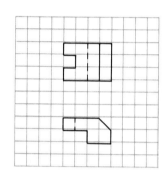

PROB. 10

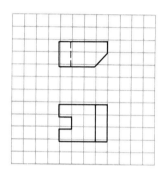

PROB. 11

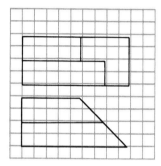

PROB. 12

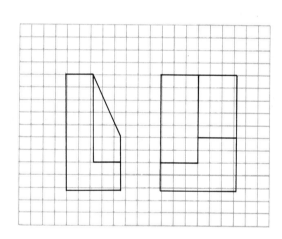

PROB. 13

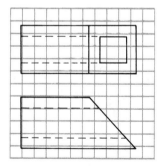

PROB. 14

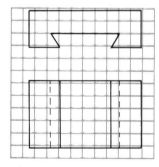

PROB. 15

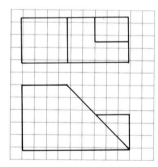

PROB. 16

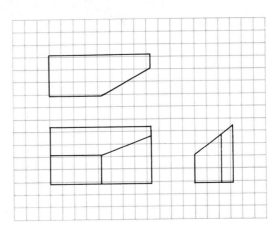

PROB. 17

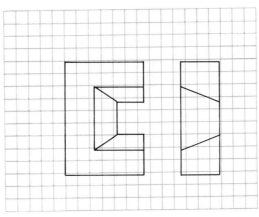

PROB. 18

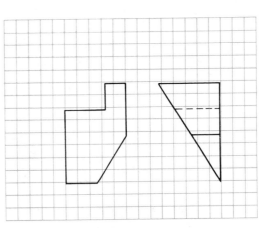

PROB. 19

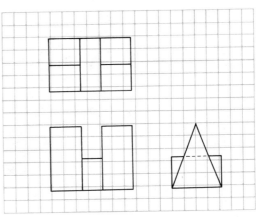

PROB. 20

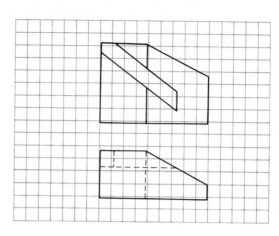

PROB. 21

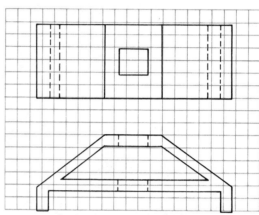

PROB. 22

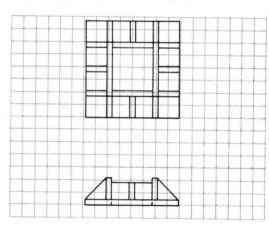

PROB. 23

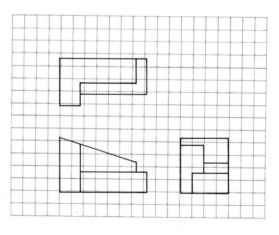

PROB. 24

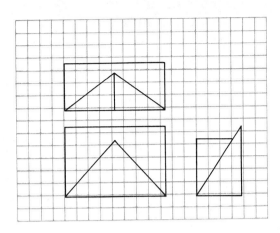

PROB. 25

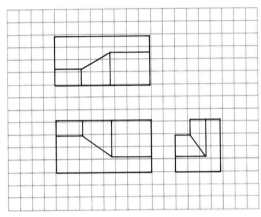

PROB. 26

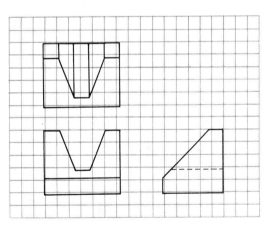

PROB. 27

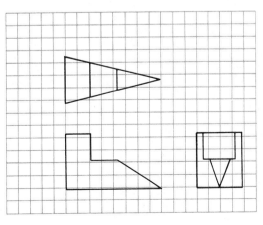

PROB. 28

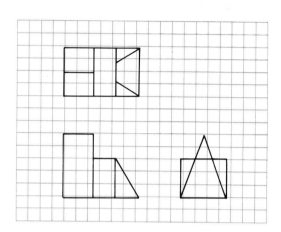

PROB. 29

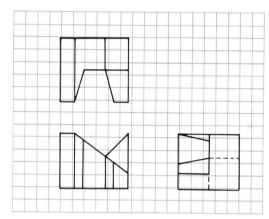

PROB. 30

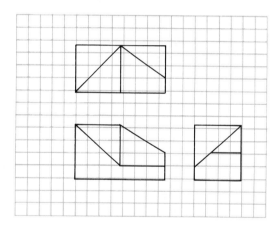

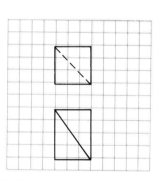

PROB. 32

PROB. 31

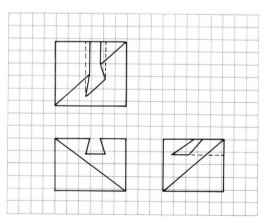

PROB. 33

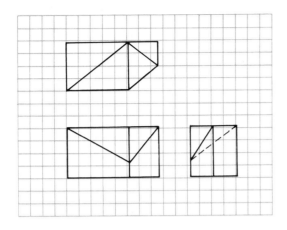

PROB. 34

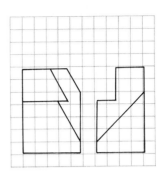

PROB. 35

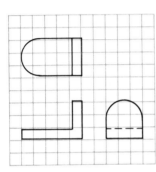

PROB. 36

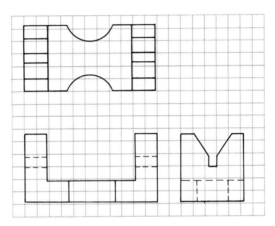

PROB. 37

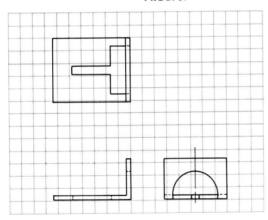

PROB. 38

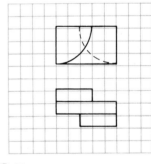

PROB. 39

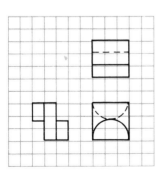

PROB. 40

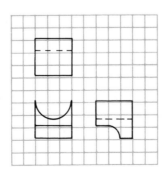

PROB. 41

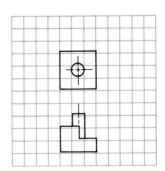

PROB. 42

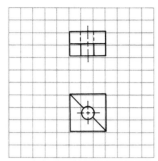

PROB. 43

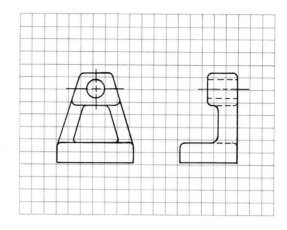

PROB. 44

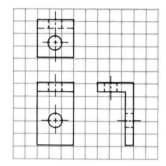

PROB. 45

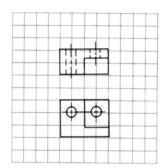

PROB. 46

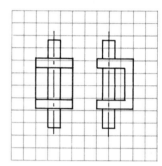

PROB. 47

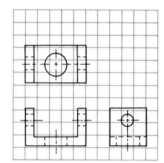

PROB. 48

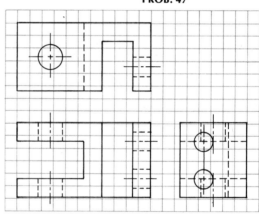

PROB. 49

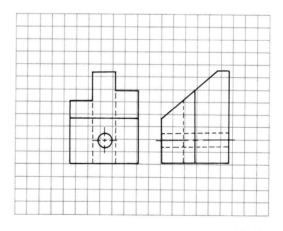

PROB. 50

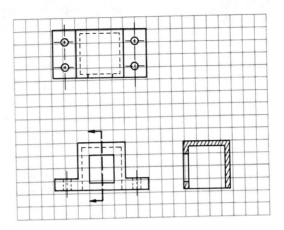

PROB. 51

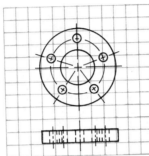

PROB. 52

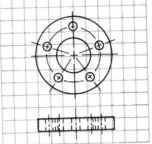

PROB. 53

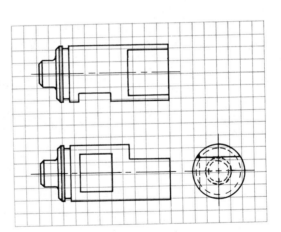

PROB. 54

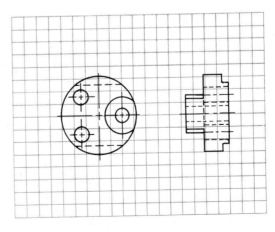

PROB. 55

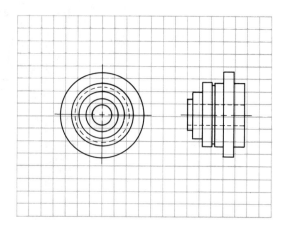

PROB. 56

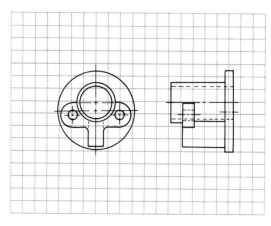

PROB. 57

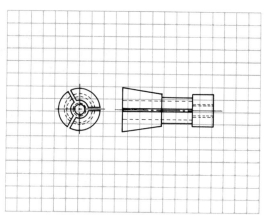

PROB. 58

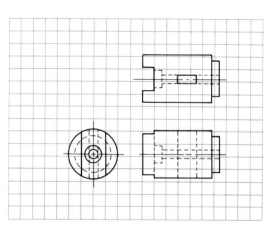

PROB. 59

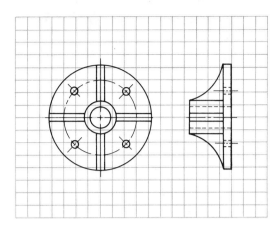

PROB. 60

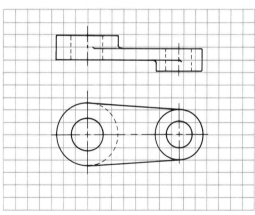

PROB. 61

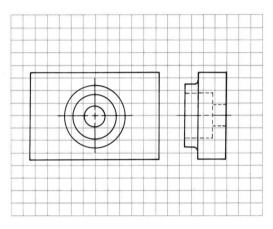

PROB. 62

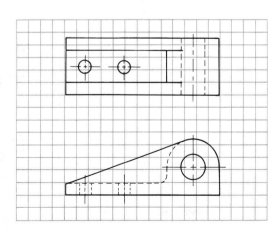

PROB. 63

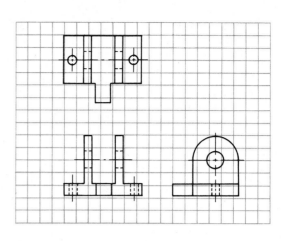

PROB. 64

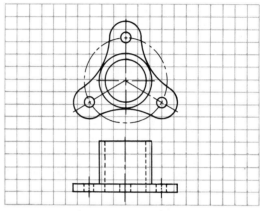

PROB. 65

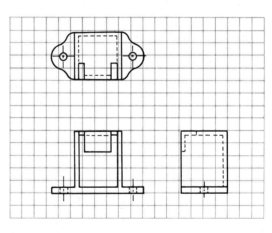

PROB. 66

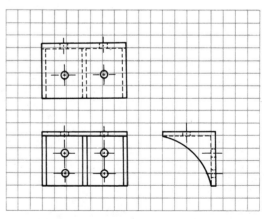

PROB. 67

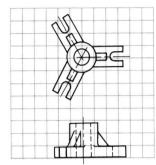

PROB. 68

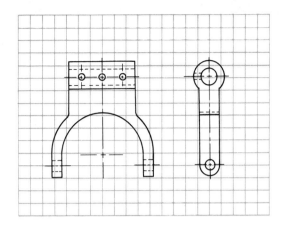

PROB. 69

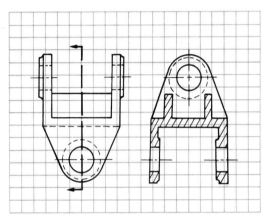

PROB. 70

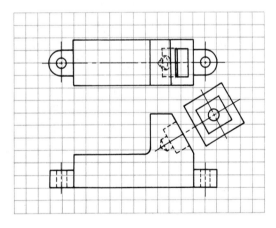

PROB. 71

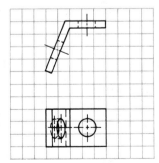

PROB. 72

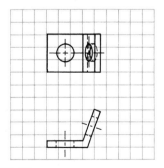

PROB. 73

PROB. 74

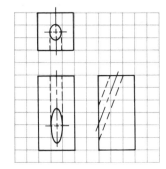

PROB. 75

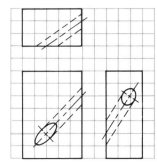

PROB. 76

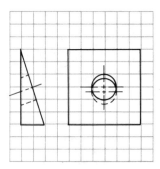

PROB. 77

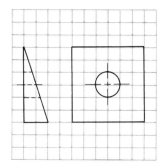

PROB. 78

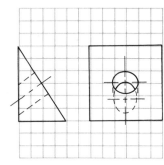

PROB. 79

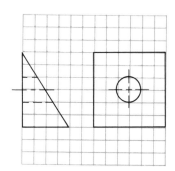

PROB. 80

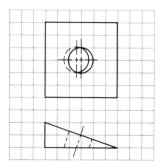

PROB. 81

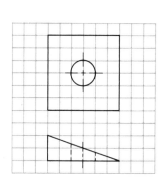

PROB. 82

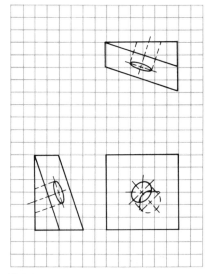

PROB. 83

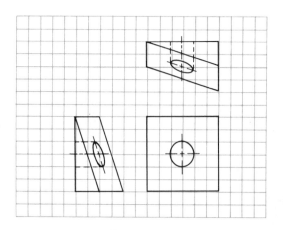

PROB. 84

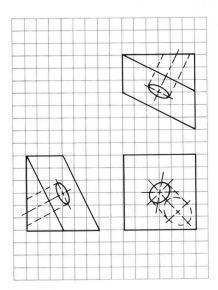

PROB. 85

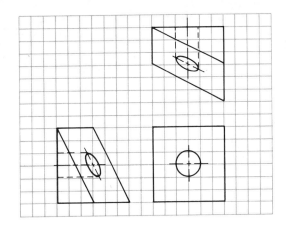

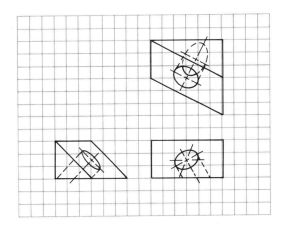

PROB. 86

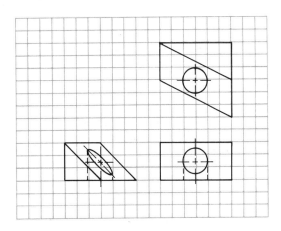

PROB. 87

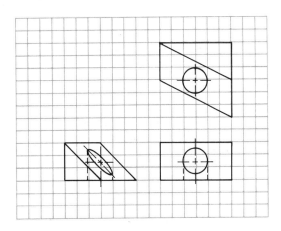

PROB. 88

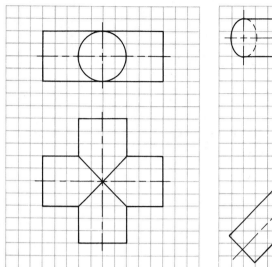

PROB. 89

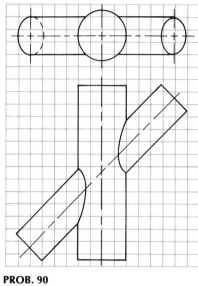

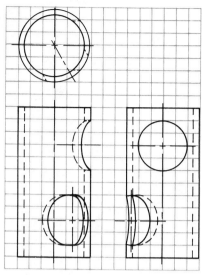

PROB. 90

PROB. 91

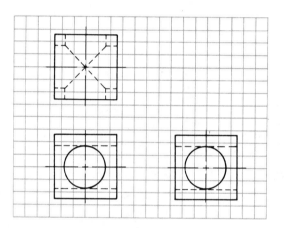

PROB. 92

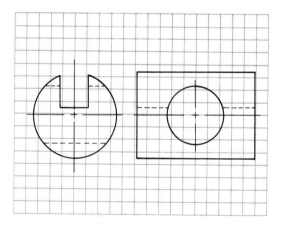

PROB. 93

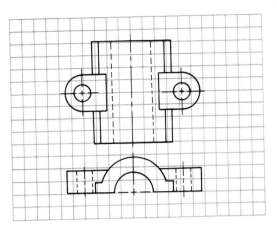

PROB. 94

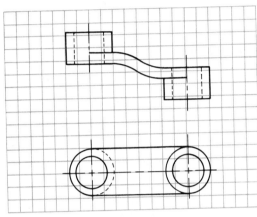

PROB. 95

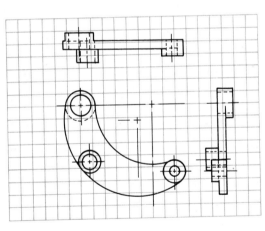

PROB. 96

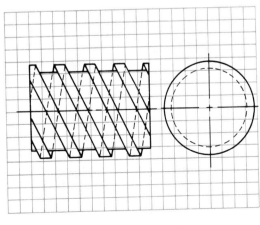

PROB. 97

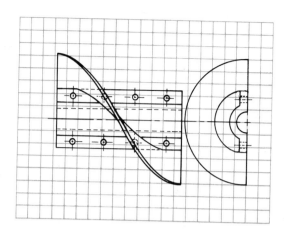

PROB. 98

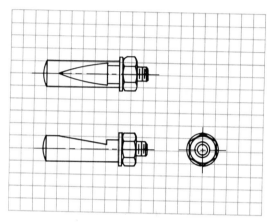

PROB. 99

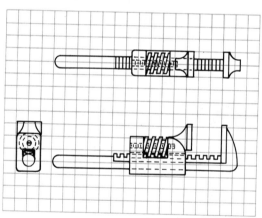

PROB. 100

Summary of Drawing Fundamentals

Technical drawings may be drawn formally with instruments, or they may be sketched freehand using only a pencil or some other marking tool. Freehand sketches are often used in developing design concepts and in planning formal drawings. Instrument drawings are normally required when it is necessary to provide accurate and detailed descriptions for manufacturing or construction.

A.1 Drawing Instruments

When making instrument drawings, specialized tools are used to draw the different types of lines required to describe an object.

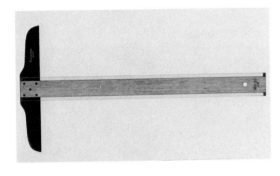

T-Square

T-square, parallel rules, and various types of drafting machines . . . used to establish a horizontal frame of reference and to draw horizontal lines.

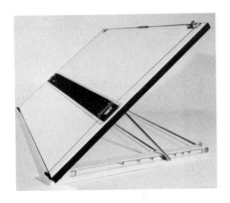

Parallel Rule

FIG. A-1

Track Type Drafting Machine

FIG. A-2

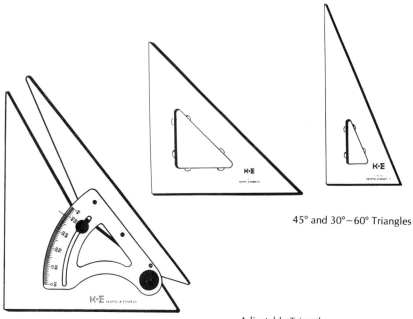

Triangles . . , used with T-squares and parallel rules to draw vertical and angled lines. These lines can be drawn directly with drafting machines.

45° and 30°−60° Triangles

Adjustable Triangle

FIG. A-3

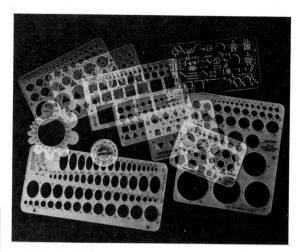

Compasses, templates, and irregular curves . . . used to draw curved lines.

Templates

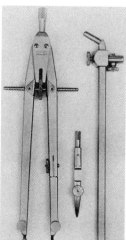

Irregular curve

Compass and Accessories

FIG. A-4

Scale

Dividers and scales . . . used to measure or lay out line lengths.

Dividers

FIG. A-5

180° Protractor

Protractors . . . used to measure or lay out angles.

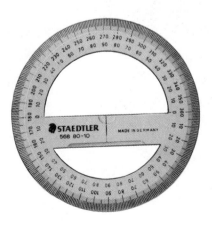

360° Protractor

FIG. A-6

Ultra-Thin Mechanical Pencil

Lead Holder

Wood Pencil

FIG. A-7

Pencils . . . used to draw lines. Many types available varying according to lead holding method, sharpening, lead diameter, and type and hardness of lead.

Rotate pencil slowly while drawing lines to maintain conical point.

Lead Grades

VERY HARD

9H   8H   7H

CONSTRUCTION LINES

6H   5H   4H   3H

FINISHED LINES

2H   H

FREEHAND SKETCHING AND LETTERING

F   HB

RENDERING AND SHADING

B   2B   3B   4B

VERY SOFT

5B   6B

FIG. A-8

Technical pens . . . used alone or in compasses to draw lines. Keep capped between uses to prevent clogging. Clean frequently.

FIG. A-9

FIG. A-10

A.2 Line Drawing Procedures

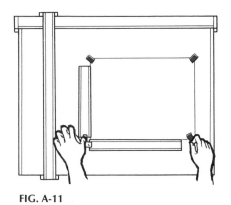

FIG. A-11

The drawing paper is lined up horizontally
. . . corners are taped to the board.

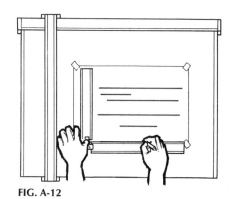

FIG. A-12

Horizontal lines are drawn directly.

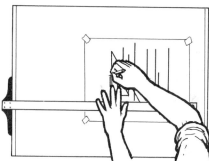

FIG. A-13

Vertical lines are drawn with a triangle placed on a T-square or parallel rule . . .

. . . or drawn directly with a drafting machine.

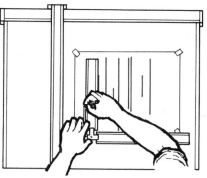

FIG. A-14

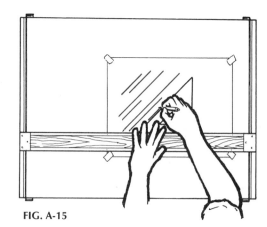

FIG. A-15

Angled lines are also drawn with a triangle

. . . or directly with a drafting machine.

FIG. A-16

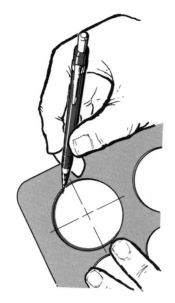

Circles must be located first with centerlines
. . . then drawn with a compass or template.

FIG. A-17

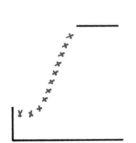

FIG. A-18

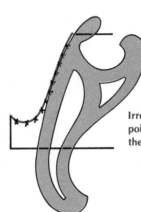

Irregular curves are located by plotting
points . . . the curve is lightly sketched . . .
then darkened in with an irregular curve.

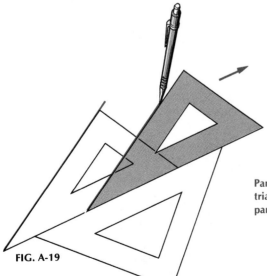

Parallel lines can be drawn by sliding
triangles on one another or on a T-square or
parallel rule.

FIG. A-19

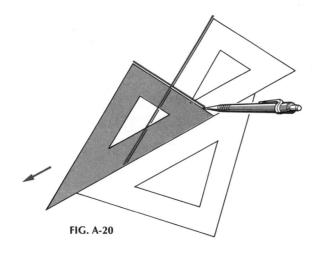

FIG. A-20

Perpendicular lines can be drawn by sliding triangles on one another or on a T-square or parallel rule.

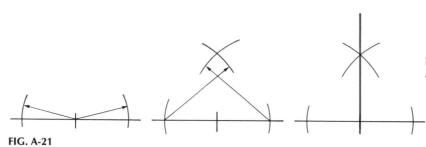

FIG. A-21

Perpendicular lines can be constructed with a compass.

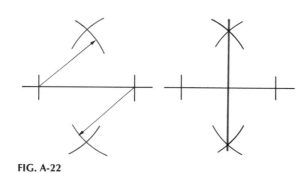

FIG. A-22

Bisecting a line with a compass.

Uniform Divisions   Non-Uniform Divisions

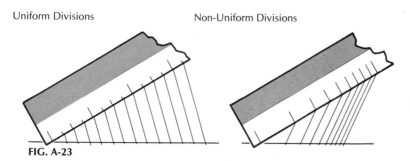

FIG. A-23

Dividing a line into parts using existing scales . . . set the scale at a convenient angle and draw parallel lines.

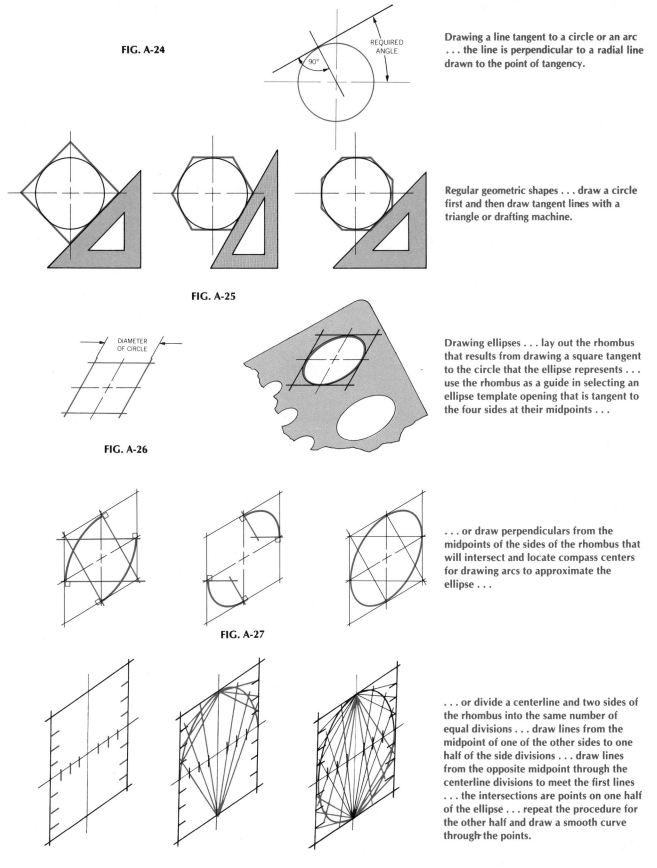

FIG. A-24

Drawing a line tangent to a circle or an arc . . . the line is perpendicular to a radial line drawn to the point of tangency.

REQUIRED ANGLE

90°

Regular geometric shapes . . . draw a circle first and then draw tangent lines with a triangle or drafting machine.

FIG. A-25

DIAMETER OF CIRCLE

Drawing ellipses . . . lay out the rhombus that results from drawing a square tangent to the circle that the ellipse represents . . . use the rhombus as a guide in selecting an ellipse template opening that is tangent to the four sides at their midpoints . . .

FIG. A-26

. . . or draw perpendiculars from the midpoints of the sides of the rhombus that will intersect and locate compass centers for drawing arcs to approximate the ellipse . . .

FIG. A-27

. . . or divide a centerline and two sides of the rhombus into the same number of equal divisions . . . draw lines from the midpoint of one of the other sides to one half of the side divisions . . . draw lines from the opposite midpoint through the centerline divisions to meet the first lines . . . the intersections are points on one half of the ellipse . . . repeat the procedure for the other half and draw a smooth curve through the points.

FIG. A-28

A.3 Lettering

Standard letter and number forms are used for clarity, repeatability, and ease of drawing. The customary sequence of pencil strokes is labeled 1, 2, 3, ...

Vertical   Inclined

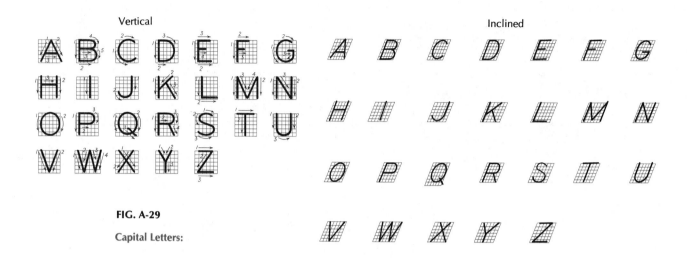

FIG. A-29

Capital Letters:

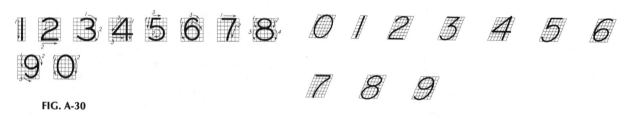

FIG. A-30

Numbers:

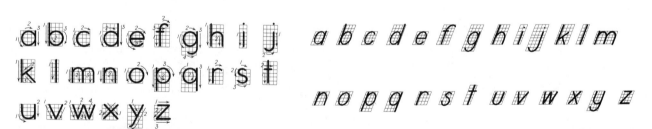

FIG. A-31

Lower Case Letters:

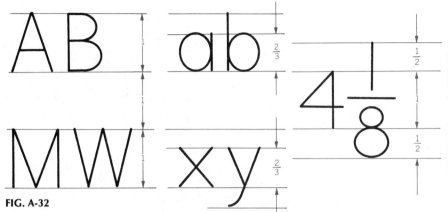

Lettering technique . . . draw light guidelines. Most engineering lettering is 3 mm (.12 in.) high with proportions as shown.

Maintain uniform slant. Do not retrace letters. Rotate pencil slightly between letters to maintain its conical point.

FIG. A-32

Letter spacing . . . maintain equal area between letters.

FIG. A-33

FIG. A-34

Word spacing . . . allow one letter width between words and after punctuation.

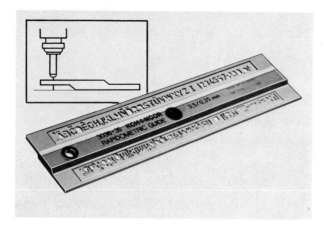

FIG. A-35

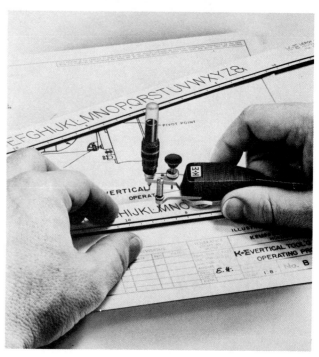

Ink lettering . . . used where greater clarity and reproducibility is required. Especially required if drawing will be reduced in size when it is duplicated. For best quality, the pen is guided by a template or held in a scriber that follows a template.

Transfer lettering . . . used in special situations where large letters and special letter forms are needed. Individual letters are pressed or rubbed onto drawing surface.

FIG. A-36

A.4 Multiview Drawing

Multiview drawings are made using the orthographic projection system. In this system the drawing on paper is the picture that the viewer sees on the surface of a transparent viewing plane placed perpendicular to the line of sight between the viewer's eyes and the object.

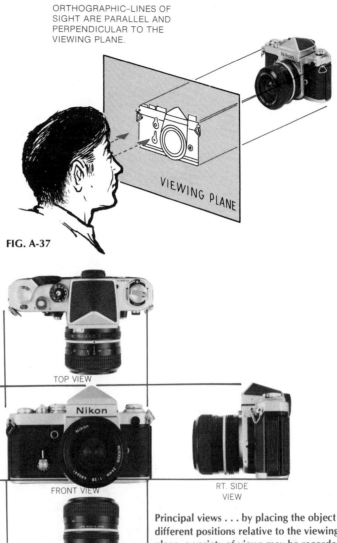

ORTHOGRAPHIC-LINES OF SIGHT ARE PARALLEL AND PERPENDICULAR TO THE VIEWING PLANE.

VIEWING PLANE

FIG. A-37

TOP VIEW

REAR VIEW   LEFT SIDE VIEW   FRONT VIEW   RT. SIDE VIEW

BOTTOM VIEW

FIG. A-38

Principal views . . . by placing the object in different positions relative to the viewing plane, a variety of views may be recorded. Principal views are obtained by positioning the object's principal faces—front and rear, top and bottom, left and right sides—parallel to the viewing plane.

Views are aligned with each other and arranged in the standard order shown so that they can be quickly recognized. Usually two or three principal views are sufficient unless the object is quite complex.

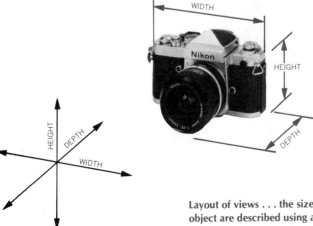

WIDTH

HEIGHT

DEPTH

HEIGHT

DEPTH

WIDTH

Layout of views . . . the size and shape of an object are described using a rectangular coordinate measuring system. The dimensions of space are width, height, and depth.

FIG. A-39

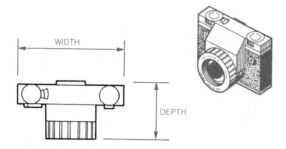

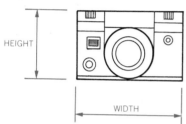

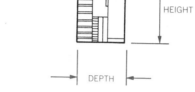

Each orthographic view shows only two dimensions of space.

FIG. A-40

FIG. A-41

Lines and surfaces cannot disappear — they must be accounted for in all views. Lines may appear true length, foreshortened, or as a point.

Planes may appear true size, distorted, or as a line. Even if distorted, the characteristic shape is retained—rectangles have four sides that are parallel in all views.

FIG. A-42

Front View Position

Selection of views . . . the object is positioned so that its most characteristic contour is seen in the "front" view position.

Draw only the minimum number of views required to completely describe the object.

The views selected should be those that show the shape of the features most clearly with the fewest hidden lines.

TYPE	WEIGHT	LINES
OBJECT (VISIBLE)	THICK	————————
HIDDEN	THIN	– – – – – –
CENTER	THIN	— – — – —
PHANTOM	THIN	— – – — – –
EXTENSION & DIMENSION	THIN	←————→
LEADER	THIN	↙
SECTION	THIN	/////////
CUTTING PLANE	THICK	↑ – – – – ↑
SHORT BREAK	THICK	～～～～
LONG BREAK	THIN	——⋀⋁——⋀⋁——

FIG. A-43

Types of lines . . . a standard "alphabet" of lines is used to describe an object on a drawing. Object lines outline the visible features. Any feature lines that are hidden are drawn using the hidden line symbol.

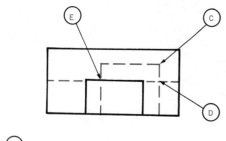

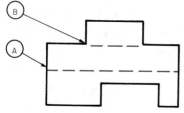

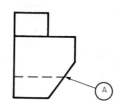

Hidden lines start and end with a dash Ⓐ . . . except when the hidden line is a continuation of a visible line Ⓑ.

Intersecting hidden lines meet at a dash Ⓒ . . . non-intersecting hidden lines do not touch. Ⓓ.

Hidden and visible lines that cross do not touch Ⓔ.

FIG. A-44

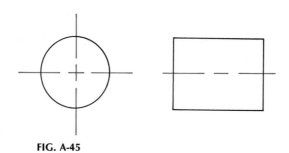

Centerlines are drawn on all views of cylindrical objects. The centerlines are broken between views.

FIG. A-45

A.5 Auxiliary Views

In multiview drawing, auxiliary views are produced when the principal faces of the object are positioned at an angle to the viewing plane. The viewer's line of sight is no longer perpendicular to a principal face. Only the line or surface to which the viewing plane is parallel is seen in its true size. By directing lines of sight at appropriate angles, auxiliary viewing planes perpendicular to the line of sight can be established. Any line, surface, angle, or distance to which the auxiliary viewing plane is parallel will appear true size in the auxiliary view which is produced.

Viewing Directions:

Principal view . . . the line of sight is perpendicular to one of the principal faces of the object.

FIG. A-46

Primary auxiliary view . . . the line of sight is at an angle to two principal faces of the object (top and front in this example).

FIG. A-47

Secondary auxiliary view . . . the line of sight is at an angle to three principal faces of the object (top, front, and right side in this example).

FIG. A-48

Layout of Auxiliary Views:

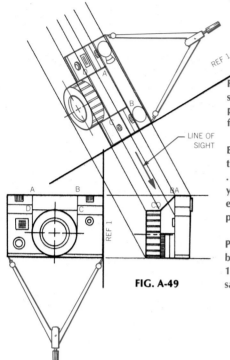

For a primary auxiliary . . . direct the line of sight at an angle to a principal view . . . draw projection lines parallel to the line of sight from the features of the principal view.

Establish reference line 1 perpendicular to the projection lines at a convenient location . . . in a view adjacent to the one from which you projected (the front view in this example), draw a mating reference line 1 perpendicular to its projection lines.

Plot points defining the features of the object by transferring distances from reference lines 1 . . . label the points to prevent error and to save time.

The example shows a line of sight directed perpendicular to an inclined plane that is seen on edge in the side view. This establishes an auxiliary viewing plane parallel to the inclined plane. The auxiliary view shows the true size of this plane and the true lengths of its lines.

FIG. A-49

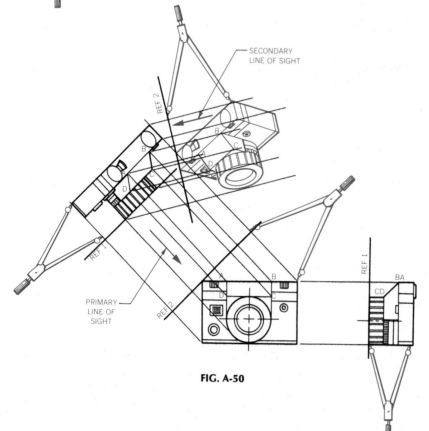

FIG. A-50

For a secondary auxiliary . . . direct a line of sight at an angle to a principal view and draw a primary auxiliary view.

Direct a second line of sight at any angle to this view . . . draw projection lines parallel to the line of sight from the features of the primary view.

Establish reference line 2 perpendicular to the secondary projection lines at a convenient location . . . in the view adjacent to the one from which you projected (the front view in this example), draw a mating reference line 2 perpendicular to the projection lines used to draw the primary auxiliary view.

Plot points defining the features of the object by transferring distances from reference lines 2. In this example the secondary auxiliary view shows a pictorial type view of the entire object.

A.6 Section Views

Section views show features that are hidden inside an object. The layout procedure for a section view is the same as that for any other type of view in multiview drawing. The object is imagined to be cut open at a selected location with the viewing plane positioned parallel to the cut surface.

Layout of Section Views:

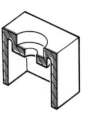

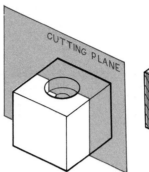

FIG. A-51

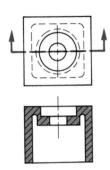

FIG. A-52

Cutting plane line . . . shows location of cut and direction of viewing. The section view is placed behind the arrows.

Section lining . . . shows the cut surface. Hidden lines are normally omitted in section views.

When several section views are drawn, or when a view must be moved out of its normal projected location, each section must be labeled.

A view must retain its proper orientation when moved and must remain behind the arrows. The section lining pattern remains constant throughout the drawing.

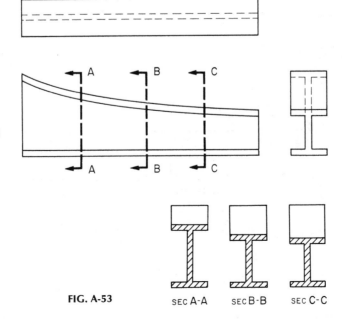

FIG. A-53

SEC A-A   SEC B-B   SEC C-C

Special Types of Section Views:

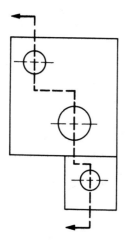
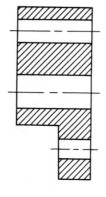

FIG. A-54

Offset section . . . the cutting plane passes through several features to reduce the number of views required. The changes in direction of the cutting plane are not shown on the section view.

Aligned section . . . symmetrical features may be revolved to avoid a distorted appearance in the section view.

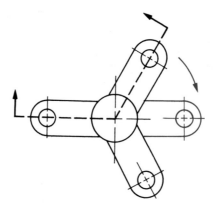

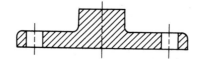

FIG. A-55

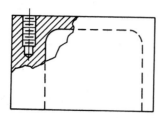

Broken out section . . . a view may be partially sectioned to show only a small feature. No cutting plane is shown.

FIG. A-56

Special Types of Section Views (cont'd)

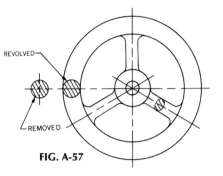

FIG. A-57

Revolved section . . . the cross-sectional shape of certain features can be shown directly on a view. The cut is assumed to be at the centerline of the section view, so no cutting plane is needed.

When a revolved section is moved outside of the view, it is called a removed section.

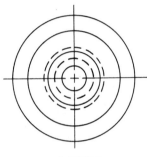

Half section . . . on a symmetrical object both inside and outside features can be shown in the same view. The cutting plane is not shown because it is always assumed to pass through the axis of symmetry. Hidden lines are often omitted in the "outside" half since the section portion shows the inside contours.

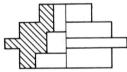

FIG. A-58

Assembly section . . . each cut part of an assembled object must be given a distinguishing section lining pattern that remains constant throughout the drawing. The patterns on adjacent parts must contrast in angle and/or spacing.

Shafts and standard parts are not sectioned when on the cutting plane.

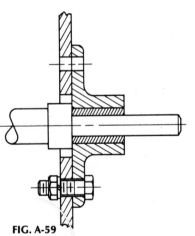

FIG. A-59

A.7 Threads and Fasteners

Fasteners and the holes associated with them frequently appear on engineering drawings. To save time, items such as these are usually drawn in a simplified or symbolic manner.

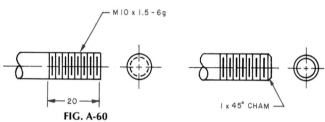

FIG. A-60

Standard threads . . . drawn symbolically unless of very large diameter. The nominal diameter of the thread is drawn to scale. The lines representing the threads are spaced for realistic appearance only.

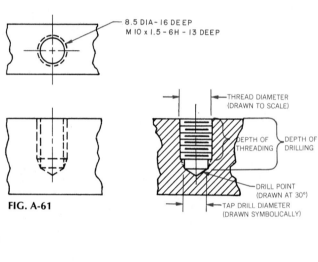

FIG. A-61

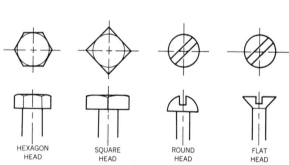

FIG. A-62   Common fasteners . . . drawn slightly simplified and oriented in the direction shown. Hidden lines are normally omitted.

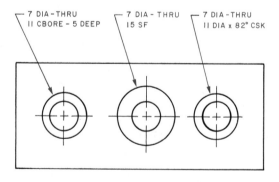

Special holes . . . often associated with fasteners.

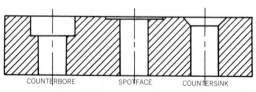

FIG. A-63

A.8 Intersections

The features of an object are composed of a series of intersecting geometric shapes. The intersection lines may be straight or curved depending on the nature of the intersecting surfaces.

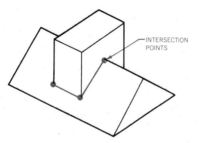

Plane surfaces . . . intersect in a straight line that joins the points of intersection of lines of one plane with the surface of the other plane.

FIG. A-64

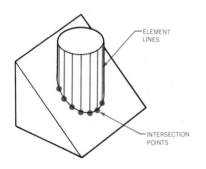

Curved surfaces and plane surfaces . . . usually intersect in a curved line that joins the points where element lines on the curved surface intersect the surface of the plane.

FIG. A-65

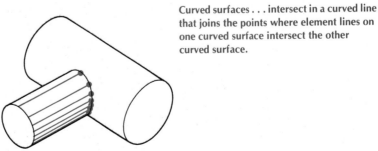

Curved surfaces . . . intersect in a curved line that joins the points where element lines on one curved surface intersect the other curved surface.

FIG. A-66

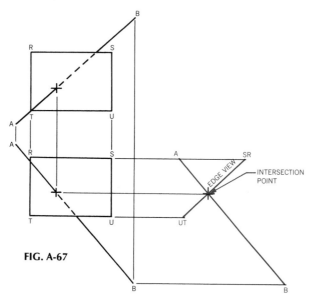

FIG. A-67

Line and a plane . . . intersect in a point. This is an important step in locating intersection lines. It is also important in locating attachment points for support wires and points where wires pass through surfaces.

If an edge view of the plane is available or is easily drawn, as with the inclined plane in Fig. A-67, the intersection point can be seen where the line passes through the edge view. The point can then be projected to other views.

If the edge view is not available, the intersection point can be found by passing the edge of a "cutting" plane through one view of the line. When the intersection line of the two planes is projected onto an adjacent view, it will cross the line at its intersection point.

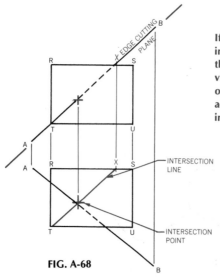

FIG. A-68

A.9 Developments

Hollow objects that are made of thin material are often formed from one flat piece of material that is folded on **bend** lines and joined on **seam** lines. The development may be either an **inside** or an **outside** pattern depending on which side of the object is uppermost on the drawing.

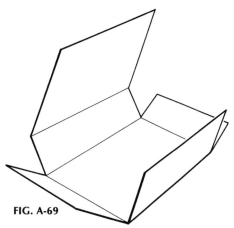

FIG. A-69

Prism Development (open ends):

Draw two views of the prism . . . one showing the edge (bend) lines in their true length . . . the other showing the edge lines as points.

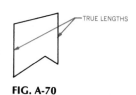

FIG. A-70

Project all points of the prism perpendicular to the edge lines. Draw a "stretch-out" line parallel to the projection lines.

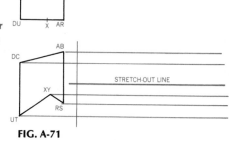

FIG. A-71

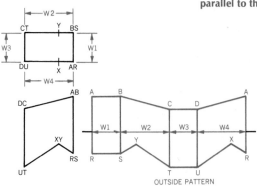

OUTSIDE PATTERN

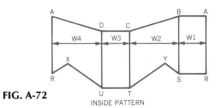

FIG. A-72 INSIDE PATTERN

Transfer the panel widths from the end view of the prism to the stretch-out line. Start at the desired seam line and proceed in the necessary order for an outside or an inside pattern.

Cylinder Development (open ends):

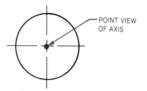

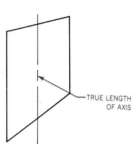

Draw two views of the cylinder . . . one showing the axis (centerline) in its true length . . . the other showing the axis as a point.

FIG. A-73

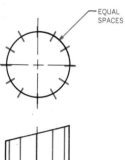

Draw equally spaced element lines on the surface parallel to the axis. These lines correspond to the edge (bend) lines of a prism.

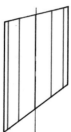

FIG. A-74

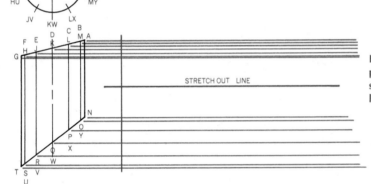

STRETCH OUT LINE

Project all points of the cylinder perpendicular to the centerline. Draw a stretch-out line parallel to the projection lines.

FIG. A-75

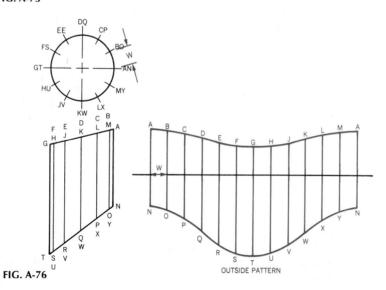

OUTSIDE PATTERN

Transfer the panel widths from the end view of the cylinder to the stretch-out line. Start at the desired seam line and proceed in the specified order for an outside or an inside pattern. Use the chords of the arcs to approximate the panel widths.

FIG. A-76

Pyramid Development (open bottom):

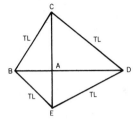

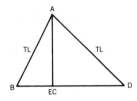

Draw two or more views of the pyramid to show the true length of all of its lines. Auxiliary views may be required to do this.

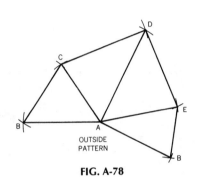

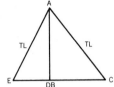

FIG. A-77

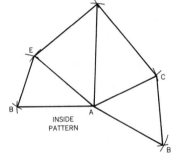

FIG. A-78

Starting at the desired seam line, lay out the true size of each triangular panel by swinging arcs with a compass set at the true length of each line. Follow in sequence in the specified order for an outside or an inside pattern.

A.10 Dimensioning

Before an object or a structure is manufactured or constructed, its shape is normally defined in a multiview drawing. The views on this drawing must also include all of the dimensions necessary to define the exact size and location of the various features. These dimensions must be stated clearly and precisely with only one possible interpretation. For machine drawing, national and international standards have been established to aid in this process.

Defining Shape:

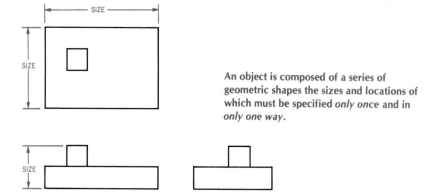

An object is composed of a series of geometric shapes the sizes and locations of which must be specified *only once* and in *only one way*.

Specify overall size (width, depth, and height) . . . in most cases.

FIG. A-79

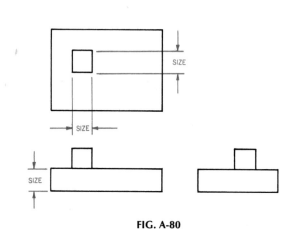

Specify sizes of individual shapes not already covered by overall dimensions. The function of the object determines which sizes to give. In this example the height of the large block was judged to be more important than that of the small block.

FIG. A-80

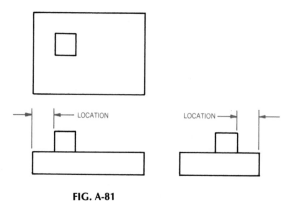

Specify locations of the individual shapes. The function of the object determines the surfaces that will be used for location.

FIG. A-81

Dimension Placement:

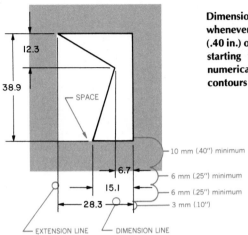

Dimensions are placed outside of the views whenever possible. Leave at least a 10 mm (.40 in.) open space around each view before starting the dimension lines that show the numerical value of each dimension. The contours of the object are extended with extension lines that start with a small space and end 3 mm (.12 in.) beyond the last dimension line. Extension lines may cross extension and object lines. Dimension lines may not be crossed.

FIG. A-82

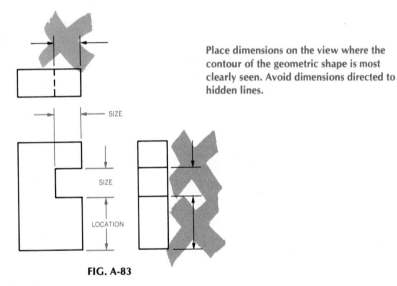

Place dimensions on the view where the contour of the geometric shape is most clearly seen. Avoid dimensions directed to hidden lines.

FIG. A-83

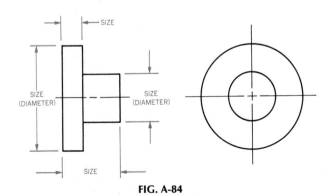

The size (diameter and length) of a solid cylinder is normally specified on its noncircular view.

FIG. A-84

Dimension Placement (cont'd)

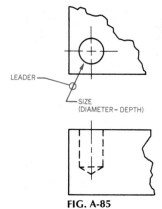

The size (diameter and depth) of a hollow cylinder (a hole) is normally specified on its circular view using a leader and a note. The leader must aim at the center of the hole with the tip of the arrow touching the circle. The horizontal portion of the leader is at least 6 mm (.25 in.) long.

FIG. A-85

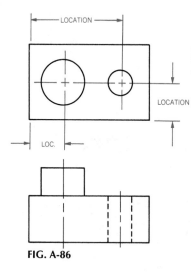

A cylindrical shape (solid or hollow) is located by its centerline in the circular view.

FIG. A-86

The size of a partial cylinder (a rounded corner) is specified by its radius in the circular view by using a leader. The leader must aim at or pass through the center of the radius. The letter "R" must follow the numerical value of the size.

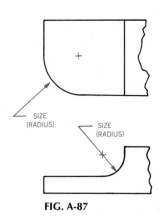

FIG. A-87

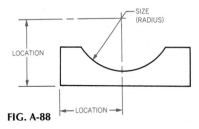

FIG. A-88

If a partial cylinder is tangent to a flat surface, location dimensions for the center of its radius are not needed. If the partial cylinder is not tangent, the center of the radius must be located.

A.11 Pictorial Drawing

A pictorial drawing system is used when it is necessary to describe an object in only one view for general information purposes. Pictorial systems vary in their ease of use, their versatility in showing an object from different viewing directions, and their degree of realism in portraying the object. Hidden lines are normally omitted in pictorial drawing because most of the important features are visible if the viewing direction is properly selected.

Axonometric Drawing:

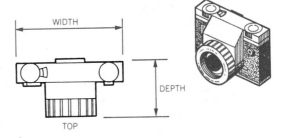

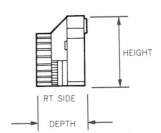

As previously discussed, in multiview drawing each view normally shows only one face of the object.

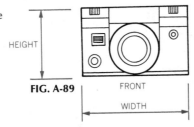

FIG. A-89

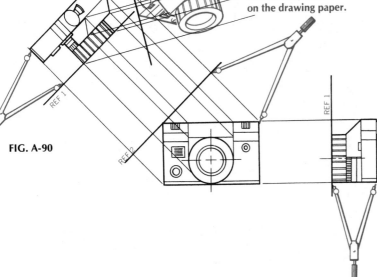

Auxiliary views are required in multiview drawing to show two or three faces in one view. This procedure is time consuming, and the auxiliary view is not realistically oriented on the drawing paper.

FIG. A-90

In axonometric drawing, however, the same view as seen in an auxiliary view can be drawn directly and in a natural position on the paper. The basic line and shape relationships of plane surfaces shown in multiview drawing are retained. Parallel lines remain parallel. Circular features appear as ellipses.

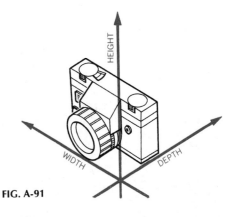

FIG. A-91

Axonometric Drawing Systems:

In axonometric drawing the object is positioned at an angle to the viewing plane. The three axonometric systems—isometric, dimetric, and trimetric—differ in the degree to which the three principal faces of the object are visible. This is done by increasing or decreasing the angle between each face and the viewing plane. As a face is tilted away from the viewing plane, its dimensions appear smaller. In drawing the view, this shortening is produced by using appropriate reducing scales on the width, height, and depth axes.

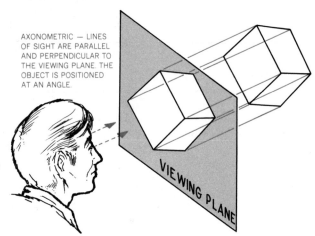

AXONOMETRIC — LINES OF SIGHT ARE PARALLEL AND PERPENDICULAR TO THE VIEWING PLANE. THE OBJECT IS POSITIONED AT AN ANGLE.

VIEWING PLANE

FIG. A-92

Isometric . . . the three principal faces are equally visible because they are positioned at the same angle to the viewing plane. The width and depth axes are drawn at 30° to the horizontal. The same scale is used on all three axes because the dimensions are equally distorted.

In practice, to save time, the dimensions along all three isometric axes are transferred directly from the multiview drawing rather than by using a reducing scale. This makes the isometric system the easiest of the axonometric systems to use.

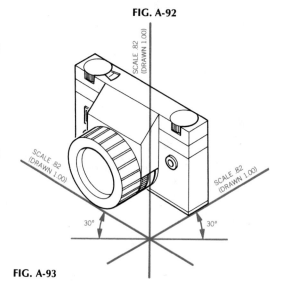

SCALE .82 (DRAWN 1.00)
SCALE .82 (DRAWN 1.00)
SCALE .82 (DRAWN 1.00)
30°   30°

FIG. A-93

Dimetric . . . two principal faces of the object are equally visible with the third face given greater or less visibility by varying its angle to the viewing plane. To obtain a better view of the top surface than in an isometric drawing, the object can be tilted up more. The width and depth scales remain equal, but the height scale is reduced.

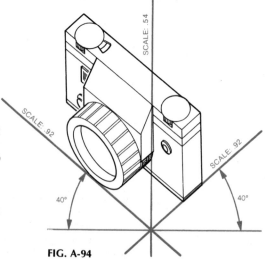

SCALE: .54
SCALE: .92
SCALE: .92
40°   40°

FIG. A-94

Axonometric Drawing Systems (cont'd)

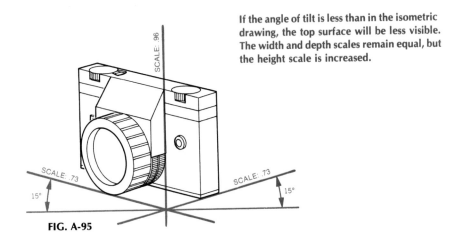

If the angle of tilt is less than in the isometric drawing, the top surface will be less visible. The width and depth scales remain equal, but the height scale is increased.

FIG. A-95

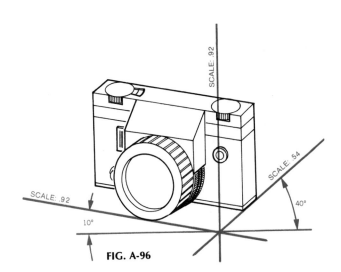

A better view of the front surface can be obtained by rotating the object so that the front is at a smaller angle to the viewing plane. In this case the depth scale varies with the degree of rotation while the width and height scales remain equal.

FIG. A-96

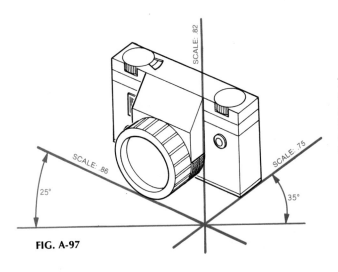

Trimetric . . . each principal face of the object is at a different angle to the viewing plane. This gives greater flexibility in positioning the three faces but is more time consuming to draw since different scales must be used on each axis.

Dimetric is more widely used than trimetric because it provides adequate views while requiring only two scales.

FIG. A-97

Layout of Axonometric Views:

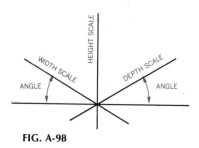

Set up the axis system desired with the required angles and scales.

FIG. A-98

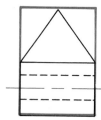
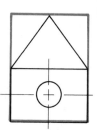

Imagine the object enclosed in a rectangular box that just touches its outermost points and surfaces.

FIG. A-99

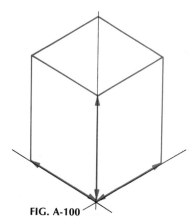

Lay out the width, height, and depth of the enclosing box along the axonometric axes. Be sure to use the correct scale for each axis.

FIG. A-100

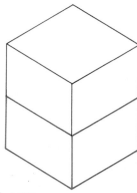

On the outline of the enclosing box draw in the surfaces of the object that are in contact with the outside faces. Omit hidden lines.

FIG. A-101

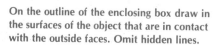

Layout of Axonometric Views (cont')

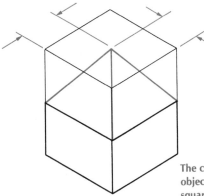

FIG. A-102

Next, draw in the surfaces of the object that fall inside the box. Locate the beginning and ending points of angled lines with measurements parallel to the width, height, and depth axes.

The circular opening on the right side of the object is drawn by laying out an enclosing square on the surface. The resulting rhombus serves as a guide for selection of an ellipse template opening that is tangent to the four sides.

A circle appearing on a surface is represented in axonometric by an ellipse the minor axis of which is parallel to the direction of a line perpendicular to the surface (the width axis in this example). A 35° ellipse template is used for circles on the principal faces of an object drawn in isometric.

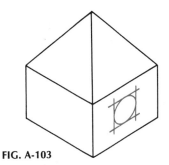

FIG. A-103

Perspective Drawing:

In perspective drawing more realistic pictorial views are produced. Although quite similar to the views produced in axonometric drawing, perspective drawing produces views that more closely duplicate how the human eye sees an object in space. Since the lines of sight are not perpendicular to the viewing plane, parallel lines on the object must be drawn so as to converge at an imaginary point in the distance. Width, height, and depth measurements must be made progressively smaller as they vanish into the distance. These variations from axonometric require additional time to draw accurately. This makes perspective drawing more suitable for artistic presentations.

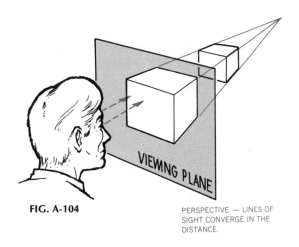

FIG. A-104

PERSPECTIVE — LINES OF SIGHT CONVERGE IN THE DISTANCE.

Perspective Drawing Systems:

The three perspective systems differ in the direction in which the object is viewed and the degree of realism produced.

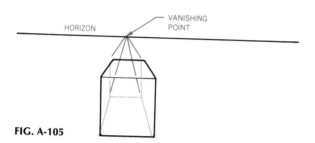

One point perspective . . . object lines parallel to the depth axis converge to a single vanishing point on the horizon.

FIG. A-105

Two point perspective . . . object lines parallel to the width and depth axes converge to two vanishing points on the horizon. This is the most commonly used perspective system.

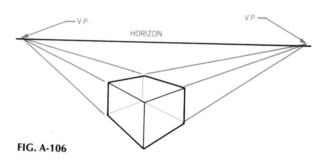

FIG. A-106

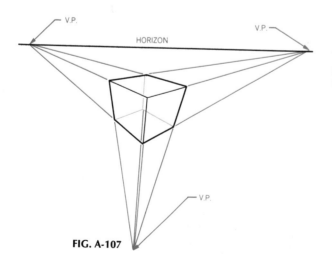

Three point perspective . . . object lines parallel to width, depth, and height axes converge to three vanishing points.

FIG. A-107

Oblique Drawing:

In oblique drawing less realistic pictorial views are produced, but an acceptable view is often produced in less time. This makes the oblique system more useful for freehand sketching than for professional illustration.

A principal face of the object is positioned parallel to the viewing plane, thus giving this face and those surfaces parallel to it an undistorted appearance. Being true size and shape makes these surfaces easier to draw. The lines of sight are parallel but at an angle to the viewing plane so that the other faces of the object can be seen.

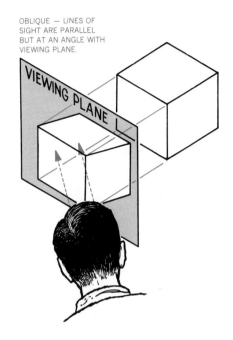

OBLIQUE — LINES OF SIGHT ARE PARALLEL BUT AT AN ANGLE WITH VIEWING PLANE.

FIG. A-108

Layout of Oblique Views:

TOP

FRONT

FIG. A-109

RT. SIDE

Orient the object so that the face having the most contours is in the "front" viewing position and can be drawn undistorted. All measurements on or parallel to the width and height axes are the same as on the multiview drawing.

The depth axis is usually drawn at 45° to the horizontal. For convenience in sketching, depth measurements are usually made to the same scale as that used for width and height. Lines parallel to the depth axis remain parallel.

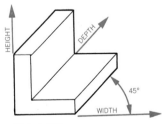

FIG. A-110

Layout of Oblique Views (cont'd)

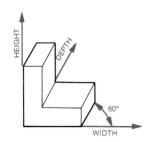

To create a more realistic appearance, depth measurements may be made to a reduced scale. The angle of the depth axis may also be changed and its scale changed accordingly.

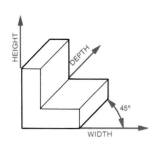

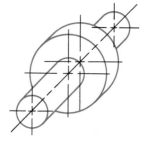

For objects that are basically rectangular, an enclosing box can be used to help in the layout. Orient the object so that circles and irregular contours appear on the undistorted front face.

FIG. A-112

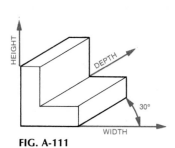

FIG. A-111

For cylindrical objects, a longitudinal centerline is laid out first . . . depth measurements are marked off on this axis to locate the centers of the circular faces.

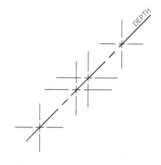

FIG. A-113

A.12 Charts and Graphs

Charts and graphs are used to portray graphically the relationship between various types of data. This comparison may be made using lines, solids, or pictures of volumes.

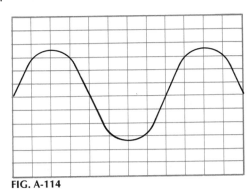

FIG. A-114

Graphs use lines to show the relationship between variables.

Bar charts use rectangular solids to compare several quantities.

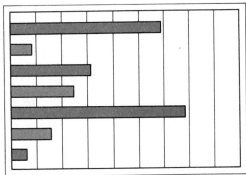

FIG. A-115

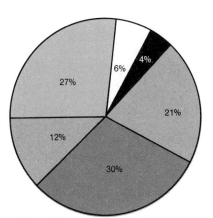

FIG. A-116

Circle ("pie") charts use solids to show the various percentages that make up a whole.

Pictographic charts use pictures or symbols to show relationships.

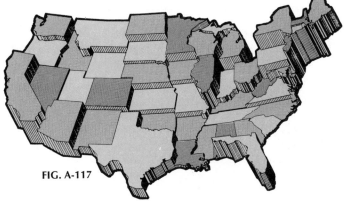

FIG. A-117

Preparing Graphs:

The quantities being compared are usually stated in order, with the dependent variable first and the independent variable second . . . the dependent is usually plotted on the vertical (ordinate) axis and the independent on the horizontal (abscissa) axis.

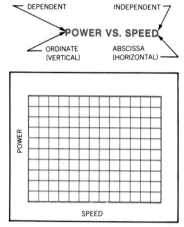

FIG. A-118

Preprinted graph paper makes the preparation of graphs much easier . . . scale divisions should be selected to produce a curve that will clearly display the functional relationship between the variables.

The scales are normally drawn inside the borders of the graph paper . . . scales must be labeled with the names of the variables and the units in which they are measured.

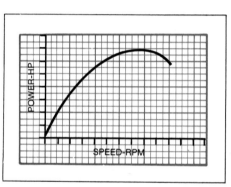

FIG. A-119

Plotted points are not usually shown on graphs of theoretical relationships.

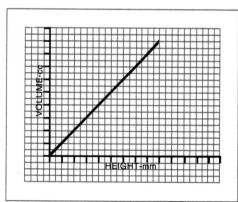

FIG. A-120

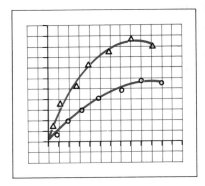

FIG. A-121

When plotting experimental data, the points are normally enclosed in small circles . . . if more than one curve is plotted on the same sheet, other geometric shapes, such as triangles and squares, can be used for identification.

The curve is usually sketched in lightly to average the points and then darkened in. The line starts and stops at the edge of each point symbol and need not pass through all points.

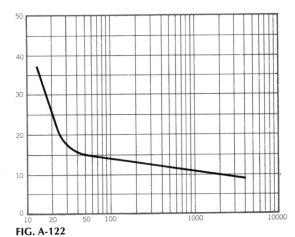

FIG. A-122

If a variable has a very large range of values, it can be compressed by plotting it on a logarithmic scale.

Semilog graph paper has uniform graduations on one axis and logarithmic graduations on the other.

Log-log paper has logarithmic graduations on both axes.

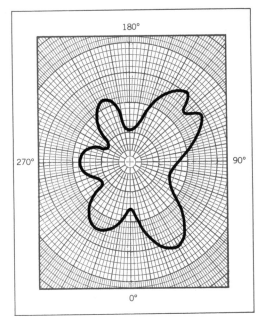

Graphs can also be plotted on polar coordinate graph paper.

FIG. A-123

Appendix B

Geometric Constructions

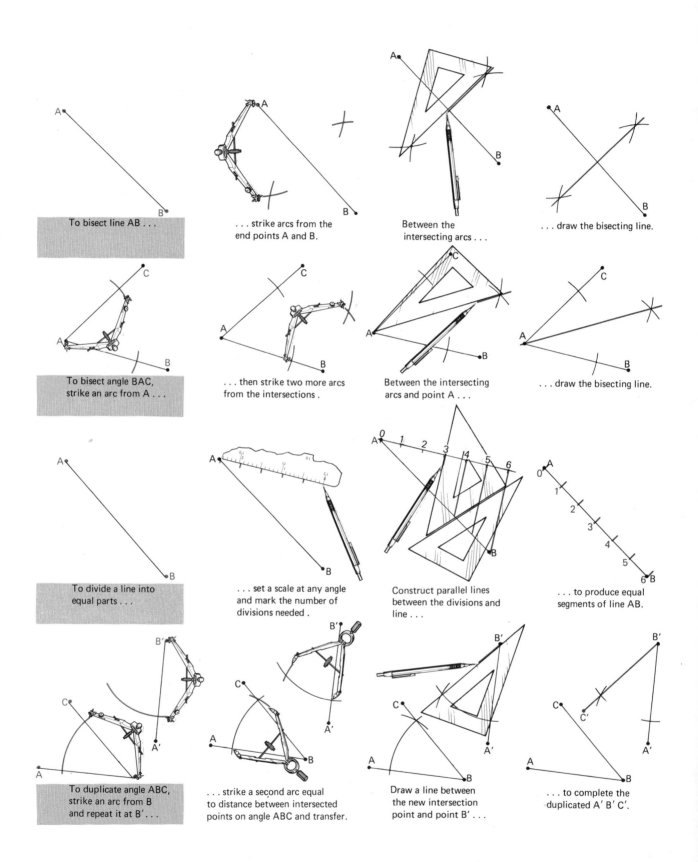

To bisect line AB . . .

. . . strike arcs from the end points A and B.

Between the intersecting arcs . . .

. . . draw the bisecting line.

To bisect angle BAC, strike an arc from A . . .

. . . then strike two more arcs from the intersections .

Between the intersecting arcs and point A . . .

. . . draw the bisecting line.

To divide a line into equal parts . . .

. . . set a scale at any angle and mark the number of divisions needed .

Construct parallel lines between the divisions and line . . .

. . . to produce equal segments of line AB.

To duplicate angle ABC, strike an arc from B and repeat it at B' . . .

. . . strike a second arc equal to distance between intersected points on angle ABC and transfer.

Draw a line between the new intersection point and point B' . . .

. . . to complete the duplicated A' B' C'.

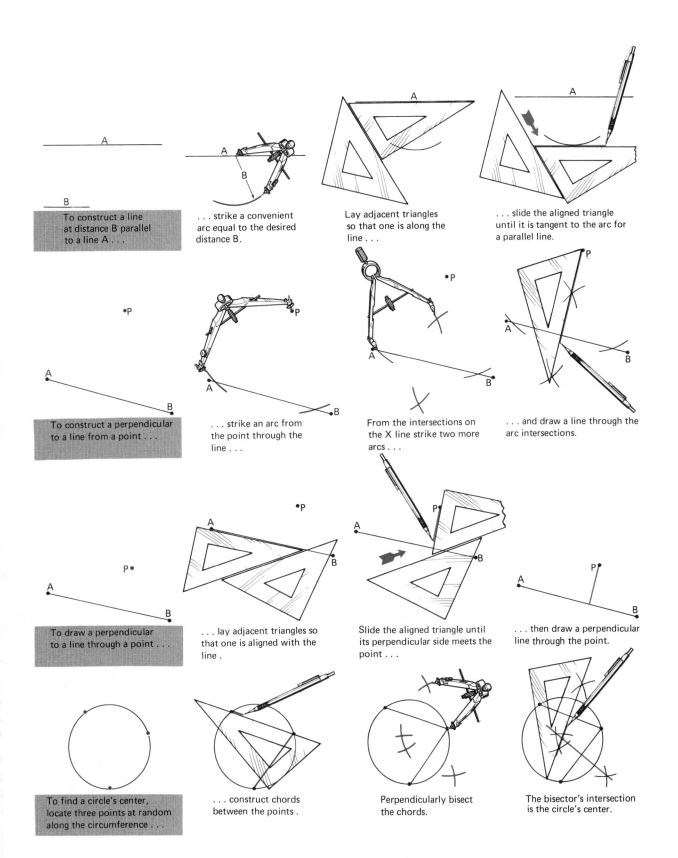

To construct a line at distance B parallel to a line A . . .

. . . strike a convenient arc equal to the desired distance B.

Lay adjacent triangles so that one is along the line . . .

. . . slide the aligned triangle until it is tangent to the arc for a parallel line.

To construct a perpendicular to a line from a point . . .

. . . strike an arc from the point through the line . . .

From the intersections on the X line strike two more arcs . . .

. . . and draw a line through the arc intersections.

To draw a perpendicular to a line through a point . . .

. . . lay adjacent triangles so that one is aligned with the line .

Slide the aligned triangle until its perpendicular side meets the point . . .

. . . then draw a perpendicular line through the point.

To find a circle's center, locate three points at random along the circumference . . .

. . . construct chords between the points .

Perpendicularly bisect the chords.

The bisector's intersection is the circle's center.

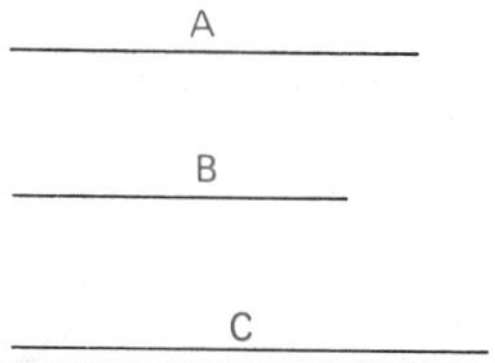

A

B

C

To construct a triangle
from three given lines . . .

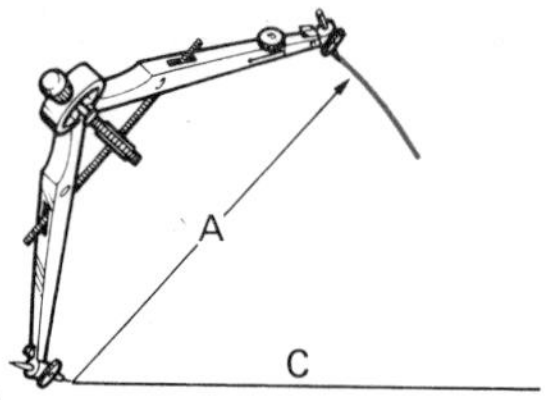

. . . strike an arc equal
in length to one line . . .

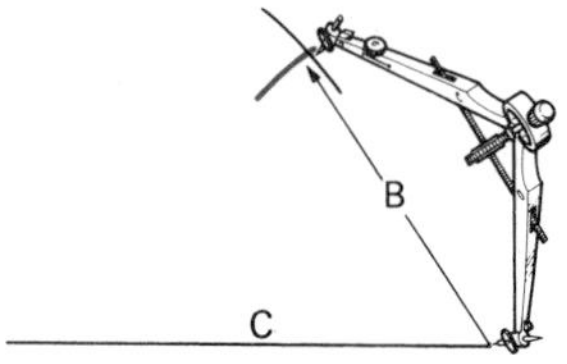

A

C

. . . then another arc equal
to the second line . . .

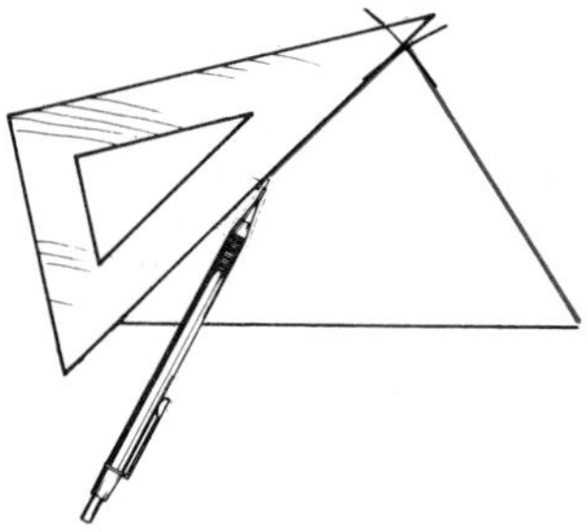

B

C

. . . and connect the end
points of the lines.

To construct an equilateral
triangle . . .

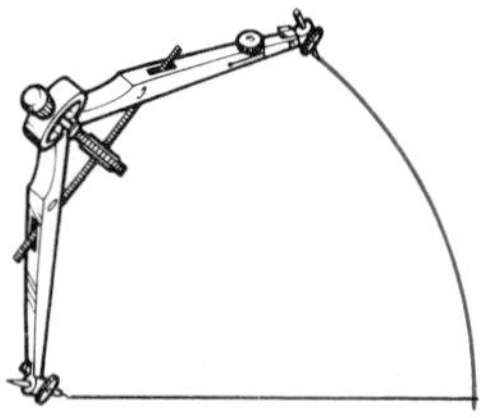

. . . strike an arc equal to
the given side . . .

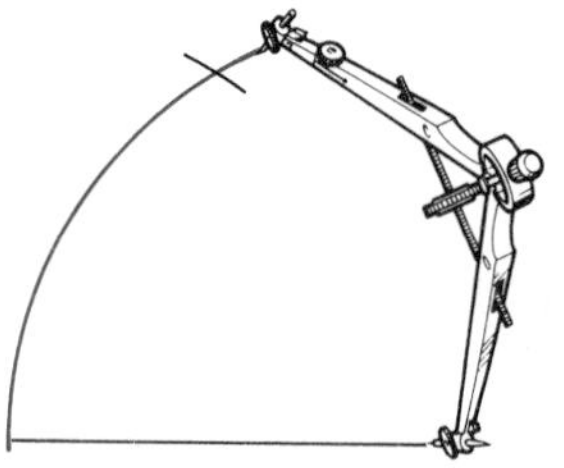

. . . strike another arc
equal to the given side . . .

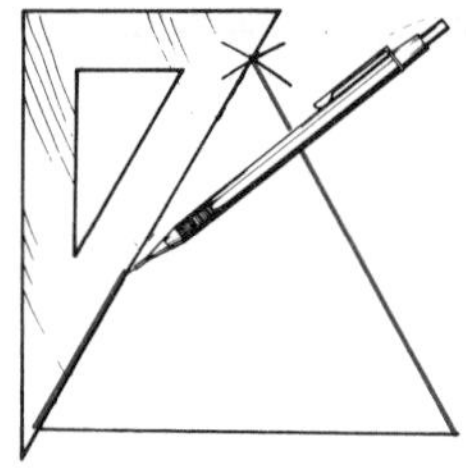

. . . connect the ends of the
given side and the arcs' intersection.

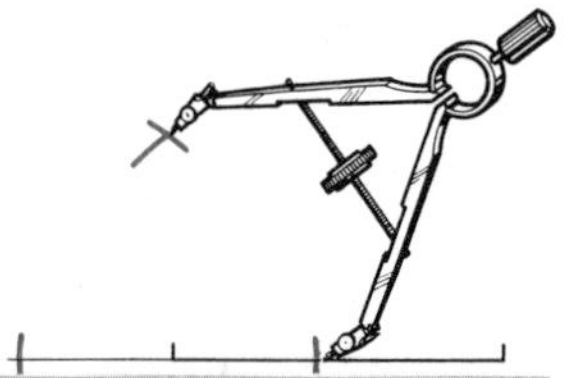

To construct a square, draw a
perpendicular at one end
of the initial side . . .

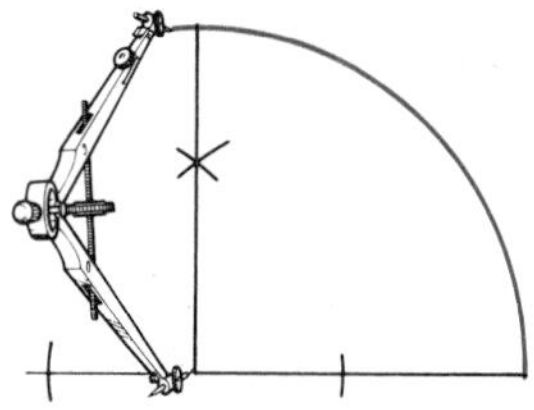

. . . strike an arc to establish
the length of the perpendicular .

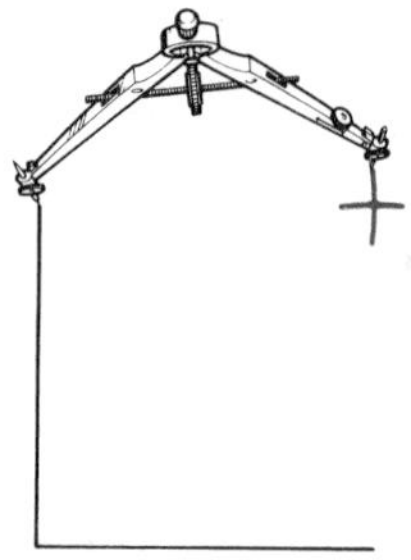

Determine the final corner
by striking arcs from the ends
of the two lines . . .

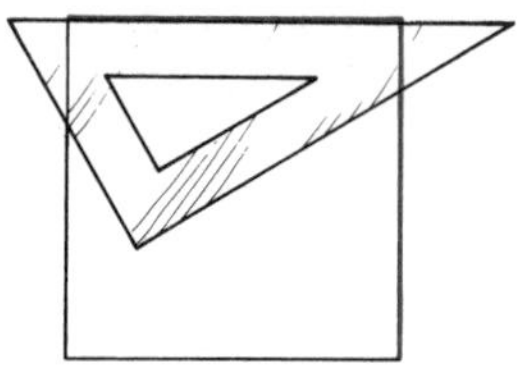

. . . connect all corners
to complete the square.

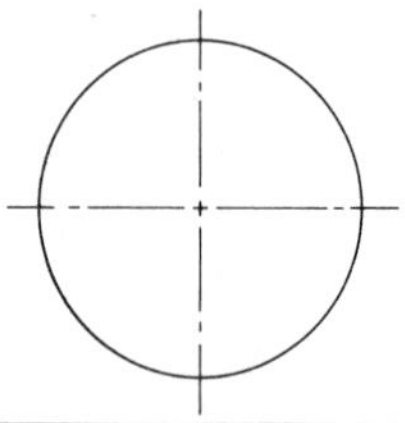

To construct a square inside
a given circle . . .

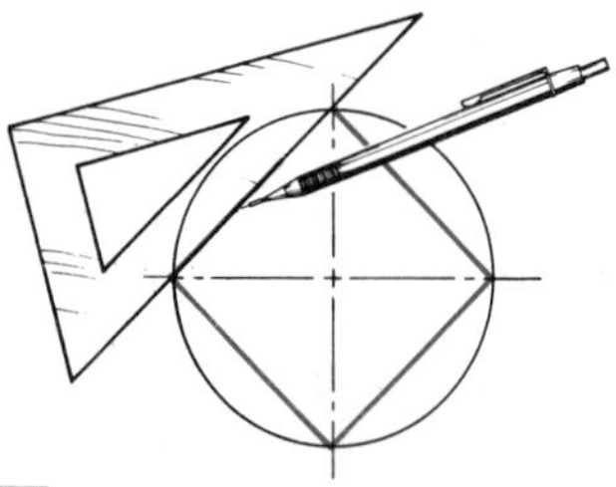

. . . draw lines' to connect the
center line and circumference
intersections.

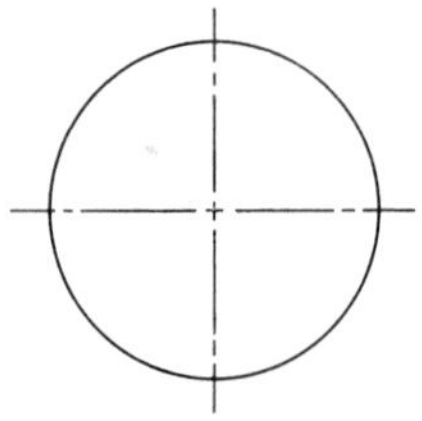

To construct a square
outside a given circle . . .

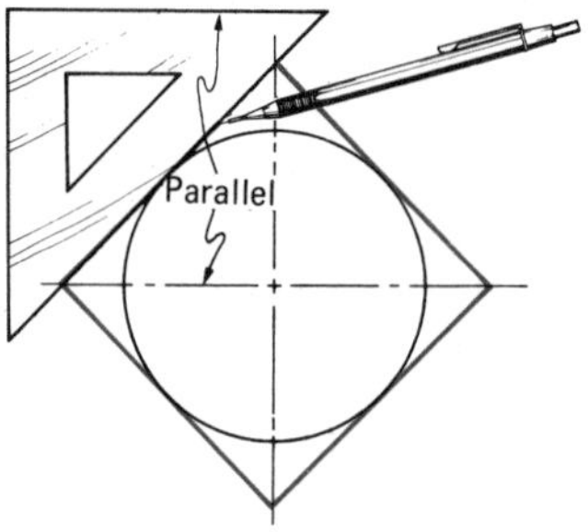

Parallel

. . . connect center line
extensions with 45° tangents.

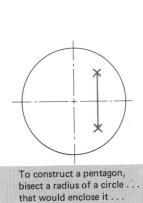

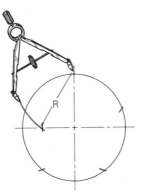

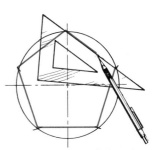

To construct a pentagon, bisect a radius of a circle . . . that would enclose it . . .

. . . using the bisected radius, strike an arc of radius A . . .

The resulting radius R is . . .

. . . used to establish the five points of a pentagon.

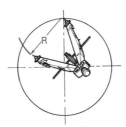

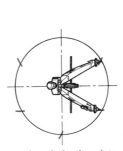

To construct a hexagon transfer the radius R of a circle that would enclose it . . .

. . . to the circumference . . .

. . . and mark the six points . . .

. . . used to establish a hexagon.

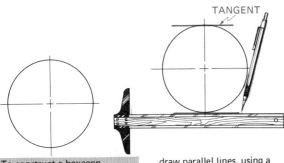

TANGENT

TANGENT

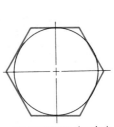

To construct a hexagon around a given circle . . .

. . . draw parallel lines, using a "T" square, that are tangent to opposite sides of the circle .

Using a 30° –60° triangle, construct two pairs of parallel lines that . . .

. . . are tangent to the circle to complete the hexagon.

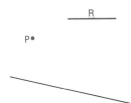

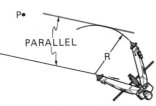

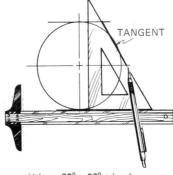

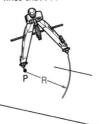

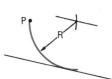

R

P•

PARALLEL

R

P•

To draw an arc of radius R tangent to a line and through a point . . .

. . . draw a parallel at distance R.

Intersect the parallel with an arc R from the point .

Using the intersection draw an arc tangent to the line through P

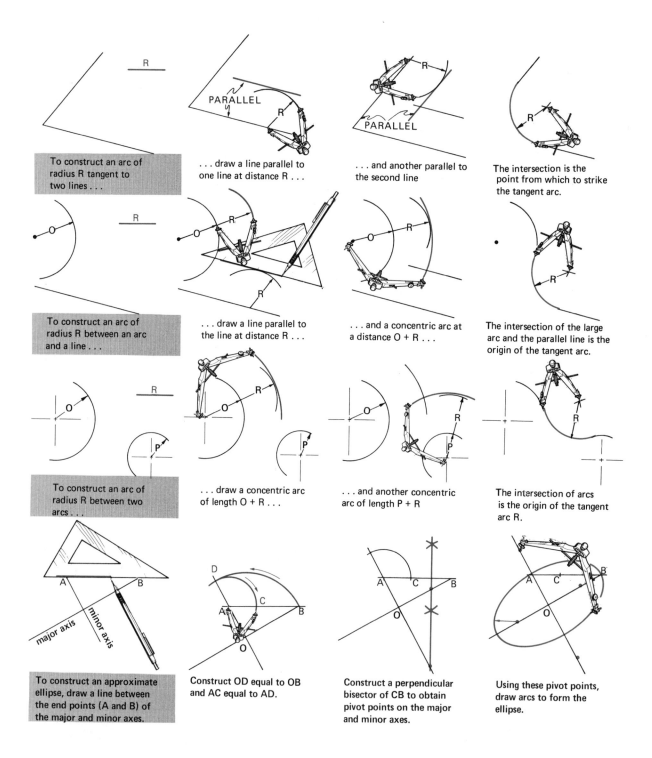

To construct an arc of radius R tangent to two lines . . .

. . . draw a line parallel to one line at distance R . . .

. . . and another parallel to the second line

The intersection is the point from which to strike the tangent arc.

To construct an arc of radius R between an arc and a line . . .

. . . draw a line parallel to the line at distance R . . .

. . . and a concentric arc at a distance O + R . . .

The intersection of the large arc and the parallel line is the origin of the tangent arc.

To construct an arc of radius R between two arcs . . .

. . . draw a concentric arc of length O + R . . .

. . . and another concentric arc of length P + R

The intersection of arcs is the origin of the tangent arc R.

To construct an approximate ellipse, draw a line between the end points (A and B) of the major and minor axes.

Construct OD equal to OB and AC equal to AD.

Construct a perpendicular bisector of CB to obtain pivot points on the major and minor axes.

Using these pivot points, draw arcs to form the ellipse.

Appendix C

Scales, Grids, and Protractors

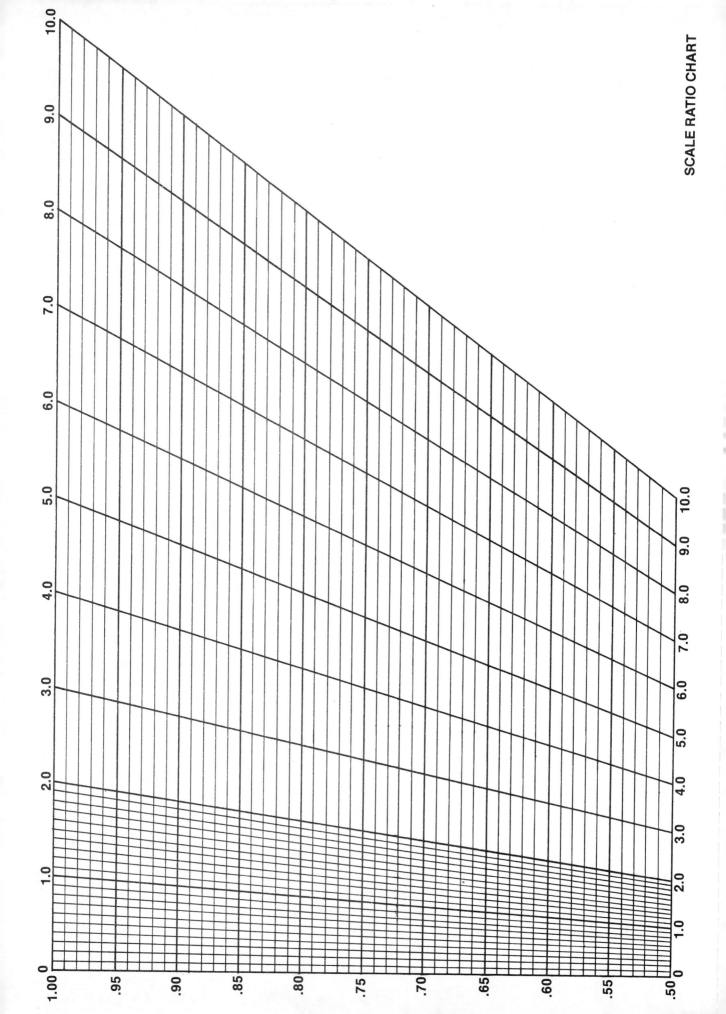

SCALE RATIO CHART

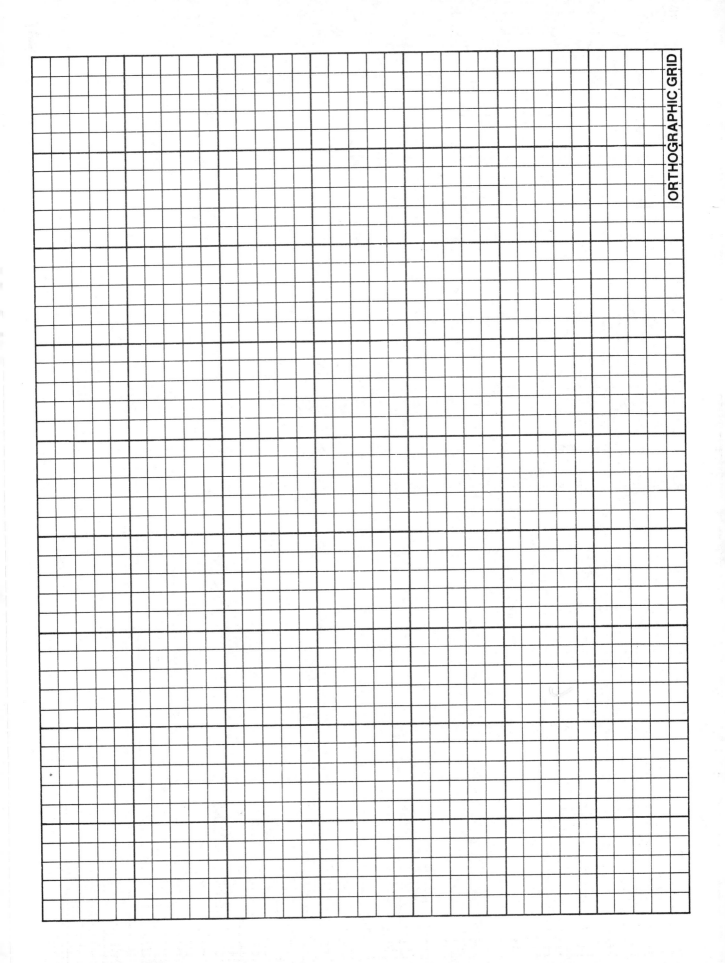

ORTHOGRAPHIC GRID

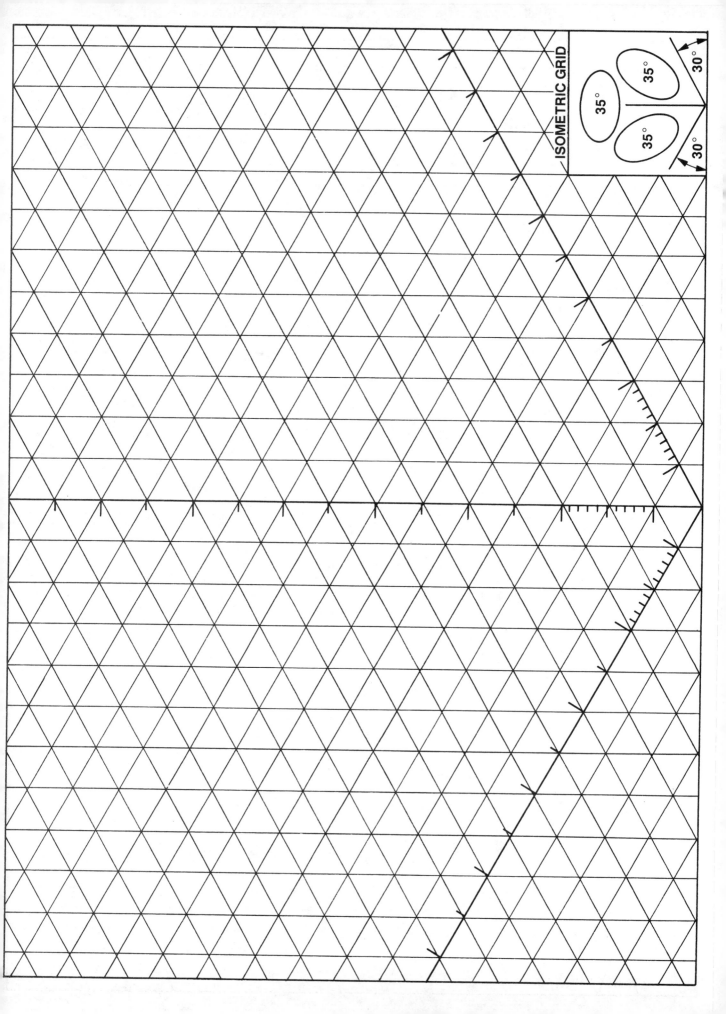

ISOMETRIC GRID

35° 35° 35°

30° 30°

DIMETRIC GRID

20°

40°   40°

20°   20°

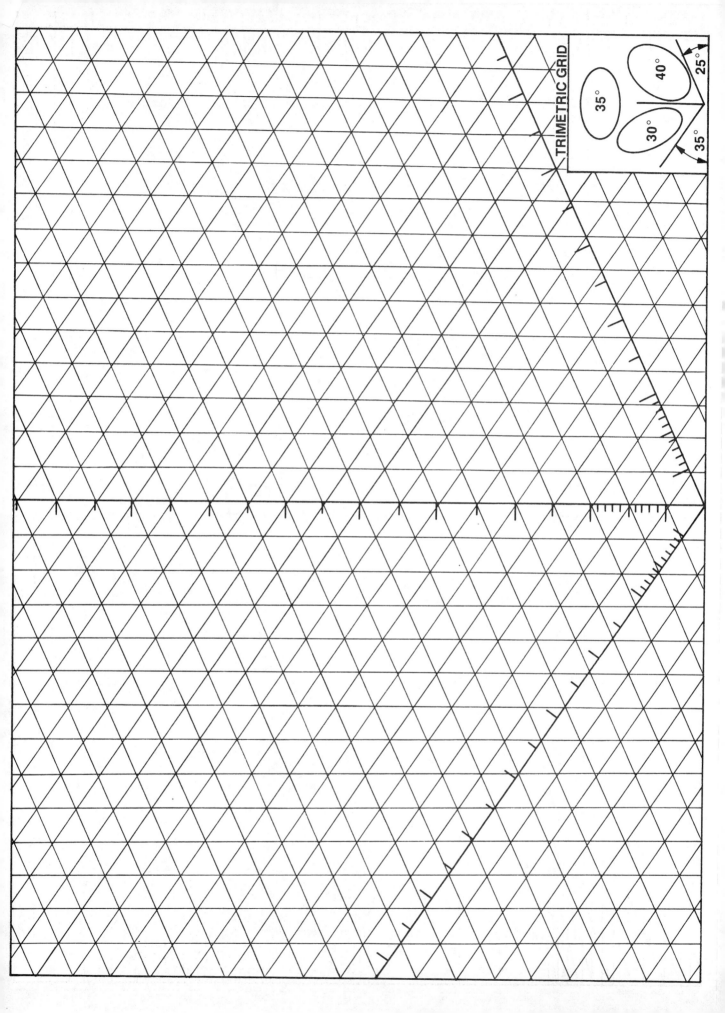

TRIMETRIC GRID

35°　　30°

40°

25°

35°

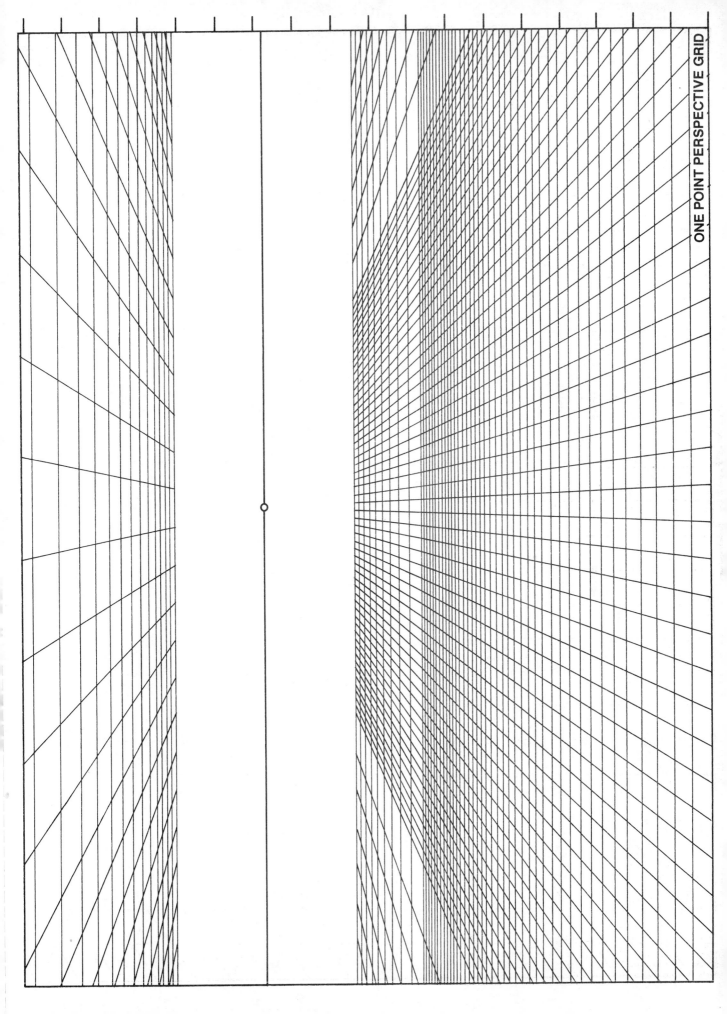

ONE POINT PERSPECTIVE GRID

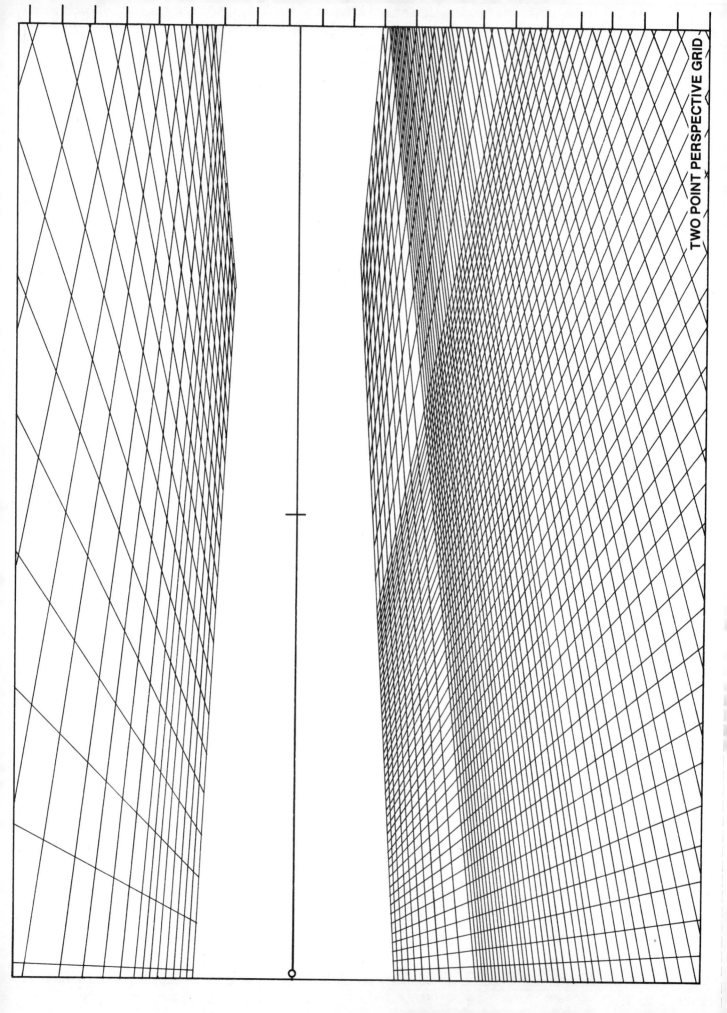

TWO POINT PERSPECTIVE GRID

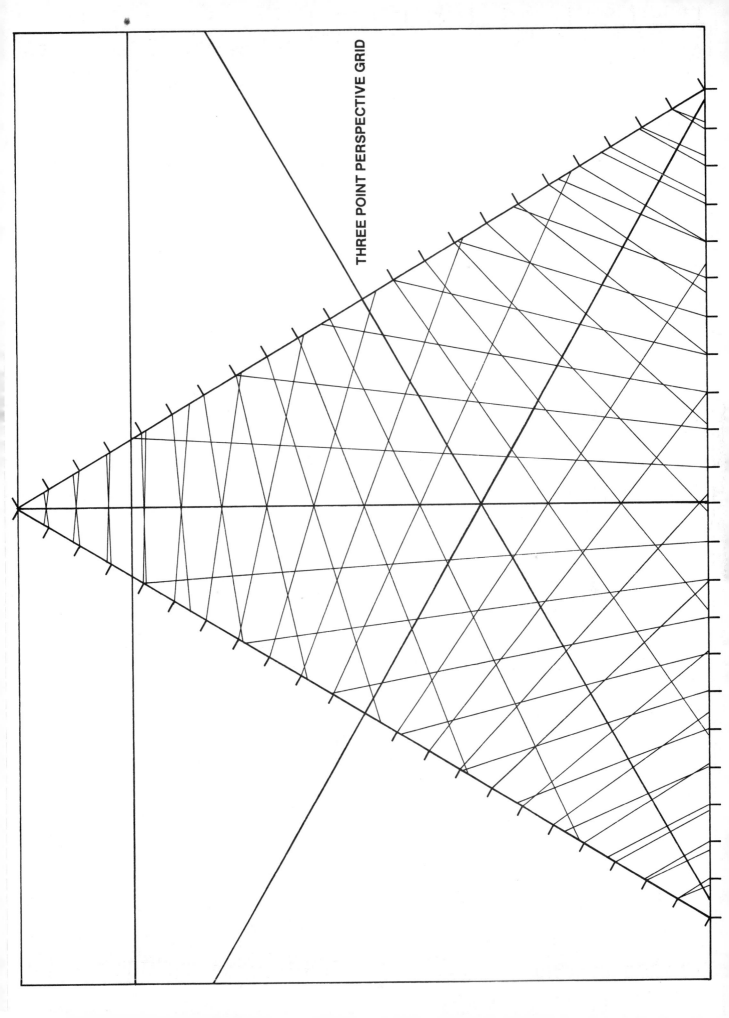

THREE POINT PERSPECTIVE GRID

OBLIQUE GRID

1.0

.7

45°

20°

1.0

1.0

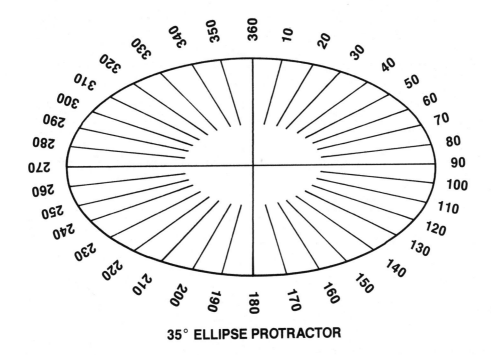

35° ELLIPSE PROTRACTOR

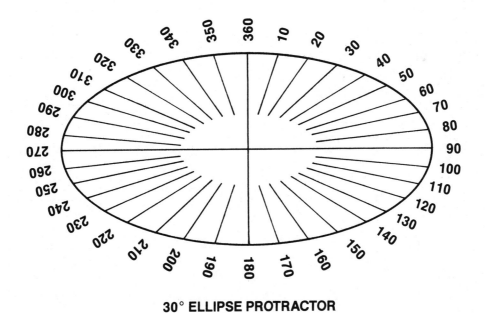

30° ELLIPSE PROTRACTOR

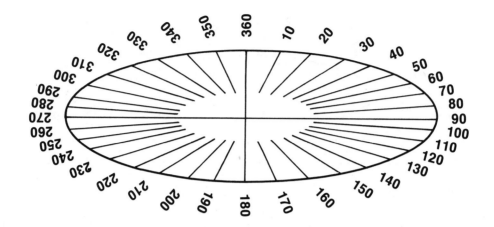

20° ELLIPSE PROTRACTOR

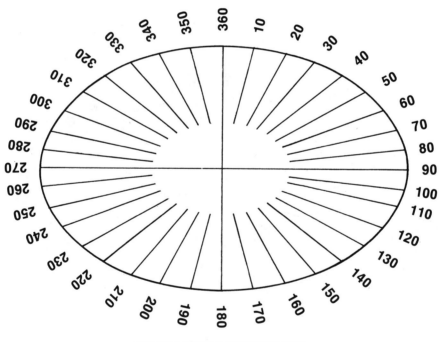

40° ELLIPSE PROTRACTOR

Appendix D

Tables and Charts

NOMENCLATURE FOR COMMON PRODUCT FEATURES

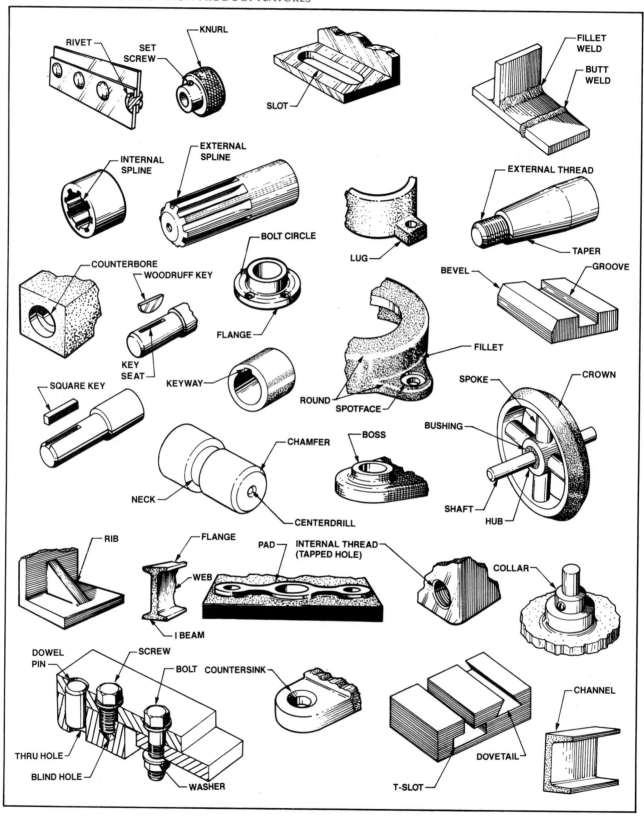

GEOMETRIC SHAPES AND FORMULAS

Figure	Shape	Formulas
Rectangle		Area = (base)(altitude) = ab Diagonal = $\sqrt{\text{(altitude)}^2 + \text{(base)}^2}$ $C = \sqrt{a^2 + b^2}$
Any triangle		Angles $A + B + C = 180°$ (Altitude h is perpendicular to base c) Area = $\frac{1}{2}$(base)(altitude)
Right triangle		Angle A + angle B = angle C = $90°$ Area = $\frac{1}{2}$(base)(altitude) Hypotenuse = $\sqrt{\text{(altitude)}^2 + \text{(base)}^2}$ $C = \sqrt{a^2 + b^2}$
Parallelogram		Area = (base)(altitude) Altitude h is perpendicular to base AB Angles $A + B + C + D = 360°$
Trapezoid		Area = $\frac{1}{2}$(altitude)(sum of bases) (Altitude h is perpendicular to sides AB and CD. Side AB is parallel to side CD.)
Regular polygon		Area = $\frac{1}{2}\begin{bmatrix}\text{Length of}\\\text{one side}\end{bmatrix}\begin{bmatrix}\text{Number}\\\text{of sides}\end{bmatrix}\begin{bmatrix}\text{Distance}\\OA\text{ to}\\\text{center}\end{bmatrix}$ A regular polygon has equal angles and equal sides and can be inscribed in or circumscribed about a circle.
Circle		AB = diameter, CD = radius $C = 2\pi$(radius) Area = π(radius)^2 = $\frac{\pi\,\text{(diameter)}^2}{4}$ $\frac{\text{arc }BC}{\text{circumference}} = \frac{\text{angle }BDC}{360°}$ Circumference (C) = π(diameter) 1 radian = $\frac{180°}{\pi}$ = $57.2958°$
Sector of circle		Area = $\frac{(\text{arc }AB)(\text{radius})}{2}$ $= \pi\frac{(\text{radius})^2(\text{angle }ACB)}{360°}$ $= \frac{(\text{radius})^2(\text{angle }ACB\text{ in radians})}{2}$
Segment of circle		Area = $\frac{(\text{radius})^2}{2}\left[\frac{\pi(\angle ACB°)}{180} - \sin ACB°\right]$ Area = $\frac{(\text{radius})^2}{2}\left[\angle ACB\text{ in radians} - \sin ACB°\right]$ Area = area of sector ACB − area of triangle ABC
Ellipse		Area = π(long radius OA)(short radius OC) Area = $\frac{\pi}{4}$(long diameter AB)(short diameter CD)

FRACTION TO DECIMAL INCH AND MILLIMETER CONVERSION CHART

4ths	8ths	16ths	32nds	64ths	to 2 places	to 3 places	to 4 places	Millimeters to 4 places	4ths	8ths	16ths	32nds	64ths	to 2 places	to 3 places	to 4 places	Millimeters to 4 places
				1/64	0.02	0.016	0.0156	0.3969					33/64	0.52	0.516	0.5156	13.0969
			1/32		0.03	0.031	0.0312	0.7938				17/32		0.53	0.531	0.5312	13.4938
				3/64	0.05	0.047	0.0469	1.1906					35/64	0.55	0.547	0.5469	13.8906
		1/16			0.06	0.062	0.0625	1.5874			9/16			0.56	0.562	0.5625	14.2875
				5/64	0.08	0.078	0.0781	1.9844					37/64	0.58	0.578	0.5781	14.6844
			3/32		0.09	0.094	0.0938	2.3813				19/32		0.59	0.594	0.5938	15.0813
				7/64	0.11	0.109	0.1094	2.7781					39/64	0.61	0.609	0.6094	15.4781
	1/8				0.12	0.125	0.1250	3.1750		5/8				0.62	0.625	0.6250	15.8750
				9/64	0.14	0.141	0.1406	3.5719					41/64	0.64	0.641	0.6406	16.2719
			5/32		0.16	0.156	0.1562	3.9688				21/32		0.66	0.656	0.6562	16.6688
				11/64	0.17	0.172	0.1719	4.3656					43/64	0.67	0.672	0.6719	17.0656
		3/16			0.19	0.188	0.1875	4.7625			11/16			0.69	0.688	0.6875	17.4625
				13/64	0.20	0.203	0.2031	5.1594					45/64	0.70	0.703	0.7031	17.8594
			7/32		0.22	0.219	0.2188	5.5563				23/32		0.72	0.719	0.7188	18.2563
				15/64	0.23	0.234	0.2344	5.9531					47/64	0.73	0.734	0.7344	18.6531
1/4					0.25	0.250	0.2500	6.3500	3/4					0.75	0.750	0.7500	19.0500
				17/64	0.27	0.266	0.2656	6.7469					49/64	0.77	0.766	0.7656	19.4469
			9/32		0.28	0.281	0.2812	7.1438				25/32		0.78	0.781	0.7812	19.8438
				19/64	0.30	0.297	0.2969	7.5406					51/64	0.80	0.797	0.7969	20.2406
		5/16			0.31	0.312	0.3125	7.9375			13/16			0.81	0.812	0.8125	20.6375
				21/64	0.33	0.328	0.3281	8.3344					53/64	0.83	0.828	0.8281	21.0344
			11/32		0.34	0.344	0.3438	8.7313				27/32		0.84	0.844	0.8438	21.4313
				23/64	0.36	0.359	0.3594	9.1281					55/64	0.86	0.859	0.8594	21.8281
	3/8				0.38	0.375	0.3750	9.5250		7/8				0.88	0.875	0.8750	22.2251
				25/64	0.39	0.391	0.3906	9.9219					57/64	0.89	0.891	0.8906	22.6219
			13/32		0.41	0.406	0.4062	10.3188				29/32		0.91	0.906	0.9062	23.0188
				27/64	0.42	0.422	0.4219	10.7156					59/64	0.92	0.922	0.9219	23.4156
		7/16			0.44	0.438	0.4375	11.1125			15/16			0.94	0.938	0.9375	23.8125
				29/64	0.45	0.453	0.4531	11.5094					61/64	0.95	0.953	0.9531	24.2094
			15/32		0.47	0.469	0.4688	11.9063				31/32		0.97	0.969	0.9688	24.6063
				31/64	0.48	0.484	0.4844	12.3031					63/64	0.98	0.984	0.9844	25.0031
1/2					0.50	0.500	0.5000	12.7000	1					1.00	1.000	1.0000	25.4000

Values or sizes that reflect common fractional increments will be expressed as decimal equivalents of the fractional increments. These values should be expressed to 2, 3, or 4 decimal places as illustrated. The number of decimal places will be determined by the tolerance required.

To avoid needless perpetuation of odd decimal numbers, this chart should not be used for new work. Instead, a value or size should be chosen having a final digit that is zero or an even number.

Source: Extracted from American National Standard Decimal Inch (ANSI B87.1-1965) with the permission of the publisher, the Society of Manufacturing Engineers, One SME Drive, Dearborn, Michigan.

INCHES TO MILLIMETERS CONVERSION CHART

Inches	mm	Inches	mm	Inches	mm	Inches	mm	Inches	mm
1	25.4	26	660.4	51	1295.4	76	1930.4
2	50.8	27	685.8	52	1320.8	77	1955.8
3	76.2	28	711.2	53	1346.2	78	1981.2
4	101.6	29	736.6	54	1371.6	79	2006.6
5	127.0	30	762.0	55	1397.0	80	2032.0
6	152.4	31	787.4	56	1422.4	81	2057.4
7	177.8	32	812.8	57	1447.8	82	2082.8
8	203.2	33	838.2	58	1473.2	83	2108.2
9	228.6	34	863.6	59	1498.6	84	2133.6
10	254.0	35	889.0	60	1524.0	85	2159.0
11	279.4	36	914.4	61	1549.4	86	2184.4
12	304.8	37	939.8	62	1574.8	87	2209.8
13	330.2	38	965.2	63	1600.2	88	2235.2
14	355.6	39	990.6	64	1625.6	89	2260.6
15	381.0	40	1016.0	65	1651.0	90	2286.0
16	406.4	41	1041.4	66	1676.4	91	2311.4
17	431.8	42	1066.8	67	1701.8	92	2336.8
18	457.2	43	1092.2	68	1727.2	93	2362.2
19	482.6	44	1117.6	69	1752.6	94	2387.6
20	508.0	45	1143.0	70	1778.0	95	2413.0
21	533.4	46	1168.4	71	1803.4	96	2438.4
22	558.8	47	1193.8	72	1828.8	97	2463.8
23	584.2	48	1219.2	73	1854.2	98	2489.2
24	609.6	49	1244.6	74	1879.6	99	2514.6
25	635.0	50	1270.0	75	1905.0	100	2540.0

Basis: 1 inch = 25.4 millimeters

Inches	mm	Inches	mm	Inches	mm	Inches	mm
.0001	.0025	.0026	.0660	.0051	.1295	.0076	.1930
.0002	.0051	.0027	.0686	.0052	.1321	.0077	.1956
.0003	.0076	.0028	.0711	.0053	.1346	.0078	.1981
.0004	.0102	.0029	.0737	.0054	.1372	.0079	.2007
.0005	.0127	.0030	.0762	.0055	.1397	.0080	.2032
.0006	.0152	.0031	.0787	.0056	.1422	.0081	.2057
.0007	.0178	.0032	.0813	.0057	.1448	.0082	.2083
.0008	.0203	.0033	.0838	.0058	.1473	.0083	.2108
.0009	.0229	.0034	.0864	.0059	.1499	.0084	.2134
.0010	.0254	.0035	.0889	.0060	.1524	.0085	.2159
.0011	.0279	.0036	.0914	.0061	.1549	.0086	.2184
.0012	.0305	.0037	.0940	.0062	.1575	.0087	.2210
.0013	.0330	.0038	.0965	.0063	.1600	.0088	.2235
.0014	.0356	.0039	.0991	.0064	.1626	.0089	.2261
.0015	.0381	.0040	.1016	.0065	.1651	.0090	.2286
.0016	.0406	.0041	.1041	.0066	.1676	.0091	.2311
.0017	.0432	.0042	.1067	.0067	.1702	.0092	.2337
.0018	.0457	.0043	.1092	.0068	.1727	.0093	.2362
.0019	.0483	.0044	.1118	.0069	.1753	.0094	.2388
.0020	.0508	.0045	.1143	.0070	.1778	.0095	.2413
.0021	.0533	.0046	.1168	.0071	.1803	.0096	.2438
.0022	.0559	.0047	.1194	.0072	.1829	.0097	.2464
.0023	.0584	.0048	.1219	.0073	.1854	.0098	.2489
.0024	.0610	.0049	.1245	.0074	.1880	.0099	.2515
.0025	.0635	.0050	.1270	.0075	.1905	.0100	.2540

Basis: 1 inch = 25.4 millimeters (rounded to 4 decimal places)

MILLIMETERS TO INCHES CONVERSION CHART

mm	Inches	mm	Inches	mm	Inches	mm	Inches	mm	Inches
1	0.0394	21	0.8268	41	1.6142	61	2.4016	81	3.1890
2	0.0787	22	0.8661	42	1.6535	62	2.4409	82	3.2283
3	0.1181	23	0.9055	43	1.6929	63	2.4803	83	3.2677
4	0.1575	24	0.9449	44	1.7323	64	2.5197	84	3.3071
5	0.1969	25	0.9843	45	1.7717	65	2.5591	85	3.3465
6	0.2362	26	1.0236	46	1.8110	66	2.5984	86	3.3858
7	0.2756	27	1.0630	47	1.8504	67	2.6378	87	3.4252
8	0.3150	28	1.1024	48	1.8898	68	2.6772	88	3.4646
9	0.3543	29	1.1417	49	1.9291	69	2.7165	89	3.5039
10	0.3937	30	1.1811	50	1.9685	70	2.7559	90	3.5433
11	0.4331	31	1.2205	51	2.0079	71	2.7953	91	3.5827
12	0.4724	32	1.2598	52	2.0472	72	2.8346	92	3.6220
13	0.5118	33	1.2992	53	2.0866	73	2.8740	93	3.6614
14	0.5512	34	1.3386	54	2.1260	74	2.9134	94	3.7008
15	0.5906	35	1.3780	55	2.1654	75	2.9528	95	3.7402
16	0.6299	36	1.4173	56	2.2047	76	2.9921	96	3.7795
17	0.6693	37	1.4567	57	2.2441	77	3.0315	97	3.8189
18	0.7087	38	1.4961	58	2.2835	78	3.0709	98	3.8583
19	0.7480	39	1.5354	59	2.3228	79	3.1102	99	3.8976
20	0.7874	40	1.5748	60	2.3622	80	3.1496	100	3.9370

Basis: 1 inch = 25.4 millimeters (rounded to 4 decimal places)

Index